SEAMUS HEANEY

SEAMUS HEANEY

The Crisis of Identity

Floyd Collins

Newark: University of Delaware Press
London: Associated University Presses

Associated University Presses
2010 Eastpark Boulevard
Cranbury, NJ 08512

Associated University Presses
Unit 304, The Chandlery
50 Westminster Bridge Road
London SE1 7QY, England

Associated University Presses
P.O. Box 338, Port Credit
Mississauga, Ontario
Canada L5G 4L8

The paper used in this publication meets the requirements of the American National Standard for Permanence of Paper for Printed Library Materials Z39.48-1984.

Library of Congress Cataloging-in-Publication Data

Collins, Floyd, 1951–
    Seamus Heaney : the crisis of identity / Floyd Collins.
        p. cm.
Includes bibliographical references and index.
    ISBN 0-87413-805-1 (alk. paper)
1. Heaney, Seamus—Criticism and interpretation. 2. Identity
(Psychology) in literature. I. Title.
PR6058.E2 Z58 2003
821'.914—dc21

                                            2002151559

PRINTED IN THE UNITED STATES OF AMERICA

For Caroline and my mother
in memoriam James Isaac Collins

Contents

Acknowledgments

THIS STUDY BEGAN AS AN ESSAY FOCUSING ON SEAMUS HEANEY'S *Selected Poems, 1966–1987.* I owe special thanks to Peter Stitt, editor of *The Gettysburg Review*, who first published my work on Heaney. His consistent support and encouragement kept me going through the writing and revision process. I am also indebted to Sidney Burris, whose interest in Heaney's work fueled my own. His expertise and advice proved invaluable throughout every stage of this project. Thanks are also due Michael Heffernan and John Guilds, who advised me during the initial stages of writing. I found previous Heaney scholarship by Neil Corcoran, Henry Hart, Phyllis Carey and Catharine Malloy, Michael Parker, and Helen Vendler especially helpful.

A number of others contributed to the making of this book. Gregory Pope provided the splendid sketch of an eleventh-century Viking torque for the book's cover design. The interlibrary loan staff members at the University of Arkansas, Quincy University, Wabash College, and Gordon College offered timely, efficient assistance in acquiring much-needed research materials. My wife, Caroline, kept a careful eye on the manuscript in every phase of its development and made occasional suggestions for improvement. Finally, I am obliged to the staff at the University of Delaware Press and Associated University Presses who helped see this book into print, especially director Donald C. Mell and assistant director Karen Druliner at the University of Delaware Press, as well as director Julien Yoseloff and managing editor Christine Retz at Associated University Presses.

Abbreviations

B	*Beowulf.* New York: W. W. Norton, 2000.
CP	*Crediting Poetry: The Nobel Lecture.* New York: Farrar, Straus, & Giroux, 1995.
CT	*The Cure at Troy.* London: Faber and Faber, 1990.
EL	*Electric Light.* New York: Farrar, Straus, & Giroux, 2001.
FW	*Field Work.* New York: Farrar, Straus, & Giroux, 1979.
GT	*The Government of the Tongue.* New York: Farrar, Straus, & Giroux, 1988.
HL	*The Haw Lantern.* New York: Farrar, Straus, & Giroux, 1987.
Poems	*Poems, 1965–1975.* New York: Farrar, Straus, & Giroux, 1980.
Pr	*Preoccupations: Selected Prose, 1966–1978.* New York: Farrar, Straus, & Giroux, 1980.
RP	*The Redress of Poetry.* New York: Farrar, Straus, & Giroux, 1995.
SA	*Sweeney Astray.* New York: Farrar, Straus, & Giroux, 1984.
SI	*Station Island.* London: Faber and Faber, 1984.
SL	*The Spirit Level.* New York: Farrar, Straus, & Giroux, 1996.
ST	*Seeing Things.* London: Faber and Faber, 1991.

SEAMUS HEANEY

1

The Crisis of Identity
and the Development of a Poetic Consciousness

AFTER TEN YEARS OF ARMED CONFLICT BEFORE THE GLEAMING CITADEL of Troy, and after another ten spent wandering the timeless Aegean, Odysseus returns to his island kingdom, Ithaca, forewarned that scores of suitors daily besiege his wife in the great hall. Fearing for his life and the patrimony of his son, Telemachus, the master strategist enters his own *megaron* disguised as a ragged wayfarer obliged by an evil fate to beg for alms among the tables. The callow young aristocrats force Odysseus to box with an idler and lout named Iros for a portion of the blood-pudding. To their surprise and abiding irritation, the older man easily proves the better pugilist. Even after dispatching his rival, Odysseus must endure the company's black caprice, as enmity deepens within the hall. Antinoös strikes the "famished tramp" on the shoulder with a stool, and Ktesippos pegs a cow's hoof at his head. Those female servants whose pubescent beauty allows them to grace the beds of the more dominant suitors offer Odysseus insults and abuse. But the grizzled veteran bides his time, concealing his identity and his rage from all save a trusted few. Only when Penelope brings out the great horn bow of Odysseus and bids the contestants shoot through "iron axe-helve sockets, twelve in a line," does the wise Ithacan make his presence known. For the first time in Western literature, the identity of the hero and the poet fuse in one sublime gesture:

> But the man skilled in all ways of contending,
> satisfied by the great bow's look and heft,
> like a musician, like a harper, when
> with quiet hand upon his instrument
> he draws between his thumb and forefinger

15

a sweet new string upon a peg: so effortlessly
Odysseus in one motion strung the bow.
Then slid his right hand down the cord and plucked it,
so the taut gut vibrating hummed and sang
a swallow's note.[1]

This extended metaphor, in which the bow becomes a harp emblematic of the epic singer, allows us a fleeting glimpse of Homer before his image is once again obscured by Odysseus. Yet the poet's subversive spirit lingers in the submerged pun, "a swallow's note": when Odysseus's second arrow strikes the insolent Antinoös "under the chin / and punch[es] up to the feathers through his throat,"[2] Homer's lethal cunning with language hits home. Unwitting participants in their own funeral games, the youthful pretenders lose the *agon* of the great bow, and their lives into the bargain. And whether or not Homer was in fact a composite figure or a solitary genius standing alone at the culmination of a centuries-old oral tradition, we have a vivid dramatization, albeit allegorical, of the struggle between aspiring poets and their great precursors. In *The Western Canon,* Harold Bloom emphatically states that "the aesthetic and the agonistic are one, according to all the ancient Greeks, and to Burckhardt and Nietzsche, who recovered this truth."[3] According to Bloom, every strong contemporary must develop his own poetic or literary identity by engaging the masters of the European tradition in the literary equivalent of a *psychomachia*, and only through a highly skillful "misprision" or "creative misreading" of his chosen predecessors can the aspiring latecomer hope to prevail: "Contemporary writers do not like to be told that they must compete with Shakespeare and Dante, and yet that struggle was Joyce's provocation to greatness, to an eminence shared only by Beckett, Proust, and Kafka among modern Western authors."[4]

Whether or not we accept the more subtle implications of Bloom's theory, the issue of identity has been a major theme throughout Western literature; indeed, the crisis of identity, in the voice of the individual who has lost his place in the culture, emerges as early as Anglo-Saxon laments like "The Seafarer." Clearly, identity is a major issue for all cultures: we derive our sense of identity from a sense of continuity or discontinuity, from our position in the larger culture, and from our sense of place. All contemporary poets struggle with the question of identity, attempting to negotiate certain remnants of High Modernism, such as T. S. Eliot's dictum regarding the extinction of the poet's personality. Those contemporary writers who find themselves in the midst of a cultural crisis—namely, a time of war or social upheaval—face even more difficult questions about identity, as they ponder the role of the artist in crisis.

The notion of identity is, at best, difficult to define. Robert Penn Warren acknowledges the elusive, multifaceted nature of the term "identity": "On this word will focus, around this word will coagulate, a dozen issues, shifting, shading into each other."[5] Seamus Heaney noted the problematic issue of Irish identity in a 1974 review of P. V. Glob's *The Mound People*: "In Ireland our sense of the past, our sense of the land and even our sense of identity are inextricably interwoven."[6] For Heaney, a number of elements of identity are inseparable. His literary identity is bound up with his family's heritage of agricultural labor, his Catholic upbringing, and his cultural ancestry, including centuries of conflict with England, as well as decades of strife between Protestant and Catholic.

In *Identity, Youth and Crisis* (1968), psychologist Erik H. Erikson explains identity as a conscious sense of individual uniqueness, a striving for continuity of experience, and a sense of belonging or solidarity.[7] Presenting human growth and identity as a series of "crises," he defines a crisis not as "a threat or a condition of imminent disaster," but rather as "a necessary turning point, a crucial moment of heightened vulnerability and potential when development must move one way or another, marshaling resources of growth, recovery, and further differentiation."[8] For the modern writer, the crisis of identity involves a continual struggle to find his own place within the community of the world and within the literary canon.

The matter of identity is especially troublesome for Irish citizens, who must confront an unwieldy cultural and historical legacy that includes both their relationship with England and the reality of political and sectarian strife in their homeland. In this respect, Ireland seems an anomaly, as Elmer Andrews observes in his discussion of "Bogland," the concluding poem of Heaney's second collection, *Door into the Dark*: "Normally, millions of years would help a country to achieve and define itself. Not so in Ireland."[9] Polly Devlin, a former Irish journalist who is also Seamus Heaney's sister-in-law, notes in *All of Us There* how a repressive, authoritarian Irish Catholic educational system affected children's sense of identity:

In this prevailing ethos, the questions asked of children differed only in their emphasis from the genuine questions asked in other systems. But emphasis makes all the difference. "Who do you think *you* are?" asked to wound, as a reprimand, or as the amazed response to what has been been interpreted as conceit, immodesty or the dreaded boldness is very different from the genuine enquiry bent on genuine exploration: "*Who* do you think you are?" . . . Why should our mentors, our teachers, our guides ask the question like this? We knew nothing of our history, of the reductive process of a way of life built on deprivation and poverty, nothing of the cruelty of a religion or a political system that made self-effacement the safest way to live and which took away from a race its ability to esteem itself. . . . Effacement and quietness became equated with goodness, no new equation in Ireland, where effacement had once contributed to survival.[10]

In *Transitions: Narratives of Modern Irish Culture* (1987), Richard Kearney observes that the cultural crisis in twentieth-century Ireland was often experienced as a conflict between the claims of tradition and modernity. Today's Irish must confront "the prevailing sense of discontinuity, the absence of a coherent identity, the breakdown of inherited ideologies and beliefs, [and] the insecurities of fragmentation."[11]

It is not surprising, then, that identity has traditionally been a concern for Irish writers: "With no continuity, no shared history, no reliable audience, the Irish writer's experience has typically been one of exposure and alienation. His is, as Thomas Kinsella says, a divided mind."[12] Interestingly, Erikson listed "the Irish expatriates" among those writers who have become "the artistic spokesmen and prophets of identity confusion," and notes the difficulty of identity for the creative artist who finds himself in the midst of a cultural crisis: "Artistic creation goes beyond complaint and exposure, and it includes the moral decision that a certain painful identity-consciousness may have to be tolerated in order to provide the conscience of man with a critique of conditions, with the insight and the conceptions necessary to heal himself of what most deeply divides and threatens him."[13] Writing in the mid to late 1960s, Erikson almost seems to foretell the extent to which identity would continue to be a problem for successive generations of Irish writers. According to Kearney, the tension between revivalism and modernism has occasioned a transitional crisis in contemporary Irish writers: "They often write as *émigrés* of the imagination, conveying the feeling of being both part and not part of their culture, of being estranged from the very traditions to which they belong, of being in exile even while at home."[14] Here Kearney takes his cue from Heaney, who casts himself as "an inner émigré" in "Singing School" and whose speaker in "The Tollund Man" paradoxically finds himself as "lost, / Unhappy and at home" in Denmark as in Ireland. Like all contemporary Irish writers, Heaney must resolve for himself the competing claims of tradition and modernity, but he must also face the specter of self-imposed exile, a repudiation of his own identity and the community to which he belongs. As Robert Penn Warren has declared, "[N]either extreme offers a happy solution. Yet there is no simple solution of half-and-half, for the soul doesn't operate with that arithmetical tidiness."[15] Contemporary Irish poets confront a difficult literary ancestry, as they explore the extremes of Yeats's Romanticism and Joyce's Modernism, Yeats's myth-making and Joyce's exile and expatriation, while simultaneously questioning themselves about identity. Small wonder that Elmer Andrews describes Seamus Heaney as "a skeptical, defensive, displaced poet, torn by conflicting dogma and troubled by the nightmare of history, constantly threatened with the dissolution of the self yet deeply suspicious of the more obvious forms of ideological control."[16]

Though Heaney's identity may not have been as profoundly influenced by experiences such as the one Polly Devlin describes above, his poetry and prose express what may at best be termed a sense of dividedness. Like many postcolonial writers, he notes the presence of conflicting influences or origins: "the voices of my education," he explains, "pull in two directions, back through the political and cultural traumas of Ireland, and out towards the urgencies and experience of the world beyond it" (*Pr* 35). Oddly enough, an education emphasizing English literature and all things English in one respect reinforced his identity: he became more sensitive to Irish influences. In an essay on Patrick Kavanagh, which originally saw print in the *Massachusetts Review* and reappeared in his second collection of critical prose, *The Government of the Tongue* (1989), Heaney describes the startling yet intimate experience of encountering Kavanagh's poems for the first time:

> I was excited to find details of a life which I knew intimately—
> but which I had always considered to be below or beyond books—
> being presented in a book. . . . Potato-pits with rime on them,
> guttery gaps, iced-over puddles being crunched, cows being milked,
> a child nicking the doorpost with a pen-knife, and so on. What
> was being experienced was not some hygienic and self-aware pleasure
> of the text but a primitive delight in finding world become word. (7–8)

The encounter with Kavanagh's work marks the beginning of his own poetic identity: "I began as a poet when my roots were crossed with my reading" *(Pr* 37). The obvious delight with which Heaney culls, rehearses, and savors the rich sensory detail of Kavanagh's verse is a sure indication of how indelibly the penknife reinscribes his own experience. He suddenly apprehends the emblems of life through an abrupt nick that cuts to the roots of consciousness.

"Digging," the first piece presented in Heaney's *Poems 1965–1975*, commemorates this initial encounter with "world become word" by recalling the deft precision of a rural laborer in the peat-bogs "Nicking and slicing neatly, heaving sods / Over his shoulder, going down and down / For the good turf" (*Poems* 4). As the man continues to negotiate this neat patchwork of ground, the turf breaks up into damp monosyllables, "the squelch and slap / Of soggy peat." Each spadeful prickles with root hairs like raw nerve endings: "the curt cuts of an edge / Through living roots awaken in my head" (*Poems* 4). Heaney's capacity to listen generously, almost passively, enables world and word to permeate one another so thoroughly that each becomes inextricably linked with the other. In "Digging," he cultivates an empathic mode of composition wherein words function as aural counters beautifully adapted to the phenomena described.

The most dynamic feature of the poem's dramatic situation, however, inheres not in its crisp imagery, but in simple autobiographical fact—the worker plying his spade with a sapper's single-minded aplomb is Heaney's grandfather. Earlier on in the piece, the poet recalls his father digging in the potato drills: "By God, the old man could handle a spade. / Just like his old man" (*Poems* 3). Raised on a farm in the townland of Mossbawn, County Derry, in Northern Ireland, Heaney must confront the crisis of identity from the very outset: "But I've no spade to follow men like them." He resolves this sense of discontinuity, eventually choosing to efface through poetry the boundaries between world and word: "Between my finger and my thumb / The squat pen rests. / I'll dig with it." Though he has called it "a big coarse-grained navvy of a poem" (*Pr* 43), "Digging" serves as an *ars poetica* for Heaney.

Heaney's designation of Kavanagh as an immediate literary forebear, one whose example would facilitate or resolve his own crisis of identity, is especially significant. Indeed, Blake Morrison asserts that "[i]f Kavanagh had not existed, Heaney would have had to invent him: he needed the example of an Irish poet through whom he could place himself—and Yeats would not serve."[17] This pronouncement seems somewhat surprising, when we consider Yeats's struggle with the problem of identity. Indeed, we may see Yeats and his successors as participating in a tradition of the crisis of identity. When Yeats's artist father moved the family from Sligo to London in 1873, a Pollexfen aunt told the boy: "You are going to London. Here you are somebody. There you will be nobody at all."[18] Perhaps as a result of this sense of his own difference, the Pre-Raphaelite dreaminess of his early poetry eulogized the bleakly beautiful countryside along the west coast of Ireland: "There midnight's all a glimmer, and noon a purple glow, / And evening full of the linnet's wings."[19] Yeats forsook the English landscapes of Matthew Arnold, resolving the discontinuity between his identity and his locale by celebrating the waterfalls around Sligo and the ancient burial cairn on the hill of Knocknarea, all of which prompted his father to comment: "We [the Yeatses] have ideas and no passions, but by marriage with a Pollexfen we have given a tongue to the sea cliffs."[20] The fledging Irish poet delved subsequently into the rich lore of Cuchulain and the Red

Branch warriors, and immediately recognized in Celtic mythology an alternative to Tennyson's Arthurian narratives and the Icelandic sagas of the thirteenth century. Yeats's determination to recount the deeds of pre-Christian Irish heroes in "Ballad and story, rann and song" ultimately led to the revival of a national literature in Ireland. But helping to create a national consciousness for his homeland did not solve Yeats's personal crisis of identity. In *The King's Threshold* (1904), a play first performed on the evening of 7 October 1903 in Molesworth Hall by the Irish National Theatre Society, Yeats lends dramatic impetus to the poet's plight when his protagonist, Seanchan, starves himself to death on the steps before the palace of King Guaire at Gort. Seanchan seeks to reassert a time-honored protocol: the right of the poet to sit on the king's great council. Dismissed by his sovereign because the "Bishops, Soldiers, and Makers of the Law" felt it beneath their dignity "[f]or a mere man of words to sit amongst them," Seanchan angrily tells the king's chamberlain:

> shake your coat
> Where little jewels gleam on it, and say,
> A herdsman, sitting where the pigs had trampled,
> Made up a song about enchanted kings,
> Who were so finely dressed one fancied them
> All fiery, and women by the churn
> And children by the hearth caught up the song
> And murmured it, until the tailors heard it.[21]

By proxy of Seanchan, Yeats insists that the glittering robes of state are but a crude variation on a theme inaugurated long ago by the "herdsman" poet. But Yeats was already beginning to weary of the unacknowledged legislator's role. In "A Coat," the final poem of his 1914 volume, *Responsibilities*, he repudiates his own part in reawakening Ireland's legendary past, at the same time rebuking those who followed him so blithely into the mist-shrouded Celtic Twilight:

> I made my song a coat
> Covered with embroideries
> Out of old mythologies
> From heel to throat;
> But the fools caught it,
> Wore it in the world's eyes
> As though they'd wrought it.
> Song, let them take it,
> For there's more enterprise
> In walking naked.[22]

However, Yeats never discarded the Romantic concept of the individual's capacity for greatness. As a result, he tended to mythologize his life and the lives of those about him. In "The Wild Swans at Coole," he broods for the first time on the great households of the Protestant Ascendancy, and his *in memoriam* for Lady Gregory's son Robert portrays the young aristocrat as the apotheosis of the Renaissance courtier: "Soldier, scholar, horseman, he, / . . . And all he did done perfectly."[23] But Yeats's crisis of identity far exceeded any need to praise the virtues of his cherished circle of acquaintance. Desiring a unique ordering principle for both his life and his art, he hearkened to William Blake's sturdy admonition: "Create a System or be enslaved by another Man's." Not surprisingly, Yeats's system began to take definitive shape shortly after his marriage to Georgianna Hyde-Lees:

> On the afternoon of October 24th 1917, four days after my marriage, my wife surprised me by attempting automatic writing. What came in disjointed sentences, in almost illegible writing, was so exciting, sometimes so profound, that I persuaded her to give an hour or two day after day to the unknown writer, and after some half-dozen such hours offered to spend what remained of life explaining and piecing together those scattered sentences. "No," was the answer, "we have come to give you metaphors for poetry."[24]

For all its esoteric symbols—the Great Wheel, the interlocking gyres or cones, the Phases of the Moon—*A Vision* was basically a more systematized reworking of certain motifs already present in Yeats's poetry. In *The Identity of Yeats* (1954), Richard Ellmann offers a succinct catalogue of themes arising from the poet's lifelong obsession with the occult:

> There are the cycles, the reincarnating souls, the possible escape from the wheel of time to a timeless state, the millennial reversal of civilizations that corresponds to the rebirth of individuals, the heroic, unconventional ethic, the unknown and problematical god, the battle between the spiritual and material worlds.[25]

According to Ellmann, the "metaphors" or symbols delineated in *A Vision* were the result of decades spent poring over hermetic, theosophical, Cabbalistic, and spiritualist tomes. Yeats not only yearned for participation in a vast imaginative tradition, but he also felt cheated of orthodox religious belief by the triumph of scientific rationalism during the nineteenth century: "I am very religious, and deprived by Huxley and Tyndall, whom I detested, of the simple-minded religion of my childhood, I had made a new religion, almost an infallible church of poetic tradition."[26] In *A Vision*, he conceived a viable matrix for his own visionary aesthetic, and the oracular voice that emerges from *The Tower* (1928) and *The Winding Stair and Other Poems* (1933) has an authority rivaled only by Eliot's *The Waste Land* (1922) and the *Four Quartets* (1944).

Yeats's development of a mythos both singular and comprehensive enabled him to write a poetry of personal transcendence. The "antithetical mask" proved an especially effective device: "for Yeats 'labour' was as much the arduous task, between poems, of remaking over and over again his poetic, imaginative self, as it was concern with rhyme and rhythms."[27] Now he could juxtapose his role as a senator in the Irish Free State Parliament—the "sixty-year-old smiling public man" of "Among Schoolchildren"—against such archetypal figures as "The Wild Old Wicked Man." In the poem "My House," section two of "Meditations in a Time of Civil War," Yeats affirms his place within the larger European culture:

> An ancient bridge, and a more ancient tower,
> A farmhouse that is sheltered by its wall,
> An acre of stony ground,
> Where the symbolic rose can break into flower.[28]

For Yeats, the rose symbolized not only his love for Maude Gonne, but also the mystic union of the masculine element (the cross) and the feminine element (the rose) within the Rosicrucian Order of the Golden Dawn. Personal and occult significations aside, the rose had more universal meanings: it embodied the theme of *carpe diem* in the Renaissance love lyric and suggested also the spiritual hierarchy represented by the tiers of the great Rose in Dante's *Paradiso*. Significantly, it now flourished in the stony soil of his own fiefdom. But the fourteenth-century Norman tower, Thoor Ballylee, became an emblem of adversity, not so much for Yeats's "bodily heirs" as for his literary descendants. Terence Brown offers a concise explanation for this adverse reaction: "Yeats's challenging legacy to [his] successors was a body of verse and a literary career charged with both a sense of the heroic and the romantic."[29] In short, Yeats's visionary poetics severely tested the resources of his imitators, prompting Frank O'Connor to observe that Yeats "had fathered more bad art and literature than any other great writer of his time."[30]

Patrick Kavanagh, in particular, deplored what he believed to be the excesses of the Irish Literary Revival, and he might well have chosen stanza six of Yeats's "The Municipal Gallery Re-Visited" as an apt illustration:

> John Synge, I and Augusta Gregory, thought
> All that we did, all that we said or sang
> Must come from contact with the soil, from that

> Contact everything Antaeus-like grew strong.
> We three alone in modern times had brought
> Everything down to that sole test again,
> Dream of the noble and the beggerman.[31]

Kavanagh's rural background occasioned his repudiation of Yeats and made him an attractive literary influence for Heaney. Born in the village of Inniskeen, County Monaghan, in 1905, Kavanagh grew up on a small farmstead, and spent half his life plowing, planting, reaping crops, and raising livestock to sell at local fairs. He considered the aristocratic image of the heroic Irish peasant fostered by Yeats and Lady Gregory an idyllic absurdity. Moreover, he felt that Synge's rural folk were rustic caricatures whose sprightly idiom lacked the raw vitality of ordinary speech. Kavanagh's realistic and unremittingly bitter long poem, "The Great Hunger" (1942), chronicles the plight of the Irish Catholic peasant: "Clay is the word and clay is the flesh / Where the potato-gatherers like mechanised scarecrows move / Along the side-fall of the hill."[32] His protagonist, Patrick Maguire, depicted as a "man who made a field his bride," eschews his sexual impulse and delays marriage until it is too late. Ironically, he lives out a round of "fourteen-hour day[s]" in a state of perpetual frustration amid the rich fecundity of his fields: "He thinks it is a potato, but we know better / Than his mud-gloved fingers probe in this insensitive hair."[33] Kavanagh's portrait of Maguire would be less likely to unnerve us, were it not for the fact that his character is sixty-five when the narrative begins. Moreover, the aging farmer is the victim of an Oedipal dilemma hardly peculiar to himself: "the peasant in his little acres is tied / To a mother's womb by the wind-toughened navel cord / Like a goat tethered to the stump of a tree."[34] In the person of Maguire's ninety-one-year-old mother, Kavanagh satirizes Yeats's romantic figure of Cathleen ni Houlihan, the wraith-like incarnation of Ireland for whom a peasant youth gladly foregoes his marriage and lays down his life:

> His mother tall hard as a Protestant spire
> Came down the stairs barefoot at the kettle-call
> And talked to her son sharply: "Did you let
> The hens out, you?" She had a venomous drawl
> And a wizened face like moth-eaten leatherette.[35]

Here Kavanagh delivers a wicked counter-thrust to the Revival's romantic pastoralism. "The Great Hunger" is decidedly iconoclastic, and renders almost ridiculous Yeats's sweeping injunction to Irish poets in "Under Ben Bulben": "Sing the peasantry, and then / Hard-riding country gentlemen."[36]

Each evening in his kitchen, Patrick Maguire "sin[s] over the warm ashes," as he desperately attempts to ease a sexual hunger almost spiritual in its intensity. Seamus Heaney, in an essay titled "From Monaghan to the Grand Canal," submits a cogent explanation of Maguire's predicament: "his sense of wonder is calloused by habit so he misses the chance to find 'health and wealth and love' in 'bits and pieces of Everyday'" (*Pr* 125). But Heaney goes further still, and credits Kavanagh with discovering a new vein of consciousness in Irish poetry:

> Kavanagh's proper idiom is free from the intonations typical of the Revival poets. His imagination has not been tutored to "sweeten Ireland's wrong", his ear has not been programmed to retrieve in English the lost music of verse in Irish. The "matter of Ireland", mythic, historical or literary, forms no significant part of his material. . . . Kavanagh forged not so much a conscience as a consciousness for the great majority of his countrymen, crossing the pieties of a rural Catholic sensibility with the *non serviam* of his original personality, raising the inhibited energies of a subculture to the power of a cultural resource. (*Pr* 115–16)

Kavanagh, like Heaney, put aside the spade for the pen, but in doing so he refused the bucolic affectations of the Revival. As Robert Fitzgerald has remarked, Yeats never had his hands in the soil,[37] but from Heaney's perspective it is crucial that Kavanagh did: Kavanagh's writings confirmed Heaney's trust in his own rural ancestry. Moreover, in "The Great Hunger," Kavanagh is "imaginatively possessed by the symbols, rituals and festivals of rural catholicism,"[38] and this is also a telling point of identification for Heaney. On the other hand, Heaney sees Yeats as "[a]n Anglo-Irish Protestant deeply at odds with the mind of Irish Catholic society" (*Pr* 106).

Perhaps because he was born in 1939, the same year that the restless warden of Thoor Ballylee crossed over into Byzantium, Heaney must bear frequent comparison to William Butler Yeats. Although Heaney is doubtless the most famous Irish poet of his generation, with at least one volume, *North* (1975), selling well into the tens of thousands, his basic conception of the artist's role contrasts sharply with the stern equestrian profile Yeats loved to project. The differences run far deeper than Heaney's failure to share Yeats's enthusiasm for *The Courtier* (1528), Castiglione's book of manners aimed at the genteel set: Heaney's inclination to take his metaphors for poetry from what he calls "the locus of the given world" distinguishes him from Yeats with regard to aesthetic philosophy. In his essay "Yeats as an Example?" he introduces a dialogue, a hypothetical exchange wherein he voices his personal objections to Yeats: "Fairies first of all. Then Renaissance courts in Tuscany and Big Houses in Galway. Then

Phases of the Moon and Great Wheels" (*Pr* 101). Heaney not only objects
to the fantastic lore of the Celtic Twilight, but also looks askance at Yeats's
later tendency to celebrate the cultural distance between the aristocratic
Protestant Ascendancy and the Catholic bourgeoisie of the new Free State.
Heaney's allusion to these lines from "Blood and the Moon" is evident: "I
declare this tower is my symbol; I declare / This winding, gyring, spiring
treadmill of a stair is my ancestral stair; / That Goldsmith and the Dean,
Berkeley and Burke have travelled there."[39] When Heaney mentions "Big
Houses in Galway," he reproves Yeats for deliberately forging a pantheon
of Anglo-Irish writers in which he conveniently includes himself. The connection is both specious and self-aggrandizing, the epitome of the equestrian posture struck in the epitaph that Yeats composed a few years before
his death: "Cast a cold eye / On life, on death. / Horseman, pass by." But
Heaney's most ardent censure is reserved for Yeats's occult vision of history:

> Why do we listen to this gullible aesthete rehearsing the delusions of an il-
> literate peasantry, this snobbish hanger-on in country houses mystifying
> the feudal facts of the class system, this charlatan patterning history and
> predicting the future by a mumbo-jumbo of geometry and Ptolomaic as-
> tronomy? (*Pr* 101)

Apocalyptic scenarios based on esoteric symbols in poems such as "The
Second Coming" do not compel Heaney's assent. Closer to his own experience and artistic temperament are these lines from Kavanagh's "The
Great Hunger": "No drama. / That was how his life happened. / No mad
hooves galloping in the sky."[40] Of course, Harold Bloom would contend
that Heaney suffers from the anxiety of Yeats's influence, and subconsciously seeks "a personalized Counter-Sublime, in reaction to the precursor's Sublime."[41] To a certain extent, this is true: much of Heaney's
aesthetic evolves from the *agon* with Yeats, as the younger poet strives to
realize a unique identity. But Heaney's fundamental objection to Yeats
stems from the latter's Neo-Platonism: "Nothing that we love over-much /
Is ponderable to our touch."[42] As Elmer Andrews observes, Heaney taps the
source of imaginative plenitude through direct contact with the empirical
world: "His preoccupation with nature's rich, palpable, organic processes,
with the feel of ooze and ripe fullness leads him through a door into the
dark—into the hidden pre-verbal recesses of being."[43]

Kavanagh's example validated Heaney's profound sense of connectedness to the soil. However, the Ulster poet's desire for an all-encompassing
vision went deeper than his agrarian roots. In "Feeling into Words,"

Heaney extracts a passage from Wordsworth's *Prelude* to clarify his long-ing for a poetry "with the aura and authenticity of archaeological finds, where the buried shard has an importance that is not diminished by the im-portance of the buried city" (*Pr* 41). But here Heaney deceives himself when he draws on Wordsworth: his motive and cue for "poetry as a dig, a dig for finds that end up being plants" actually derives from James Joyce. In his six-hundred page study on Modernism, *The Pound Era* (1971), Hugh Kenner asserts that "a cosmos had altered" the moment German ar-chaeologist Heinrich Schliemann's spade struck a limestone citadel deep in the mound of Hissarlik in April 1870: "'Troy' after Schliemann was no longer a dream, but a place on the map."[44] Indeed, the low promontory in present-day northwest Turkey still overlooks the plain above the glittering Dardanelles, the rumored site of Homer's legendary Troy for over three thousand years. Now, for the first time in our age, heroes of flesh and blood quickened the dactylic hexameter of the *Iliad*. Schliemann's discovery and the artifacts unearthed there brought details of the life Homer described to light, connecting world and word in a way that would have far-reaching ef-fects on modern writers. Kenner cites especially the new premium placed on "particularity" in poetry—the hard, clear, precise images urged by T. E. Hulme and Ezra Pound. Acknowledged or not, Heaney's aesthetic essen-tially derives from this impulse.

The great bastion subsequently unearthed by Wilhelm Dorpfeld on the eastern circuit of Troy VI became a symbol for the primacy of the human spirit in twentieth-century literature—from Yeats's Thoor Ballylee to Joyce's Martello Tower in *Ulysses*. Of course, the Ionian bard's "great tower of Ilion" also presaged the apocalypse in Eliot's *The Waste Land:* "Falling towers / Jerusalem Athens Alexandria / Vienna London." Hence-forth, war would be waged on a scale that would dwarf the Greek confed-eration assembled by Agamemnon on the shores of Asia Minor. But Kenner goes a step beyond Eliot's "historical sense" when he implies that Homer's poetry provides the cornerstone of archaeology as well as West-ern literature. Schliemann took from the rubble at Hissarlik lance heads of "pitiless bronze" (an alloy of copper and tin worried from the rocky terrain at Cyprus), wooden spindle whorls, electrum pins, sixteen thousand bits of gold stitched into a diadem that supposedly adorned the head and shoul-ders of the Spartan queen, Helen. To Kenner, it seems a revelation "to imagine what it might mean to believe that the *Odyssey* was composed by a real person in touch with the living details of real cities, real harbors, real bowls and cups and pins and spoons, real kings, real warriors, real houses."[45] Indeed, he emphasizes that "Joyce's was the archaeologist's Homer":

> During his [Joyce's] young manhood archaeology had been turning Homer
> into just such an organizer of information as the novelist had also become,
> and this Homer . . . presented a world as real as Dublin's bricks.[46]

An extraordinarily talented writer of middle-class origins and Catholic
background, Joyce provided a strong alternative to Yeats for two generations of Irish poets. Although Joyce led an expatriate's life in Trieste,
Zurich, and Paris, he declared a year before the publication of *Ulysses*: "I
always write about Dublin, because if I can get to the heart of Dublin, I can
get to the heart of all the cities of the world. In the particular is contained
the universal."[47] Kavanagh's faith in the parochial as a means of transcending the merely provincial—"a road, a mile of kingdom, I am a king / Of
banks and stones and every blooming thing"—owes much to Joyce:
"Joyce's faithful descriptions of nonpoetic aspects of the city encouraged
Irish poets, urban and rural, to create from the actual details of their own
lives."[48] When Joyce invokes the particular, he has in mind the corporeal
world as opposed to the refining fires of Yeats's "artifice of eternity."
Yeats's Byzantium is not a real city, but an idealized depiction of martyrs
caught up in a blaze of gold leaf on the walls of Hagia Sophia. Like Kavanagh before him, Heaney has a deeper affinity for Joyce than for Yeats.
According to Robert Fitzgerald,

> His [Heaney's] work was and would be incarnational, conceived in an ob-
> jective and substantial world and embodied in forms respectful of it, no
> matter how various with learning and linguistic art the music of the spirit
> might become. For such a writer a good poem can be autotelic and au-
> tonomous only after a manner of speaking, for it owes its life above all to
> the life of men and only necessarily, if you like, to the life of poetry; it is
> utterance and artifact on equal terms.[49]

Heaney's first-person speaker in *Death of a Naturalist* can certainly ex-
trapolate to the marvelous, but he is a thoroughgoing Aristotelian. His
imagination evolves through the succession of its actualizations; hence, his
growth depends on contact with the physical world.

   Joyce's vast permutations with language in *A Portrait of the Artist as a
Young Man* (1916), *Ulysses* (1922), and *Finnegans Wake* (1939) have also
had a powerful impact on Heaney's development as both Irishman and
poet. *A Portrait of the Artist* is first and foremost a history of the evolution
of Stephen Dedalus's mind, an evolution that takes place as his imagination uncovers the nexus between language and the phenomenal world.
Early in the Christmas dinner scene, young Stephen recalls how Protestant

children jeer at the litany of the Blessed Virgin: "*Tower of Ivory*, they used to say, *House of Gold*! How could a woman be a tower of ivory or a house of gold?" Ironically, he brings the metaphors of the litany to life when he conjures the image of a young Protestant girl with whom he is forbidden to play:

> Eileen had long white hands. One evening when playing tig she had put her hands over his eyes: long and white and thin and cold and soft. That was ivory: a cold white thing. That was the meaning of *Tower of Ivory*.[50]

In *Preoccupations*, Heaney remembers his first contact with "words as bearers of history and mystery," and it seems hardly coincidental that he lists, among other things, "the litany of the Blessed Virgin that was part of the enforced poetry in our household: Tower of Gold, Ark of the Covenant, Gate of Heaven, Morning Star" (45). If these lines bespeak a shared Catholic heritage, the nod to Joyce is also unmistakable. Heaney recounts his early tendency to relish the sensual textures of words, an inclination he would refine further with Joyce's influence:

> my mother used to recite lists of affixes and suffixes, and Latin roots, with their English meanings, rhymes that formed part of her schooling in the early part of the century. Maybe it began with the exotic listing on the wireless dial: Stuttgart, Leipzig, Oslo, Hilversum. Maybe it was stirred by the beautiful sprung rhythms of the old BBC weather forecast: Dogger, Rockall, Malin, Shetland, Faroes, Finisterre . . . None of these things were consciously savoured at the time but I think the fact that I still recall them with ease, and can delight in them as verbal music, means that they were bedding the ear with a kind of linguistic hard-core that could be built on some day. (*Pr* 45)

Interestingly, Heaney's mother keeps the "Latin roots" of English words, origins that cannot be severed even by the "curt cuts" of the peat-laborer's spade in "Digging." Moreover, we are tempted to apply a typical Joycean transposition to the final place-name in the "exotic" secular litany on the wireless, thus converting "Hilversum" to "Silverhum." But Heaney's delight in the physical world would ultimately quell any incipient tendency to indulge in what Helen Vendler terms "pure linguistic revel."[51] Like Joyce in *Ulysses*, Heaney is a manipulator of the harmonic relations of language—phonetic, syntactical, and referential—as well as the complex orchestration of associated images:

When they said *Carrickfergus* I could hear
the frosty echo of saltminers' picks.
I imagined it, chambered and glinting,
a township built of light.

("The Singer's House," FW 27)

Joyce once contended that "a lyric is a simple liberation of a rhythm," but Heaney's percussive strokes glean from a Gaelic place-name a "township" reminiscent of Kubla Khan's "pleasure dome with caves of ice." Indeed, Coleridge's splendid edifice is undercut by echoes of a subsistence hard-won from the glinting minerals of the earth. Still, it is important to point out that Heaney's aptitude for defamiliarizing the English of the literary tradition derives not solely from books, but also from the subversive potential of the Northern dialect, which Polly Devlin describes in *All of Us There*:

Almost every sentence we speak contains a word or expression, a twist or a phrase, a rearrangement of order, an irony or a bitterness which gives our speech great potency. . . . The words we use are important. Our antique daily vocabulary seems to hang with more freight and meaning in each sentence than the pale nimble English we hear when we go out of the district to gentler or future places.[52]

Words such as *hoke* ("to root"), *march* ("boundary"), and *prog* ("provender") comprise an idiom to which Heaney has ready access. Speaking of his first encounter with Keats's "To Autumn," he remarks, "I had a vague satisfaction from 'the small gnats mourn / Among the river sallows', which would have been complete if it had been 'midges' mourning among the 'sallies'" (*Pr* 26).

Clearly, Heaney inherited a difficult literary ancestry. Yeats's occult obsessions and the pseudo-history expounded in *A Vision* made him an unlikely role model, the heroic dimensions of his own struggle with the crisis of identity notwithstanding. Moreover, his later condemnation of the Catholic middle class, whom he labeled "paudeens," did not endear him to Heaney. But Joyce presented certain problems, too. In an incisive and somewhat vitriolic article entitled "The Trouble with Seamus," James Simmons remarks of Heaney: "He is very tender of family pieties."[53] To the extent that family and communal life are vital components of his personal and poetic identity, Heaney would doubtless concur with Simmons. His combination of self-effacement and pride in his father's spadework contrasts sharply with Joyce's recapitulation of his own father's talents by proxy of Stephen Dedalus:

—A medical student, an oarsman, a tenor, an amateur actor, a shouting politician, a small landlord, a small investor, a drinker, a good fellow, a storyteller, somebody's secretary, something in a distillery, a taxgatherer, a bankrupt and at present a praiser of his own past.[54]

Joyce believed that he could achieve the requisite objectivity of the artist only by complete detachment from the life of the community; his "*non serviam*," like Stephen Dedalus's, included the ties of family, church, and state. On the contrary, family life proves an integral part of Heaney's early writing; nor is he prone to reject Catholicism or nationality outright. Born and raised in Derry, one of the six Unionist and predominantly Protestant counties in Northern Ireland, Heaney was obliged from the beginning to face a more complex milieu than his Dublin predecessor.

The conflict of origins occurs early in Heaney's history, embodied in his family's farm, located between Castledawson and Toome:

Our farm was called Mossbawn. *Moss,* a Scots word probably carried to Ulster by the Planters, and *bawn,* the name the English colonists gave to their fortified farmhouses. Mossbawn, the planter's house on the bog. Yet in spite of this Ordnance Survey spelling, we pronounced it Moss bann, and *bán* is the Gaelic word for white. . . . In the syllables of my home I see a metaphor of the split culture of Ulster. (*Pr* 35)

Heaney thus describes himself as "symbolically placed between the marks of English influence and the lure of the native experience, between 'the demesne' and 'the bog'" (*Pr* 35). Yet a genuine sense of divisiveness pervades Heaney's experience as well, in the form of the sectarian strife ever-present in the North. Between 1945 and 1951, he attended the nearby primary school at Anahorish, an institution that enrolled both Catholic and Protestant children. There Heaney felt the first tremor of the current Troubles in the terse cadences of taunt-rhymes hurled back and forth between factions on the playground: "'Up the long ladder and down the short rope / To hell with King Billy and God bless the Pope.'"[55] The sectarian violence that erupted in Belfast during the summer of 1969 directly affected his sense of identity, and troubled him deeply even very early in his poetic career. In an interview with Seamus Deane, Heaney reveals that his earliest poems addressed the larger cultural crisis, citing as an example the poem "Docker," which appeared in his first book: "[M]y first attempts to speak, to make verse, faced the Northern sectarian problem." In his early work, however, "the private county Derry childhood part" of his identity over-shadowed "the slightly aggravated young Catholic male part."[56] Indeed, more than most poets, Heaney's poems reflect a search for a personal and cultural identity, an attempt to come to terms with his spiritual, historical, and literary heritage.

Heaney so excelled in his secondary school studies at St. Columb's College, Derry, that he was awarded one of twelve state scholarships available in Northern Ireland, and continued his formal education at Queen's University, Belfast. Despite the fact that the curriculum emphasized British literature to the near exclusion of Irish letters, Heaney ultimately gained from the experience. In a lecture delivered at Oxford University on 23 November 1993, he makes the following acknowledgment:

> there was . . . nothing deleterious to my sense of Irishness in the fact that I grew up in the minority in Northern Ireland and was educated within the dominant British culture. My identity was emphasized rather than eroded by being maintained in such circumstances. (*RP* 202)

If the young Heaney became more open to Irish influences, he also took advantage of what the dominant culture had to offer. As one who sought to define the nature of the poet in the Preface to the second edition of *Lyrical Ballads* (1800), and subsequently undertook to trace the development of a poetic consciousness in the posthumously published *Prelude* (1850), Wordsworth was the perfect model for a young practitioner such as Heaney. Heaney's immediate affinity for Wordsworth's celebration of shepherds, ploughmen, reapers, and fishermen emerges in his own early poems about diviners, thatchers, and blacksmiths: "Witnessing the grace, dignity, and creative energy embodied in such figures, both poets humbly sought an 'objective correlative' for their own artistic purposes [and] spiritual endeavors."[57] Even more important was the perceived corollary between the teeming rural landscape of South Derry and Wordsworth's nineteenth-century Lake District in the region of Cumberland and Westmorland:

> I could record with no reluctant voice
> The woods of autumn, and their hazel bowers
> With milk-white clusters hung; the rod and line,
> True symbol of hope's foolishness, whose strong
> And unreproved enchantment led us on
> By rocks and pools shut out from every star,
> All the green summer, to forlorn cascades
> Among the windings hid of mountain brooks.[58]

Perhaps less sylvan than the environs of Wordsworth's Windermere, Heaney's demesne of flax-dams, salmon streams, and rhyming wells is likewise the product of a sacramental vision. Describing Wordsworth's method of composition in "The Makings of Music," he limns a process similar to his own: "What we are presented with is a version of composition as listening, as a wise passiveness, a surrender to energies that spring within the centre of the mind" (*Pr* 63). Wordsworth's example would also enable Heaney to postpone the inevitable *agon* with Yeats until a more fortuitous time.

Another English poet whose influence Heaney felt even before he left St. Columb's was Gerard Manley Hopkins. Born into a High Church Anglican family at Stratford in Essex, Hopkins, after a period of prolonged spiritual turmoil, converted to Catholicism under the sponsorship of John Henry Newman in 1866. Ordained by the Jesuits in 1877, Hopkins spent much of his remaining life attempting to reconcile his priestly duties with his poetic avocation. That Heaney internalized Hopkins's personal crisis of identity is doubtful, but he definitely came under Hopkins's spell in other ways. Through Hopkins, Heaney first encountered the "principle of individuation" elucidated by the Franciscan philosopher Duns Scotus (1266–1308):

> All medieval philosophers were concerned with how human beings could come to know the universal; Scotus believed that they could do so by apprehending an individual object's essence, which he named its "this-ness" (*haecceitas*); and that such apprehensions and intuitions ultimately reveal God. By directing such intuitions of nature towards God man can perfect his own *haecceitas*, his will.[59]

If Hopkins borrowed from Scotus a doctrine that would allow him to reconcile the objective world with the universal truths of the Church, Heaney caught from Hopkins the "consonantal fire struck by idea off language" (*Pr* 84). The first stanza of "As Kingfishers Catch Fire, Dragonflies Draw Flame" speaks to the essence of every object in the ringing alliterative cadences of Cynewulf:

> As kingfishers catch fire, dragonflies draw flame;
>   As tumbled over rim in roundy wells
>   Stones ring; like each tucked string tells, each hung bell's
> Bow swung finds tongue to fling out broad its name;
>
> Each mortal thing does one thing and the same:
>   Deals out that being indoors each one dwells;
>   Selves—goes itself; *myself* it speaks and spells,
> Crying *What I do is me: for that I came.*[60]

From Hopkins, Heaney learned the meaning of the Old English word for poet, *scop* or "shaper." In "The Fire i' the Flint," Heaney declares: "His [Hopkins's] own music thrusts and throngs and it is forged" (*Pr* 87).

While still in his early twenties, Heaney chanced on Ted Hughes's *Lupercal* (1960) in the Belfast Public Library. Until then, the idea of poetry as a lifetime endeavor had seemed remote from his experience. Hughes's artisanal vigor, the raw vitality hammered into each stanza of his verse, echoed the rich consonantal music of Hopkins. But "View of a Pig" compelled Heaney's interest on yet another level, as he notes in an interview with James Randall:

> in my childhood we'd killed pigs on the farm, and I'd seen pigs shaved, hung up, and so on . . . [S]uddenly, the matter of contemporary poetry was the material of my own life. I had had some notion that modern poetry was far beyond the likes of me—there was Eliot and so on—so I got this thrill out of trusting my own background, and I started about a year later, I think.[61]

Hughes was a virtual contemporary, only nine years older than Heaney; the rude muscularity of his speech and his rural landscapes reinforced the younger man's immediate experience as no other poet since Kavanagh. After graduation from Queen's College, Heaney came under the tutelage of Philip Hobsbaum, a fervent apologist for Hughes since his days at Cambridge. Hobsbaum encouraged Heaney to avoid the mincing syntax and studied gentility of The Movement poets in England, urging Hughes's robust diction and brutal *weltanshauung* as an alternative. Throughout Heaney's career, critics have commented on the similarities between his bogland and Hughes's primeval moors, although the connection is often tenuous and does not extend much beyond Heaney's first few volumes.

To acquire a singular identity through an achieved voice is the ultimate goal of every serious poet. In his first collection, Heaney strives to assimilate his various influences—Kavanagh, Wordsworth, Hopkins, Hughes— even as he shapes an aesthetic identity uniquely his own. Because Heaney traces the development of a poetic consciousness from childhood to young adulthood, Wordsworth emerges as the presiding genius of *Death of a Naturalist* (1966). Indeed, the title poem in its very progression recalls these lines from Book One of *The Prelude*: "Fair seed-time had my soul, and I grew up / Fostered alike by beauty and by fear."[62] In "Death of a Naturalist," Heaney remembers his childhood encounter with a flax-dam that "festered in the heart" of the community. Rank with decaying vegetable matter, each spring the dam seems about to burst the "strong gauze" cerements woven by teeming bluebottles. Despite the unpleasant odor, seductions abound in this place: "There were dragon-flies, spotted butterflies / But best of all was the warm thick slobber / Of frogspawn that grew like clotted water" (*Poems* 5). Here, the speaker dips frogspawn from the pond:

> I would fill jampotfuls of the jellied
> Specks to range on window-sills at home,
> On shelves at school, and wait and watch until
> The fattening dots burst into nimble-
> Swimming tadpoles.

Strategically swollen with plosives, as in "jampotfuls" and "tadpoles," Heaney's alliterative cadences move inexorably from the slow dilation of the eggs to a miniature bang of creation. Evidently the boy's free-ranging imagination intuitively rejects the naturalist doctrine stating that scientific laws are adequate to account for all phenomena. The metamorphosis from "jellied / Specks" to polliwogs appears to be spontaneous, and enables him to contrive his own myth of retribution. He flees, conscience-stricken, when he blunders one day into the presence of adult frogs at the flax-dam:

> Right down the dam gross-bellied frogs were cocked
> On sods; their loose necks pulsed like sails. Some hopped:
> The slap and plop were obscene threats. Some sat
> Poised like mud grenades, their blunt heads farting.
> I sickened, turned and ran. The great slime kings
> Were gathered there for vengeance and I knew
> That if I dipped my hand the spawn would clutch it.
>
> (*Poems* 6)

The tiny galaxies suspended in primal ooze have become a palpable threat. Apparently, delving into these waters was, from the beginning, what Wordsworth termed "an act of stealth / And troubled pleasure." Seeing the spawn's mysterious potential magnified into a fearful potency, the young "naturalist" abandons his trove to the volatile "slime kings." This episode marks Heaney's introduction to the ominous discords of nature; at the same time, it insists upon the tenuous capacity of language to embody and contain those discords. He calls the bullfrogs "mud grenades," raw earth metaphorically charged with the promise of violence and chaos.

Of course, a certain element of pastoral nostalgia underlies Heaney's description of this traumatic childhood incident. Flax-dams were already beginning to disappear in his youth, as E. Estyn Evans described in *Irish Folk Ways* (1957): "All processes are now mechanized apart from a little high-quality hand-loom weaving in Ulster, and very little flax is home-

grown even in the traditional linen districts."[63] The flax-dam, so rich with a
fecundity born of decay, has been effectively displaced in all but Heaney's
memory. Thus the memory of the poet becomes the living memory of a
landscape long since yielded to the posturings of "gross-bellied frogs . . .
cocked / On sods." Although the harlequinesque "slime kings" arise in part
from the psychic depths of a child, "Death of a Naturalist" reminds us of
Heaney's very real affinity for the rhythms of rural life. Its nostalgic setting
and subject matter recall his self-effacement in "Digging," his manifest
pride in the self-sufficiency of his forebears. The grandfather who "cut
more turf in a day / Than any other man on Toner's bog" was even then part
of a dying breed; Evans observed in 1957 that "[s]killed 'slanesmen'
[spademen] are becoming scarce."[64] In "The Barn," also narrated from a
child's point of view, instruments of agrarian toil resemble medieval battle-
tackle in Hrothgar's hall: "The musty dark hoarded an armoury / Of farmyard implements, harness, plough-socks." Awe and curiosity blend, as
tools acquire an almost heraldic gleam in the breathless dark: "A scythe's
edge, a clean spade, a pitch-fork's prongs: / Slowly bright objects formed
when you went in." Once again the boy's sense of well-being is threatened
when nature intrudes on the stronghold of his imagination:

> Then you felt cobwebs clogging up your lungs
>
> And scuttled fast into the sunlit yard.
> And into nights when bats were on the wing
> Over the rafters of sleep, where bright eyes stared
> From piles of grain in corners, fierce, unblinking.
>
> (*Poems* 7)

It must be emphasized that the perspective belongs to a child, not only
when the speaker valorizes the farmyard implements but also when he de-
monizes the inevitable encroachments of nature. Stagnant, dust-choked
webs, homing bats, and fire-eyed rodents may not be conceits of an unschooled intelligence, but the implied danger is exaggerated: "I was chaff /
To be pecked up when birds shot through the air-slits." Heaney conflates
the fearsome gnawers in the dark and the sacked grains of the harvest in the
last line: "The two-lugged sacks moved in like great blind rats." Unfortunately, the pun on "lugged" betrays too much cleverness; moreover, the
earlike projections or lugs fail to complete the metaphoric transition from
bulging granary sacks to outsized rats.

   "An Advancement of Learning" and "Blackberry-Picking" both recount significant "spots of time" wherein the poet's consciousness moves
from childhood towards adolescence. In the first poem, the youthful pro-

THE CRISIS OF IDENTITY

tagonist overcomes his earlier timidity and revulsion in the presence of
vermin by facing down a rat on a narrow bridge. The first two stanzas
appear innocuous, but they set the tone for the ordeal to come:

> The river nosed past,
> Pliable, oil-skinned, wearing
>
> A transfer of gables and sky.
> Hunched over the railing,
> Well away from the road now, I
> Considered the dirty-keeled swans.

(Poems 8)

The river is almost sentient, its waters so oily that reflected images, "gables
and sky," take on a viscous sheen. The "dirty-keeled" swans are a long way
from Coole Park; indeed, were the speaker less visually intent, we might
expect the sort of epiphany experienced by Patrick Kavanagh in the
summer of 1955: "I sat on the bank of the Grand Canal . . . and let the water
lap idly on the shores of my mind. My purpose in life was to have no purpose."[65] Young Heaney is purposive to an unprecedented degree when the
pliant surface of his reverie breaks: "a rat / Slimed out of the water and /
My throat sickened." He establishes an awkward "Bridgehead" (8), refusing to retreat before his enemy: "He trained on me. I stared him out // For-
getting how I used to panic / When his grey brothers scraped and fed"
(Poems 9). Here the boy enacts a significant rite of passage, overcoming
the inchoate fears of childhood; the knob-skulled rat flees, and he crosses
the bridge to a new level of self-awareness.

"Blackberry-Picking" hints at the approach of adolescence, introducing
a rustic version of the carpe diem motif, as Heaney and his companions
plunder brambles popped with ripe clusters during August. The subject
matter becomes more poignant than cheerful if juxtaposed against Evans's
contention that the Great Famine made such fare unpalatable to country-
folk: "So bitter is the folk-memory of these times that useful wild sources
of food are now neglected and despised; for example, wild berries of all
kinds."[66] The lure of forbidden fruit is one thing, a craving for the despised
quite another. Still, "Blackberry-Picking" has sources closer to home for
Heaney than Wordsworth's "Nutting," as evidenced by this brief passage
from Kavanagh's autobiography, The Green Fool:

> Up here the blackberries grew in wonderful abundance, good ones the size
> of big plums. I filled my can to the brim in a short time . . . My bare legs
> were raw with briar scratches . . . My hands were blue with berry-dye and
> my face as well—we used to stain our faces with the first blackberry.[67]

"Blackberry-Picking" is perhaps the most sensual poem in *Death of a Naturalist*. Heaney's youthful protagonist plucks the lush fruit greedily, and the first "glossy purple clot" squelches all misgivings with its intoxicating sweetness:

> You ate that first one and its flesh was sweet
> Like thickened wine: summer's blood was in it
> Leaving stains upon the tongue and lust for
> Picking. Then red ones inked up and that hunger
> Sent us out with milk-cans, pea-tins, jam-pots
> Where briars scratched and wet grass bleached our boots.
>
> (*Poems* 10)

Words such as "flesh," "sweet," "wine," "blood," "tongue," and "lust" connote not only a sacramental joy, but also nascent sexual longing. Heaney mimics the tinkling of sunlit berries in tin cans through the repetition of short *i* sounds. Tactile images link "bramble jam" to libidinal pricklings: "Our hands were peppered / With thorn pricks, our palms sticky as Bluebeard's." But a childhood nemesis reappears, as the wild fruit picked from the tangle of briars in adjoining fields soon falls prey to pestilence and rot: "We hoarded the fresh berries in the byre. / But when the bath was filled we found a fur, / A rat-grey fungus, glutting on our cache." Subconsciously, the poet's youthful imagination inverts the literal value of the adjective-noun combination, "rat-grey," endowing a parasitic mold with a seemingly malign intelligence. The metamorphosis from "fungus" to "rat" gains aural resonance from the participle "glutting." Here enlargement of consciousness is enacted by a vital "interchange between mind and nature."[68] For the first time, Heaney associates mutability with a palpable evil: plucked from its bush, "[t]he fruit fermented, the sweet flesh would turn sour." "Blackberry-Picking" foreshadows both the sensuality and the concern with mutability that pervade his work.

"Death of a Naturalist," "The Barn," "An Advancement of Learning," and "Blackberry-Picking" all relate significant incidents in the growth and development of Heaney's psyche; as such, they comprise a verse *bildungsroman* remarkably similar to Wordsworth's *Prelude*. The identity of the young poet is evolving, still being shaped by day-to-day experience, and only "Blackberry-Picking" deals with ritual or communal behavior. Moreover, form answers content in this poem about random foraging amid bushes and briars, as Heaney makes use of comparatively sprawling verse paragraphs rather than strict stanzaic patterns. But the poet senses firmer footing on cultivated ground. "Follower," for example, consists of six carefully plotted octosyllabic quatrains that illustrate superbly what Auden meant by the "farming of a verse":

> My father worked with a horse-plough,
> His shoulders globed like a full sail strung
> Between the shafts and the furrow.
> The horses strained at his clicking tongue.
>
> An expert. He would set the wing
> And fit the bright steel-pointed sock.
> The sod rolled over without breaking.
> At the headrig, with a single pluck
>
> Of reins, the sweating team turned round
> And back into the land. His eye
> Narrowed and angled at the ground,
> Mapping the furrow exactly.
>
> *(Poems* 14)

The deliberately measured stanzas rhyming *abab*, the adroit play on the Latin *versus* (literally, "turning") in the ninth line, the scintillant arrangement of vowels in "steel-pointed sock": all of these elements converge like neat furrows on a far horizon. If Heaney plods studiously in his father's "hobnailed wake," mingling the plowman's craft with his own, the focus of identity remains twofold. The polished lines and sophisticated linguistic topography also emphasize his schooling in the ancient pastoral tradition handed down from Virgil's *Georgics*. Still, "Follower" is anything but idyllic; it also depicts the boy's initiation into a grueling daily round:

> I wanted to grow up and plough,
> To close one eye, stiffen my arm.
> All I ever did was follow
> In his broad shadow round the farm.
>
> *(Poems* 14)

The plough angling into the earth resembles the gnomon on a sundial; the father shadows it even as the son follows him, marking time. The poem builds on the clockwise motion that derives in part from tradition: "[t]he ploughman . . . turn[s] his horses with the sun, from left to right, to invoke its blessing on the work."[69] But Heaney claims he did not measure up to this ritual labor; indeed, he was always "tripping, falling." Now his father must struggle along after the poem's deftly turned lines: "But today / It is

my father who keeps stumbling / Behind me, and will not go away"
(*Poems* 15). With wry humor, the poet remembers in *Preoccupations* the
widening gap between his interests and those of his father:

> The oil lamp is lit and a neighbour called Hugh Bates is interrupting
> me. "Boys but this Seamus fellow is a great scholar. What book are you
> in now, son?" And my father is likely wringing what he can from the
> moment with "He's as bad as Pat McGuckin this minute." Pat Mc-
> Guckin was a notorious bachelor farmer—a cousin of ours—who was
> said to burn his scone like King Alfred every time he lifted a book. (*Pr*
> 21–22)

Obviously, when Heaney wrote "Follower," he sought to narrow the gap
between his literary efforts and the family's agrarian tradition, to resolve
his own identity through a sense of spiritual and familial kinship. Less
humbly aspiring than the author of "Digging," he paces off his own tract of
ground.

"Mid-Term Break," a brief elegy for a younger brother struck and killed
by an automobile when Heaney himself was only fourteen, dramatizes his
growing crisis of identity perhaps better than any other poem in *Death of a
Naturalist*. A boarder in St. Columb's College, young Heaney senses the
slow encroachment of a funereal atmosphere as he waits sequestered "in
the college sick bay / Counting bells knelling classes to a close." Few lines
in Heaney's *oeuvre* register so emphatically the influence of Hopkins's alliterative prosody. The dolorous homecoming heightens his feelings of estrangement in subtle and unexpected ways: "In the porch I met my father
crying— / He had always taken funerals in his stride— / And Big Jim
Evans saying it was a hard blow." Set apart by his book learning, Seamus
alone is struck by the unintentional albeit cruel double entendre lurking beneath the conventional expression of sympathy. The irony continues to be
situational, until the young scholar mounts the stairway to view his
brother's corpse:

> Next morning I went up into the room. Snowdrops
> And candles soothed the bedside; I saw him
> For the first time in six weeks. Paler now,
>
> Wearing a poppy bruise on his left temple,
> He lay in the four foot box as in his cot.
> No gaudy scars, the bumper knocked him clear.

(Poems 18)

Snowdrops and candles scarcely imply a melting tenderness once Heaney allows himself the dark pun on his sibling's wound. "Poppy" suggests a livid welt that cannot be mollified, but also evokes Morpheus, the Greek god of dreams. Already he perceives the awful power of language both to mar and beatify. Heaney's closure is metronomically concise, almost hypnotic in its effect: "A four foot box, a foot for every year."

"Follower" and "Mid-Term Break" momentarily suspend the family pieties that Simmons claims Heaney so carefully protects. He portrays both parents as vulnerable to the vicissitudes time and misfortune bestow, especially when he evokes his mother's "angry tearless sighs" over the accidental death of her four-year-old. But Heaney usually stresses the positive side of growing up, especially the intimate activities of hearth and home. In "Churning Day," he expounds something ineffable at the heart of rural family life, describing the richest of ritual tasks in minute detail. He begins with surface and texture, as milk curdles in fired clay urns: "A thick crust, coarse-grained as limestone rough-cast, / hardened gradually on top of the four crocks / that stood, large pottery bombs, in the small pantry" (*Poems* 11). In the first line, *k* sounds break up frictionless continuates, specifically *r*, emulating the coarse grain of risen cream. The plosives in line three, *p* and *b*, are swollen with short *o* sounds, giving the brittle crocks a volatile cast. They pout at the brim when Heaney employs a typically Joycean inversion: "Out came the four crocks, s*pi*lled their heavy *lip* / of cream, their white insides." Slowed by commas, syntax accentuates the sensual ooze of such bounty, even as the liquid is tipped into a hooped churn. The poet's mother then takes soundings with the thick wooden staff:

> My mother took first turn, set up rhythms
> that slugged and thumped for hours. Arms ached.
> Hands blistered. Cheeks and clothes were spattered
> with flabby milk.

> Where finally gold flecks
> began to dance. They poured hot water then,
> sterilized a birchwood-bowl
> and little corrugated butter-spades.

> (*Poems* 11)

Torpid *u* sounds in "slugged and thumped" become an earnest conjuration, and the milk quickens into a "yellow curd" that Heaney glosses as "coagulated sunlight." The butter congeals in voiced stops, "*g*ilded *g*ravel," an alchemy compounded of patience and toil. Heaney then adorns the finished product with a familial and cultural imprimatur: butter "in soft printed slabs was piled on pantry shelves" (*Poems* 12). In *Irish Folk Ways*, Evans states that butter-prints were once hand-carved, and he offers an illustration of one bearing a rye head cut deep as any hieroglyph.[70] Interestingly, "The Butter-Print," a poem written thirty years after "Churning Day," opens with these two lines: "Who carved on the butter-print's round open face / A cross-hatched head of rye, all jags and bristles?" (*SL* 53). In "Churning Day," the meticulously carved stamp confers identity; it is the one aesthetic gesture in a process that begins with "the hot brewery of gland, cud and udder" and culminates in "soft printed slabs." It validates the tradition of self-sufficiency and familial containment that Heaney holds dear:

> And in the house we moved with gravid ease,
> our brains turned crystals full of clean deal churns,
> the plash and gurgle of the sour-breathed milk,
> the pat and slap of small spades on wet lumps.
>
> (*Poems* 12)

As Henry Hart notes, the word "gravid" derives from the Latin *gravis*, meaning "heavy," and also from *gravidus*, or "pregnant":

> A sense of grace pervades the house, conjoined with a sense of gravity, of the heavy weight of the world that submits to human shape only after strenuous labor. The making of a child, the making of butter, the making of a culture, or the making of a poem are one for Heaney. Anxiety is purged in the pain of labor, although the splendor of the final artifact never occludes the memory of its arduous process.[71]

No less a partisan of Heaney's work than Philip Hobsbaum labels his aural technique in "Churning Day" a sort of "Heaney-speak," a mannerism highly susceptible to parody. Nothing could be further from the truth. Hobsbaum ignores the subtle modulation of phonetic and visual imagery, the Joycean particularity that emerges in this poem. Like Joyce, Heaney trusts the mystery to arise from the commonplace, transmuting "gold flecks" to light incarnate.

The most accomplished poems in *Death of a Naturalist* focus on the poet's quest for identity in terms of personal, familial, and cultural experience. As Heaney seeks to recover the numinous moments of childhood and first youth, he turns to agrarian objects once near at hand—spades, plows, churns, scythes, pitchforks—investing them with a significance both local and universal. He thus restores to timeworn pastoral emblems the gleam of actual use. But what of national identity, the inevitable pitfall of the Irish writer who spurns expatriatism as an easy solution to centuries of abuse and exploitation? Rather than blithely consolidate his early success by rehearsing the theme of personal growth and development to the exclusion of all others, Heaney confronts the matter of Ireland in "At a Potato Digging" and "For the Commander of the 'Eliza.'" Both poems deal with the Great Famine of 1845–49, which accounted for the deaths of one million people and the eventual immigration of an additional one and a half million. The historian Cecil Woodham-Smith states that the population of Ireland between 1779 and 1841 increased by an astounding 172 percent because of the simple cultivation and abundant yield of the annual potato crop:

> [T]here was an abundant supply of incredibly cheap food, easily obtained, in the potato, and the standard of living of the time was such that a diet of potatoes was no great hardship. With the addition of milk or buttermilk potatoes form a scientifically satisfactory diet, as the physique of the pre-famine Irish proved. Arthur Young contrasted the Irishman's potato diet favourably with the contemporary English labourer's bread and cheese. [72]

The fungus *Phytophtora infestus*, shipped from America in a dank hold stocked with infected tubers, destroyed the staple of Irish life in September 1845. Occasionally potatoes festered in the drills, but more often the crop went bad after harvesting: "fine-looking tubers had become a stinking mass of corruption."[73] Heaney begins "At a Potato Digging" with the chilling image of contemporary laborers descending on the long drills:

> A mechanical digger wrecks the drill,
> Spins up a dark shower of roots and mould.
> Labourers swarm in behind, stoop to fill
> Wicker creels. Fingers go dead in the cold.
>
> Like crows attacking crow-black fields, they stretch
> A higgledy line from hedge to headland.
>
> (*Poems* 21)

Heaney grafts his opening lines to Kavanagh's "The Great Hunger"; however, the potato gatherers that the older poet once likened to "mechanised scarecrows" have been supplanted by "a mechanical digger." A hint of foreboding lingers in the word "mould," and certain locutions, such as "swarm," imply infestation. Indeed, the laborers become winged scavengers in stanza two, a metaphorical blight potentially as ominous as the "rat-grey fungus" of "Blackberry-Picking." Heaney surpasses Kavanagh in bitterness when the rituals and festivals of rural Catholicism that provided Patrick McGuire with occasional solace give way to numb obeisance: "Processional stooping through the turf // Recurs mindlessly as autumn. Centuries / Of fear and homage to the famine god." In section two, Heaney describes the potatoes as "knobbed and slit-eyed tubers" consigned to the cold clay: "To be piled in pits; live skulls, blind-eyed." A terrible resurrection occurs in section three:

> Live skulls, blind-eyed, balanced on
> wild higgledy skeletons
> scoured the land in 'forty-five,
> wolfed the blighted root and died.
>
> (*Poems* 22)

Heaney brings a mad hilarity, born of sheer despair, to this loose-jointed *danse macabre*. Each syllable of the Irish colloquialism, "higgledy," articulates the specter of starvation, recalling the living skeletons with skin stretched thin as parchment in 1845. It also harks back to the first application of "higgledy" in section one, thus suggesting that the whole countryside still moves to the footloose and frantic rhythms of the famine years: "A people hungering from birth, / grubbing, like plants, in the bitch earth, / were grafted with a great sorrow." In section four, Heaney returns to the present, a time of comparative plenty. The workers take "Brown bread and tea" for lunch, but remember the former seasons of dearth and hunger with a placating gesture: "Then, stretched on the faithless ground, spill / Libations of cold tea, scatter crusts" (*Poems* 23). The poem marks Heaney's first attempt to extract a vital myth from a national tragedy. In light of historic events, he sees the potato as a *memento mori* peculiar to his native soil. Firmly rooted in the matter of Ireland, "At a Potato Digging" foreshadows the vast excavations of *North*.

Heaney also bases "For the Commander of the 'Eliza'" on an incident that took place during the Great Famine, citing as his epigraph a passage from Cecil Woodham-Smith. The poem relates how the commander of a British revenue cutter patrolling off the coast of West Mayo refused aid to a boatload of starving refugees, placing obedience to Whitehall above human necessity. Heaney's persona strives for the detached reportage typical of a ship's log ("I tacked and hailed the crew / in Gaelic"), but his official intonation breaks down when he recalls the abject horror of the moment:

> O my sweet Christ,
> We saw piled in the bottom of their craft

> Six grown men with gaping mouths and eyes
> Bursting the sockets like spring onions in drills.
> Six wrecks of bone and pallid, tautened skin.
>
> (*Poems* 24)

The speaker and his men, aware of the food shortage but well-fed themselves, are shocked by the apparition:

> understand my feelings, and the men's,
> Who had no mandate to relieve distress
> Since relief was then available in Westport—
> Though clearly these poor brutes would never make it.
>
> (*Poems* 24)

The refugees react violently to being refused food, which ostensibly allows the commander to rationalize his decision: "I saw they were / Violent and without hope." He adheres to policy and "clear[s] off": "Less incidents the better." Yet the experience continues to haunt him:

> Next day, like six bad smells, those living skulls
> Drifted through the dark of bunks and hatches
> And once in port I exorcised my ship
> Reporting all to the Inspector General.
>
> (*Poems* 25)

The Inspector-General of the Coastguard Service, Sir James Dombrain, responds with direct and immediate action, as the commander relates: "Sir James, I understand, urged free relief / For famine victims in the Westport Sector / And earned tart reprimand from good Whitehall" (*Poems* 25). Apparently, Sir Randolph Routh, senior officer of the Commissariat in Dublin, considered Dombrain's sympathy for the natives' plight a nuisance to sound government:

> Sir James Dombrain, Inspector-General of the Coastguard Service, who had served on relief during the famine of 1839 . . . "very inconveniently", wrote Routh, "interfered." He "prevailed" on an officer at the Westport depot to issue meal, which he gave away free; he also "prevailed" on the captain of the Government steamship, *Rhadamanthus*, to take 100 tons of meal, intended for Westport, to the Coastguard Station at the Killeries. "The Coast Guard with all their zeal and activity are too lavish," wrote Routh to Trevalyan.[74]

Though Heaney leaves us to determine for ourselves whether the commander of the *Eliza* was aware of Sir James's humanitarian instincts prior to making his report, we must ask if the commander is merely trying to assuage his conscience for refusing immediate aid to the desperate men in the rowboat. Certainly, he dehumanizes them, describing their lingering presence in his imagination as "six bad smells" to be eventually "exorcised." However, Heaney clarifies the commander's true feelings through yet more subtle phrasing. Although his report procures an ultimate good, something the persona of this dramatic monologue wishes us to understand, he actually seeks to absolve himself of any responsibility for the wretched men who rowed out to his ship. His earlier invocation, "O my sweet Christ," dwindles to pure cant, as Heaney suggests in the poem's ambiguous closure:

> Let natives prosper by their own exertions;
> Who could not swim might go ahead and sink.
> "The Coast Guard with their zeal and activity
> Are too lavish" were the words, I think.
>
> (*Poems* 25)

Do the words "Let natives prosper by their own exertions" belong solely to the commander or to Whitehall? In this context, it is impossible to determine, though subsequent lines reveal the exact words of British officials, as the speaker is able to recall them. The axiom "sink or swim" is strictly metaphorical in most contexts, but here it is peculiarly appropriate to the persona's state of mind. Like the speaker of Browning's "My Last Duchess," he stands convicted out of his own mouth. We cannot mistake Heaney's aggrieved identification with the Irish refugees, but much of his anger is subsumed by his approach. "For the Commander of the 'Eliza,'" as Elmer Andrews has noted, "relies on its controlling ironic mode to contain the indignation of the aggravated young Catholic poet, and this prevents the poem from bleeding off into tendentious polemic."[75]

In "Docker," written years before the 1969 outbreak of sectarian strife in Belfast, Heaney satirizes a Unionist shipyard foreman:

> That fist would drop a hammer on a Catholic—
> Oh yes, that kind of thing could start again;
> The only Roman collar he tolerates
> Smiles all round his sleek pint of porter.
>
> (*Poems* 30)

The poet taps the subject of trouble long brewing with alarming prescience. What seems a cunningly benign image—the foaming porter likened to a "Roman collar" with a play on "choler"—leaves a bitter aftertaste when we consider subsequent events. Michael Parker refers to Heaney's Protestant docker as "a Unionist cousin" of the callow, brutal miner in Ted Hughes's "Her Husband."[76] Indeed, both poets depict a man who is prone to domestic violence, and Heaney occasionally adopts the obdurate rhythms of Hughes: "Mosaic imperatives bang home like rivets." But the resemblance remains superficial. Hughes's "Thistles" and "The Warriors of the North," both about the Viking presence in Iron Age England, are the poems that actually provide Heaney with metaphors for the current Troubles in Ireland. Heaney's need to comprehend the violence between Protestant and Catholic factions will be central to his crisis of identity at mid-career. "Docker" anticipates, however obliquely, the concerns of the future.

The love lyrics near the end of *Death of a Naturalist* imply a progression toward full sexual maturity and adulthood. In "Lovers on Aran," Heaney blurs the metaphorical boundaries of self, comparing sexual union to the sea carving out an imposing headland: "Did sea define the land or land the sea? / Each drew new meaning from the waves' collision. / Sea broke on land to full identity." In "Scaffolding," he compares the heady ramparts of romantic love to a temporary structure:

> Masons, when they start upon a building,
> Are careful to test out the scaffolding;
>
> Make sure that planks won't slip at busy points,
> Secure all ladders, tighten bolted joints.
>
> And yet all this comes down when the job's done
> Showing off walls of sure and solid stone.
>
> So if, my dear, there sometimes seem to be
> Old bridges breaking between you and me
>
> Never fear. We may let the scaffolds fall
> Confident that we have built our wall.
>
> *(Poems 38)*

Perhaps the analogue between lovers and the careful craftsman bespeaks a meditated emotion, a detachment inappropriate to the love lyric. For the young poet in Heaney, however, the lofty rhetoric of Yeats's "old high way of love" is a platform for courtship, and more properly belongs to the *Breton lai* of the fifteenth century. Heaney's architectonic metaphor in "Scaffolding" conjoins tenor and vehicle in a manner reminiscent of Donne, Herrick, Herbert, and other Metaphysical poets. He foregoes his

penchant for sensuality, opting instead for an introspection unusual in a
man still in his twenties, though Buttel calls Heaney's early love poems
"undistinguished," while Simmons labels them "stiff and priggish, an em-
barrassment."[77] Simmons, at least, would probably prefer the Confessional
excesses of John Berryman.

Heaney closes *Death of a Naturalist* with "Personal Helicon," a return
to childhood obsessions, but also a synoptic glimpse into the future:

> As a child, they could not keep me from wells
> And old pumps with buckets and windlasses.
> I loved the dark drop, the trapped sky, the smells
> Of waterweed, fungus and dank moss.
>
> (*Poems* 40)

In *Preoccupations*, Heaney remarks of the earlier "Digging": "This was
the first place where I felt I had done more than make an arrangement of
words: I felt that I had let down a shaft into real life" (41). The well, so
prominent in Celtic history and lore, now becomes Heaney's subterranean
bastion, a sunken stronghold more ancient than Thoor Ballylee. Just as
Schliemann's Troy disgorged innumerable artifacts, sacred waters in Ireland have relinquished golden torcs, intricately wrought brooches, bronze
fibulae, spear ferrules, and linked bridle bits, usually intended as votive of-
ferings.[78] Heaney's compulsion to delve downward into the earth will
eventually lead to the bogs and fens of *North*, those repositories of racial
and cultural memory. But in the first four stanzas of "Personal Helicon," he
is content to recall and savor the rank odors of strange ferns and mosses, to
listen for the "rich crash" of a plummeting bucket like a bell tone at ves-
pers. He remembers the richness of sumps, "A shallow one under a dry
stone ditch / Fructified like any aquarium," as well as the pristine redound-
ings of deeper shafts: "Others had echoes, gave back your own call / With
a clean new music in it." Heaney concludes his "Personal Helicon" with an
eloquent disclaimer:

> Now, to pry into roots, to finger slime,
> To stare, big-eyed Narcissus, into some spring
> Is beneath all adult dignity. I rhyme
> To see myself, to set the darkness echoing.
>
> (*Poems* 40)

The poet puts aside the narcissistic impressions of childhood that confuse
the insubstantial mirror-image with a corporeal presence. No longer inertly

receptive, his mind is an active agent capable of locating the subtler boundaries between subject and object. To "rhyme," here a metonym for poetry
as opposed to aural mimesis, is to probe the depths of the racial unconscious through the rapt inflections of language.

Commenting on Heaney's second collection, *Door into the Dark*,
Thomas Foster states that it "has proven troublesome for critics, since it is
neither a clear beginning nor an arrival."[79] While many of the agrarian
themes prominent in the first book are rehearsed from a strictly adult perspective, Heaney foregrounds the search for identity in poems that equate
the artist with the artisan of pre-industrial cultures. Moreover, the confrontation with Yeats intensifies. "The Forge" begins where "Personal Helicon" left off:

> All I know is a door into the dark.
> Outside, old axles and iron hoops rusting;
> Inside, the hammered anvil's short-pitched ring,
> The unpredictable fantail of sparks
> Or hiss when a new shoe toughens in water.
> The anvil must be somewhere in the centre,
> Horned as a unicorn, at one end square,
> Set there immoveable: an altar
> Where he expends himself in shape and music.
> Sometimes, leather-aproned, hairs in his nose,
> He leans out on the jamb, recalls a clatter
> Of hoofs where traffic is flashing in rows;
> Then grunts and goes in, with a slam and flick
> To beat real iron out, to work the bellows.
>
> (*Poems* 49)

Earlier on, Heaney acknowledged his debt to the "short-pitched" consonantal music of Hopkins and Hughes, but he also claimed this terse idiom
as intrinsically his own: "[T]he Ulster accent is generally a staccato consonantal one. Our tongue strikes the tangent of the consonant rather more
than it rolls the circle of the vowel" (*Pr* 45). On the one hand, the "unpre-
dictable fantail of sparks" links the sonnet to the "golden birds" forged in
the smithies of Yeats's Byzantine emperor. On the other, Heaney's black-
smith scorns to deal in intricate adornment, preferring the sibilant "hiss" of
incandescent iron cooling out of its element to a new hardness. But Heaney
gropes too insistently after the mysterious when he asserts that the anvil or
"altar" is "Horned as a unicorn." Such a horn is helix-shaped, its baroque
spiral more nearly resembling the Yeatsian cornucopia or "Horn of Plenty."
The simile is simply too precious to be mimetically effective. Hence, "the

centre" where the smith so lavishly expends himself will not hold. Because of one strained image, Heaney fails in his first direct *agon* with Yeats. The "bellows" that his smith works intimates but faintly the Minotaur that stirs at the heart of every genuine craftsman's labyrinth.

A far more successful poem, "Thatcher" portrays an Old World craftsman whose ostensible "Midas touch" evolves from an orthodoxy or system become anachronistic in the present century. Keeper of his own "bag of knives" and "well-honed blades," he represents the last holdout against the commodity fetishism so prevalent in an age of mass production:

> Bespoke for weeks, he turned up some morning
> Unexpectedly, his bicycle slung
> With a light ladder and a bag of knives.
> He eyed the old rigging, poked at the eaves,
>
> Opened and handled sheaves of lashed wheat-straw.
> Next, the bundled rods: hazel and willow
> Were flicked for weight, twisted in case they'd snap.
> It seemed he spent the morning warming up.

> *(Poems* 50)

Right away Heaney sets the tone, striking a balance between the thatcher's cumbersome baggage and the lightness with which he carries it in the half-chime of *morning / slung*. He infuses verbs with tactile vigor, telescoping "eyed" into "poked" through parallel structure. Indeed, Heaney achieves complete empathy with his subject by bestowing on words the same sedulous care that the thatcher extends to his materials. The past participle "lashed," for example, reinforces and invigorates the aspirate quality of "wheat-straw." By blending fricatives and aspirates with stops, as in "willow," "flicked," "twisted," Heaney tests the fiber of language, just as the thatcher tries each rod for pliability and strength. But all of this is prelude for a converging harmony:

> Then fixed the ladder, laid out well-honed blades
> And snipped at straw and sharpened ends of rods
> That, bent in two, made a white-pronged staple
> For pinning down his world, handful by handful.
>
> Couchant for days on sods above the rafters,
> He shaved and flushed the butts, stitched all together
> Into a sloped honeycomb, a stubble patch,
> And left them gaping at his Midas touch.

> *(Poems* 50)

The final touch might be best described as spellbinding. Heaney compares the thatch to a "honeycomb"—both organic and symmetrical, it is like a bee's waxwork mosaic, each cell charged with langorous honey. The echo is Frostian, reasserting his famous maxim from "Mowing": "The fact is the sweetest dream that labor knows." Moreover, Heaney has fashioned a splendid Counter-Sublime to the mandarin metalworkers of Yeats's "Sailing to Byzantium" and "Byzantium."

Heaney's need to identify with a national myth at this point in his career materializes in the poem "Requiem for the Croppies." A piece commemorating peasant insurrectionists who died in the rebellion touched off by the promise of French landings at Killala in 1798, "Requiem" anticipates his later concern with political and sectarian strife in Northern Ireland. According to Heaney,

> "Requiem for the Croppies" . . . was written in 1966 when most poets in Ireland were straining to celebrate the anniversary of the 1916 Rising. . . . I did not realize at the time that the original heraldic murderous encounter between Protestant yeoman and Catholic rebel was to be initiated again in the summer of 1969, in Belfast, two months after the book was published. (*Pr* 56)

Ironically, he chooses a variation of the sonnet, a form appropriated from the Italian and ultimately perfected in English by renowned proponents of the Empire such as Sir Philip Sidney and Edmund Spenser:

> The pockets of our greatcoats full of barley—
> No kitchens on the run, no striking camp—
> We moved quick and sudden in our own country.
> The priest lay behind ditches with the tramp.
> A people, hardly marching—on the hike—
> We found new tactics happening each day:
> We'd cut through reins and rider with the pike
> And stampede cattle into infantry,
> Then retreat through hedges where cavalry must be thrown.
> Until, on Vinegar Hill, the fatal conclave.
> Terraced thousands died, shaking scythes at cannon.
> The hillside blushed, soaked in our broken wave.
> They buried us without shroud or coffin
> And in August the barley grew up out of the grave.
>
> (*Poems* 54)

What is most astonishing is the way in which Heaney employs a stock device taken from the Elizabethan sonnet—the martial metaphor—and transforms it into a consummate expression of organic form. The scythes that the rebellious farmers brandish at Loyalist militia and British troops are not only weapons, but also standards of battle, emblems of an agrarian culture. Mowed down by grapeshot manufactured in English industrial towns, the rebels become human compost nourishing a crop unwittingly sown by their conquerors. In the last line, Heaney equates insurrection with resurrection, as the barley hoists a spiky memorial to the dead. Of course, Yeats proclaimed prior to the protracted Somme offensive in 1916 that only poems celebrating the "joy of combat" constituted a valid engagement with the subject of war. Heaney, well-acquainted with Wilfred Owen's verse and Yeats's adamant condemnation of the young officer's often realistic approach, almost certainly had the Irish laureate in mind when he wrote "Requiem for the Croppies."

Heaney closes *Door into the Dark* with "Bogland," broaching a vast tract of psychic terrain only hinted at in "Digging." The poem begins by conceding the lack of a cultural myth commensurate to that of the American West: "We have no prairies / To slice a big sun at evening." But the negation is momentary, and Heaney almost immediately posits the bog as a potential defining myth for Ireland:

> They've taken the skeleton
> Of the Great Irish Elk
> Out of the peat, set it up
> An astounding crate full of air.
>
> Butter sunk under
> More than a hundred years
> Was recovered salty and white.
> The ground itself is kind, black butter
>
> Melting and opening underfoot,
> Missing its last definition
> By millions of years.
>
> (*Poems* 85)

Extinct native fauna, "the Great Irish Elk" dwarfs the American bison, and belongs more to the realm of paleontology than living memory. Yet Heaney's personal recollection of the vaulted rib cage and enormous span of antlers proves intrinsically communal: "[W]hen I was at school the skeleton of an elk had been taken out of a bog nearby and a few of our neighbours had got their photographs in the paper, peering out across its antlers" (*Pr* 54). We should not be surprised, therefore, that when Heaney shifts to archaeology, he offers us the most domestic and ostensibly perishable of artifacts, "the yellow curd" of "Churning Day." Indeed, the ground itself is both pliant and nurturing, a "kind, black butter":

> They'll never dig coal here,
>
> Only the waterlogged trunks
> Of great firs, soft as pulp.
> Our pioneers keep striking
> Inwards and downwards,
>
> Every layer they strip
> Seems camped on before.
> The bogholes might be Atlantic seepage.
> The wet centre is bottomless.

(Poems 85–86)

The coal that fueled the British industrial revolution will never be culled from the bogs, although peat has sustained the "creatural existence" of the Irish hearth for centuries:

> I have sat at fires which, it was claimed, had not been allowed to go out for over a century, or for as far back as family memory could go. It is to the fireside seat that the visitor is invited, for this is the place of honour, and it is around the fire that tales of old time are told. The magic of the open fire, playing upon the fancies of generations who have gathered round it, has engendered a host of beliefs and portents. The fire can give warning of wind and weather, of lucky and unlucky visitors, of marriage and death. Above all, it is a shrine to which ancestral spirits return, a link with the living past.[80]

It seems altogether appropriate that the bogs stoke Heaney's imagination; however, a significant departure also occurs. Heaney dares to go back beyond tribal memory to the source of the racial unconscious. The peat bog becomes both graveyard and reliquary, a repository not only for Celtic artifacts but also for the turbulent pre-Christian civilizations of northwestern Europe. Later poems such as "The Tollund Man," "Bog Queen," "Grauballe Man," "Punishment," and "Kinship" will emerge from Heaney's "answering myth," a myth based on empirical fact rather than the occult machinations of Yeats's Great Wheel. If the "wet centre is bottomless," it also holds up to archaeological scrutiny. With "Bogland," Heaney makes his first decisive move in the *agon* with Yeats, "reclaiming the bogs both as a subject for poetry and as a central metaphor that will organize that poetry."[81]

In his early career, then, Heaney struggles to develop his own identity, seeking to understand and reconcile a number of conflicts both personal and cultural: his own divergence from his family's tradition of rural labor, the sense of dividedness between English and native influences in his own environment, divisiveness between Irish Protestants and Catholics (ignited once again shortly after the publication of *Door into the Dark*), and his reluctance to emulate without qualification the literary predecessors of his native land. On a personal level, his "inability" to follow in his ancestors' path as a rural laborer occasioned certain feelings of guilt and discomfort about writing, as he acknowledged in 1981:

> there is indeed some part of me that is entirely unimpressed by the activity, that doesn't dislike it, but it's the generations, I suppose, of rural ancestors—not illiterate, but not literary. They in me, or I through them, don't give a damn.[82]

Death of a Naturalist and *Door into the Dark* reflect Heaney's attempts to resolve such discontinuities, to assuage the attendant feelings of discomfort, and to justify his chosen avocation. Poems such as "Digging," "Follower," "Churning Day," and "Thatcher," with their affinities for the rhythms of rural life, their celebrations of his biological forebears, and their identification with skilled craftsmen, reveal a profound desire for spiritual and familial kinship, a yearning which pervades Heaney's poetry throughout his entire career. Yet that longing is expressed equally in "At a Potato Digging," "For the Commander of the 'Eliza,'" and "Requiem for the Croppies," poems that confront the brutal reality of Ireland's past, as Heaney seeks "to contain the aggravation of the young Catholic male, and to understand the historic deprivation of his people in more fundamental terms than those offered by the particular momentary strategies of politics."[83] Heaney's determination to derive his metaphors for poetry from the locus of the given world represents a resolve to be true to his own experience as well as his own gifts, to "dig" with whatever tool is best fitted to his talents. Thus, at this point in his career, he rejects what he considers the excesses of Yeats—the romantic pastoralism of the Celtic Twilight, the occult vision of history, the aristocratic tendency to romanticize the peasant, and, of course, Neoplatonism. Heaney opts instead for a more archaeological approach, seeking the particularity and precise imagery espoused by Joyce and other Modernists. After "Requiem for the Croppies," his task becomes "a search for images and symbols adequate to our predicament" (*Pr* 56), a longing to develop, through poetry, his own myth of Irish national identity.

2
Heaney's Response to the Troubles:
History, Myth, and the Bog Poems

Before Seamus Heaney's *Wintering Out* and *North*, the bogs of Ireland were scarcely a subject for poetry, much less a central or organizing metaphor. For Yeats, bogs were merely an incidental part of the Irish landscape, mentioned only in passing in the title poem of *The Tower* (1928), when drunken men venture out in search of a young beauty, "A peasant girl commended by a song." The quest has tragic consequences:

> But they mistook the brightness of the moon
> For the prosaic light of day—
> Music had driven their wits astray—
> And one was drowned in the great bog of Cloone.[1]

Not surprisingly, Yeats's bog recedes almost immediately after the inebriated wanderer is swallowed in its mire. Perhaps this fact, among others, prompted Denis Donoghue to comment that Yeats "invented another country, calling it Ireland."[2] Four and a half decades after *The Tower*, the bog emerges in the work of Seamus Heaney as a viable subject for poetry, a fecund source of cultural identity. In Heaney's bog poems, as Elmer Andrews notes, "'the mythical and the mystical spring naturally out of the mundane and the colloquial.'"[3] Within fifty years, the bog moves from backdrop to foreground: indeed, in Heaney's crisis of identity, the bog takes the position of dominant metaphor. Just as Yeats's mysterious "instructors" provided him with "metaphors for poetry," the waterlogged turf first visited in "Bogland" would afford Heaney access to the "images and symbols adequate to our predicament."

55

When Heaney has recourse to the phrase "our predicament," he refers specifically to the current Troubles that began in earnest after the Protestant "siege" of Bogside (Derry) in August 1969, an incident that resulted in the British government sending troops to Northern Ireland. Although the army's avowed purpose was to protect the Catholic minority in Ulster from attacks by Protestant gangs, the Provisional faction of the I.R.A. "exploited military insensitivity in order to redirect Catholics' indignation from their Protestant neighbours towards Britain and its 'army of occupation.'"[4] Anglophobia peaked among Catholics in the aftermath of "Bloody Sunday," 30 January 1972, when thirteen people were killed by British soldiers stationed in Derry. The victims were Civil Rights Association marchers who called for the elimination of anti-Catholic discrimination in local government, housing, and employment. As a result, Whitehall immediately imposed "Direct Rule," serving only to intensify the I.R.A.'s "Brits out" policy with regard to the six counties of Northern Ireland. The ensuing twenty-five years of sectarian strife in Ulster, referred to by Heaney as "our predicament," comes ominously to life in a brief vignette from *Preoccupations*:

> Everywhere soldiers with cocked guns are watching you—that's what they're here for—on the streets, at the corners of streets, from doorways, over the puddles on demolished sites. At night, jeeps and armoured cars groan past without lights; or road-blocks are thrown up, and once again it's delays measured in hours, searches and signings among the guns and torches. As you drive away, you bump over ramps that are specially designed to wreck you at speed and maybe get a glimpse of a couple of youths with hands on their heads being frisked on the far side of the road. Just routine. Meanwhile up in the troubled estates street-lights are gone, accommodating all the better the night-sights of sniper and marksman.
>
> If it is not army blocks, it is vigilantes. They are very efficiently organized, with barricades of new wood and watchmen's huts and tea rotas, protecting the territories. If I go round the corner at ten o'clock to the cigarette machine or the chip shop, there are the gentlemen with flashlights, of mature years and determined mien, who will want to know my business. (*Pr* 30–31)

In his description of a Belfast neighborhood less turbulent than most, Heaney foregoes eloquence, yet succinctly conveys the common misery of its citizens. The crisis of identity endemic to the time and place cannot be fixed by the narrow beam of a battery-packed torch flicked on at various checkpoints; signatures and searches seldom confirm anything other than mutual distrust. Caught between the violence of the Provisional I.R.A. and

Protestant paramilitary groups such as the Ulster Volunteer Force, Heaney is necessarily obliged to ponder the personal and cultural polarities of Catholic and Protestant, Republican and Unionist, native Celt and Anglo-Saxon. Like Yeats before him, Heaney pursues cultural continuity along mythic lines; however, he continues to derive his metaphors from the empirical world rather than occult or legendary sources.

The poems in the three volumes delineating the early middle phase of Heaney's career—*Wintering Out, Stations,* and *North*—tend to foreground the search for identity within a larger cultural milieu. Heaney wrests from the mire of the peat-bogs in Jutland an Iron Age corpse bearing mute testimony to centuries of ritual violence in northwest Europe. "The Tollund Man," the watershed poem of *Wintering Out,* is a harsh depiction of ritual sacrifice to the cult of a pre-Christian Germanic earth goddess, Nerthus. As Heaney has remarked in an interview with James Randall, when he first happened on the human face preserved in the umber-brown seepage of Tollund Fen in central Denmark, the experience was sobering: "The Tollund Man seemed to me like an ancestor almost, one of my old uncles, one of those moustached archaic faces you used to meet all over the Irish countryside."[5] For the poet, the boneless and leathery faces photographically reproduced in P. V. Glob's *The Bog People* (1969) resembled death masks displayed in a family shrine dating back several millennia. According to Glob, archaeological evidence for the violent propensities of the cultures of northwest Europe emanates not only from bogs in Denmark and Ireland, but also from the fens and marshes of England, Scotland, Wales, Norway, and Sweden.[6] Thus, the title for Heaney's fifth collection, *North,* becomes the central metaphor for an age-old racial violence extending from pre-Christian Scandinavia to contemporary Belfast.

Heaney's *agon* with Yeats looms large in *Wintering Out* and *North,* as he embraces an aesthetic methodology ostensibly similar to his predecessor's. In "Myth and Motherland," Richard Kearney divulges the more laudable underpinnings of Yeats's Celtic mythos:

> Yeats' recourse to the legendary images of Celtic mythology may be interpreted as an attempt to make peace between the opposing interests of class, creed and language. It was a plea for a cultural *continuity* based on a homogenous Ancient Irish Sect which *preceded* all contemporary disputes. In its way, it was a plea for Tone's ideal of a common Irish tradition embracing "Protestant, Catholic and Dissenter."[7]

Yeats's determination to forge a national identity for Ireland depended on a vicarious return to the legendary past. Much as Heaney would later be inspired by P. V. Glob, Yeats nurtured an enthusiasm for Standish O'Grady's

History of Ireland: Critical and Philosophical (1881), in which the author urged the cultural importance of "Cuchulain and Emain Macha" over "Brian Boru and Kincora." Indeed, O'Grady contends that heroic legends embody "the ambition and ideals of the people and, in this respect, have a value far beyond the tale of actual events and duly recorded deeds, which are no more history than a skeleton is a man."[8] By reembroidering the legends of the Red Branch warriors for the Abbey Theatre, Yeats provided a badly needed forum for an Irish national literature and also supplied an answering myth to Tennyson's Arthurian romance. Yeats's poetry and drama enabled his countrymen to recover the vision of a uniquely Irish culture, and for this reason he is justly celebrated as Ireland's foremost poet of decolonization. But was Cuchulain too idealized a figure to serve as a "befitting emblem of adversity"? According to E. Estyn Evans in *The Personality of Ireland* (1973), "There is a deep conviction, in this far western isle, that man has fallen from grace, that the golden age lies in the past, and that national glory can be restored to an imaginary state of purity if men act like the heroes of their legends."[9] More than a few of the young men who joined the Easter Rebellion of 1916 saw themselves as reenacting Cuchulain's fateful stand at the Gap of the North. Yeats acknowledges as much by proxy of the choral singer who rings down the curtain on *The Death of Cuchulain* (1939):

> What stood in the Post Office
> With Pearse and Connolly?
> What comes out of the mountain
> Where men first shed their blood?
> Who thought Cuchulain till it seemed
> He stood where they had stood?[10]

As a heroic ideal stressing Irish identity and cultural continuity, Cuchulain eventually proved too stubbornly ethnocentric. Indeed, Evans goes so far as to ascribe the factional temper of Ireland today to the glamorized violence of the Ulster Cycle:

> The north thus tended to form a distinct cultural region or group of regions, behind its frontier belt of drumlins and, if we can believe the heroic tales, its leaders—the Men of Ulster—were prepared to defend it to the end against the Men of Ireland. In the words attributed to the Ulster warriors: "We will hold our ground though the earth should split under us and the sky above on us." Fragmentation, regional rivalries and the resultant tensions have contributed a great deal to the character of Ireland.[11]

Initially appropriated by the Catholic lower-middle-class as a role model for opposing British imperialism, Yeats's Cuchulain now serves as the hallowed archetype for a Protestant paramilitary group known as the Ulster Defence Association. In fact, the U.D.A. has pledged to demolish the Cuchulain statue in the Dublin G.P.O., should the Irish Republic's army ever cross the border into Northern Ireland.[12] Ironically, Yeats's original desire to develop a national identity that would result in cultural continuity has since degenerated into the slogan "Six into Twenty-six won't go."

Yeats's determination to employ his gift for mythopoeia on behalf of Ireland was commendable in itself, but the ultimate failure of the Revival to shore up the fragmented society may have been inevitable. His ambivalence toward certain of his countrymen emerges in a letter to Katharine Tynan, even as he waxes eloquent on the possibilities of a national literature:

> Irish Catholics among whom had been born so many political martyrs had not the good taste, the household courtesy and decency of the Protestant Ireland I had known, yet Protestant Ireland seemed to think of nothing but getting on in the world. I thought we might bring the halves together if we had a national literature that made Ireland beautiful in the memory, and yet had been freed from provincialism by an exacting criticism, a European pose.[13]

The aristocratic hauteur that characterized Yeats's later career appears to be present already. Moreover, if we look closely at the source of his inspiration, we see that the Ulster Cycle is even more narrowly concerned with the upper strata of society than later Anglo-Norman literature. Heroic poetry always underscores the values of the ruling class. Yeats's obsession with the "great men" theory of history and myth caused him to exalt the individual at the expense of the cultural norm. On the other hand, Heaney's mythic North shuns the bardic ideal in favor of an approach that hews closer to documented history and the archaeological record. The Vikings of "North" and "Viking Dublin: Trial Pieces" are "neighbourly, scoretaking / killers, haggers / and hagglers, gombeen-men." Olaf Tryggvason and Harald "Bluetooth" never once don chain mail byrnies or boar-crested helmets; indeed, they never appear. Unlike Yeats, who plucks fabulous tales of Conchubar and Cuchulain from the incorporeal air, Heaney emphasizes the role that the Ostmen (Dublin Vikings) played as colonizers and traders, basing his poems on the archaeological digs at Wood Quay: "[E]xcavators found a number of wooden vessels, textiles, bronze pins, pieces of ironwork, bone combs, and coins of Dublin minting from both the Viking and the Norman periods."[14] In contrast to Yeats's Ulstermen, the Vikings were among the most easily assimilated peoples in European history:

> So evident is the similarity of the Viking and old Celtic designs that a person with no impressions of Celtic art beyond those acquired from seeing the more frequently reproduced pages of old manuscripts would detect it.[15]

In the eighth, ninth, and tenth centuries, the Viking influence included not only Ireland and England, but also extended from the Jutland peninsula to the Byzantine Empire. Here is the "European pose," a synthesis of diverse cultures, which Yeats sought in bardic legend, and which Heaney fully realizes by resorting to "the locus of the given world." In the title poem of *North*, the longship's "swimming tongue" tells Heaney to "trust the feel of what nubbed treasure / your hands have known." For Heaney, mythopoeic vision begins with empirical truth: "archaeological researches yield evidence even more trustworthy than that of written chronicle, while the ground itself . . . is the fullest and most certain of documents."[16]

Inspired by P. V. Glob's archaeological discoveries, Heaney concocts a Counter-Sublime not only to Yeats's Cuchulain, but also to his Cathleen ni Houlihan, the "indigenous territorial numen" of Ireland, who appears on the eve of the 1798 French landings at Killala in the theater production that bears her name. According to Yeats, his play was the result of a dream as distinct as a vision: "She was Ireland herself, that Cathleen ni Houlihan for whom so many songs have been sung and about whom so many stories have been told and for whose sake so many have gone to their death."[17] In the guise of the Poor Old Woman, the apparition lures the peasant youth Michael into her service on the eve of his wedding. She lives in the hope of "[g]etting my beautiful fields back" and "putting the strangers out of my house,"[18] demanding nothing less than than the life's blood of Ireland's young men before she can become once again "a young girl" with "the walk of a queen."[19] A fertility figure, she is the embodiment of the land to which the ancient Celtic chieftains felt bound in a symbolic marriage. But she proves always as ethereal as Yeats's dream, an insular spirit mired in the political disputes that Heaney wishes to transcend. His Tollund Man and Grauballe Man, however, arise from the bogs of Central Jutland, tangible victims of the earth goddess Nerthus, who is several times mentioned in Tacitus's *Germania*. Subjected to radiocarbon dating and found to be over two thousand years old, the Iron Age bog corpses belong to a tribal memory that includes all the peoples of northwest Europe. Resisting the heroic dimensions of Yeats's Cathleen ni Houlihan, Heaney devises a counter-myth of ritual sacrifice revealing not only "beauty and atrocity" but also the timeless burden of hooded victims "slashed and dumped" (*Poems* 191). In *Transitions: Narratives in Modern Irish Culture,* Richard Kearney remarks: "If the bog [in Heaney's poetry] becomes a symbol of national consciousness, it is not in the manner of an insular, self-righteous nationalism."[20] On the contrary, Heaney equates continuity with psychic affinities more ancient than medieval Christendom, as the bogs become a metaphor for the racial unconscious that joins Ireland to a pagan milieu.

Yeats endeavored to redeem Ireland from the contingencies of a difficult history, but his failure to present his homeland with an enduring national myth can be traced back to his idealism. At once mystical and wonderfully primitive, his Cuchulain achieved cult status during the Revival. However, admiration for the folk idol led to riots at the Abbey Theatre when J. M. Synge's *Playboy of the Western World* (1907) exposed the credulity of a debilitated society for whom the heroic ideal was a cultural mainstay. Declan Kiberd views Synge's Christy as a reaction to the height of the Revival, a sly caricature of the Cuchulain myth:

> For Synge, as for James Connolly, the worship of past heroes was nothing other than an evasion of present mediocrity; and his play uncompromisingly suggests that the cult of Cuchulain, or of anyone else for that matter, is more a confession of impotence than a spur to self-respect.[21]

The same crowd that vigorously applauded Cathleen ni Houlihan as an icon of Irish political martyrdom bridled at a play that held up before their gaze "the cracked lookingglass of a servant."[22] As Synge's *Playboy* demonstrates, certain Irish writers realized well before the end of the Revival that the ideal mythical figure had outlived its usefulness. Synge, Joyce, and others thus shifted to a verisimilitude much more viable and authentic in the modern world, if less palatable to the masses. Irish writers in the latter half of the twentieth century followed suit, and Seamus Heaney is probably the most singular example. Grounded in the real world, Heaney's bog victims and scoretaking Norsemen reflect both past and present in a hard light: "report us fairly, / how we slaughter / for the common good" ("Kinship," *Poems* 200). Heaney offers various images of a culture in crisis, and his explanation for Ireland's current dilemma involves an adroit coupling of history and myth. The picture is not a pretty one, nor is it meant to be. Critics who would accuse Heaney of mistaking his private ills for public evils need only glimpse the gutted taverns and boarded-up shop-fronts of Belfast. In both *Wintering Out* and *North,* Heaney's crisis of identity evolves primarily from a fragmented society.

Heaney's determination to challenge Yeats notwithstanding, Joyce emerges as the tutelary spirit of *Wintering Out.* In *Ulysses,* Stephen Dedalus declares his own crisis of identity to a fellow inmate of the Martello tower: "I am a servant of two masters . . . an English and an Italian." When Haines, an Englishman, queries Dedalus about servitude to Italy, Stephen minces few words: "The imperial British state . . . and the holy Roman catholic and apostolic church."[23] While Heaney continues to be less bitter than Joyce about Catholicism, much of the poetry in *Wintering Out* chafes at the yoke of British imperialism and the Protestant Ascendancy. Always attuned to aural nuance, Heaney begins to explore etymologies with the intention of consolidating Irish tradition and subverting British dominance. Moreover, the archaeological impulse acquired from Joyce remains paramount: "Etymology, in Heaney's hands, lays bare the poetic fossil within the linguistic ore."[24] By delving into the history and origins of words, Heaney makes good his initial promise in "Digging."

In *Wintering Out*, Heaney revives the traditional *dinnseanchas*, short Celtic poems or brief anecdotes that "relate the original meanings of place-names and constitute a form of mythical etymology" *(Pr* 131). Many *dinnseanchas* are embedded in the *Táin*, the most famous one resulting from a single combat between the white-horned bull of Ai plain, Finnbennach, and the dark bull of Cualigne, Dub. The brown bull gores the white one, and wanders the countryside with entrails on his horns: "He drank at Ath Luain, and left Finnbennach's loins there—that is how the place was named Ath Luain, the Ford of the Loins."[25] Heaney opts for less spectacular effects. The title of "Anahorish" derives from the Gaelic *Anach Fhior Uisce*, and means "the place of clear water":

> My "place of clear water,"
> the first hill in the world
> where springs washed into
> the shiny grass
>
> and darkened cobbles
> in the bed of the lane.
> *Anahorish*, soft gradient
> of consonant, vowel-meadow,
>
> after-image of lamps
> swung through the yards
> on winter evenings.
> With pails and barrows
>
> those mound-dwellers
> go waist-deep in mist
> to break the light ice
> at wells and dunghills.
>
> *(Poems* 94)

The first six lines imply a prelapsarian grace, a pristine harmony that echoes Dylan Thomas's "Fern Hill." But when Heaney invokes the actual name, the aspirate *h* in "Anahorish" unleashes clear water like a pump. We see a vaporous light moving through mist, and it leads us back to the original inhabitants of the land, ancient "mound-dwellers" who fracture thin cataracts of ice that separate past and present. Heaney not only reclaims a vigorous landscape, he also awakens the primordial music of consonant and vowel in this place. Of course, "Anahorish" is an Anglicized version of the Gaelic original, but the word prompts Heaney to enact in verse the essential crisis of being located "between 'the demesne' and 'the bog.'" In *The Poetry of Resistance*, Sidney Burris points out the subversive potential of "Anahorish":

> In a poem such as "Anahorish," Heaney imagines that the name itself possesses ineffable powers of cultural sovereignty. Irish place-names in the United Kingdom become for Heaney subversive incantations that both glorify his Celtic lineage and establish its integrity in British Northern Ireland. The poem dexterously appropriates a landscape politically British in its legal demarcation but linguistically Irish in its nomenclature.[26]

Even more phonetically precise than "Anahorish," "Toome" betrays undertones of the turbulence prevalent in Northern Ireland. Heaney begins by deftly enunciating hollow velar sounds that resemble subterranean thunder: "My mouth holds round / the soft blastings, / *Toome, Toome*." But the ominous tremors have more to do with intonation than detonation: "under the dislodged // slab of the tongue / I push into a souterrain." Like limestone rough-cut and tenuously fitted, the tongue in its cavern gives way to a hoard of archaeological relics:

> prospecting what [is] new
> in a hundred centuries'
>
> loam, flints, musket-balls,
> fragmented ware,
> torcs and fish-bones
> till I am sleeved in
>
> alluvial mud that shelves
> suddenly under
> bogwater and tributaries,
> and elvers tail my hair.

> (*Poems* 104)

Embedded flints glitter in the dark soil: some lit neolithic bonfires; others ignited the powder trains of eighteenth-century muzzle-loaders. In the tomblike hand-hewn cave, fish-bones mingle like delicate filigree with Viking torcs hammered out of Bulgar gold. An underground chamber first constructed in Ireland during the late Bronze Age (1000–500 B.C.), Heaney's souterrain has been a cache for the plunder of medieval sea-brigands and a munitions dump for Wolfe Tone's United Irishmen.[27] By speaking the word *Toome*, Heaney takes soundings that yield artifacts from the long and diverse history of Ireland. Moreover, the particularity of his imagery lends impetus to the poem's epic sweep. "Elvers" (immature eels) spring from "alluvial mud," giving the speaker a gorgonlike aspect, the semblance of ancient godhead. According to Anne Ross's *Pagan Celtic Britain* (1967), the Celts of both England and Ireland "seem truly to have venerated a 'god head,' and they imbued the 'tête coupée' with all the qualities and powers most admired and desired by them—fertility, prophecy, hospitality, wisdom and healing."[28] Dislodged with one push in "Toome," the "slab of the tongue" reveals the arcane heritage of Europe's northwestern islands, and proves as resonant an image as the "starlit Stonehenge" of Thomas Hardy's "Channel Firing." Heaney thus devises a mythic etymology and recovers a vibrant cultural identity common to all factions in the North.

Elsewhere, Heaney resurrects an aural dimension of poetry that embodies his variant of Eliot's "auditory imagination": "that feeling for word and syllable reaching down below the ordinary levels of language, uniting the primitive and civilized associations words have accrued" (*Pr* 81). In "Gifts of Rain," he sifts through the detritus of alluvial waters, letting the river Moyola speak its own name:

> The tawny guttural water
> spells itself: Moyola
> is its own score and consort,
>
> bedding the locale
> in the utterance,
> reed music, an old chanter
>
> breathing its mists
> through vowels and history.

(Poems 103)

Heaney plays the vowel notes in "Moyola," "score," and "consort" off glottal stops, conjuring "reed music" older than any bone-whistle or flute.

Untold generations have been drawn to its "antediluvian lore." Indeed, Heaney claims that the river "spells" or enchants itself, a bit of double-en- tendre reminiscent of Joyce in *Finnegans Wake*. In the title poem of *Station Island* (1984), he will describe Joyce's words as "cunning, narcotic, mimic," a voice "eddying with the vowels of all rivers." Like the Dublin expatriate, Heaney craves primordial song, an elemental harmony prior to the strictly referential qualities of language. Yet "Gifts of Rain" retains a local flavor, inasmuch as the Moyola River runs through the county of Heaney's origins. In an interview with Seamus Deane, the poet explains how the place-name poems of *Wintering Out* momentarily assuaged his personal crisis of identity, resolving his sense of conflicting or divided ori- gins:

> I had a great sense of release as they were being written, a joy and devil- may-careness, and that convinced me that one could be faithful to the nature of the English language—for in some senses these poems are erotic mouth-music by and out of the anglo-saxon tongue—and, at the same time, be faithful to one's own non-English origin, for me that is County Derry.[29]

But Heaney's variations on the *dinnseanchas*, once so vital to the Celtic literary tradition, provide only a temporary respite from the cultural dis- continuities of Ulster. Educated in a public school system that privileged *Beowulf* over the *Táin*, Heaney laments the routing of Gaelic vowels by the consonantal harshness of English in the first section of "Traditions":

> Our guttural muse
> was bulled long ago
> by the alliterative tradition,
> her uvula grows
>
> vestigial, forgotten
> like the coccyx
> or a Brigid's Cross
> yellowing in some outhouse.
>
> (*Poems* 109)

The supple, lambent flow of the Gaelic vowel or "guttural muse" has been quelled in the throat. Moreover, Heaney implies that the "uvula," the pen- dant lobe of flesh in the soft palate, is now "vestigial," an atrophied organ of speech. He compares the fading of the Gaelic language to a St. Brigid's Cross "yellowing" in a byre. Significantly, Brigid was an Irish-born saint, and her crosses took the form of lozenges or swastikas woven from rushes uprooted, but not cut. The intricately wrought charms were believed "to protect the house and the livestock from harm and fire."[30] That these pastoral talismans eventually failed to work on either the local or national level is manifest in the sarcastic tone of section two:

> We are to be proud
> of our Elizabethan English:
> "varsity," for example,
> is grass-roots stuff with us;
>
> we "deem" or we "allow"
> when we suppose
> and some cherished archaisms
> are correct Shakespearean.
>
> (*Poems* 109)

Of course, the spoken English of the "sovereign mistress," Elizabeth I, could hardly be "grass-roots" for a people who plaited the St. Brigid's Cross from rushes rooted in native soil. Heaney goes on to relate how maligned the Irish actually were Shakespeare's day:

> MacMorris, gallivanting
> round the Globe, whinged
> to courtier and groundling
> who had heard tell of us
>
> as going very bare
> of learning, as wild hares,
> as anatomies of death:
> "What ish my nation?"
>
> (*Poems* 110)

Perhaps the original stage Irishman, MacMorris exclaims against his own country in act 3, scene 2 of *Henry V*: "What ish my nation? Ish a villain and a bastard, and a knave, and a rascal!"[31] Heaney's closure answers the question of nationality through another literary character, Joyce's Leopold Bloom: "much / later, the wandering Bloom / replied, 'Ireland,' said Bloom, / 'I was born here. Ireland.'" Bloom, however, is a complex figure, plagued by his own crisis of identity. Gently ostracized by friends at Paddy Dignam's funeral in the Glasnevin chapter of *Ulysses*, he later suffers outright verbal abuse from a coterie of drunken blackguards in Barney Kiernan's pub. Because of his Jewish ancestry, Bloom is interrogated about his nationality:

—What is your nation if I may ask? says the citizen.
—Ireland, says Bloom. I was born here. Ireland.
   The citizen said nothing only cleared the spit out of his gullet and, gob, he spat a Red bank oyster out of him right in the corner.[32]

Perverse and inarticulate, the "citizen" summons the pith of corruption from his gullet at the idea of Bloom's claiming Irishness. He is the embittered product of Tudor incursions, a twentieth-century victim of Elizabeth's Act of Uniformity "[that] enforced English by means of the church onto a largely uncomprehending and resentful Gaelic population."[33] We need not wonder why Heaney mourns the passing of the "guttural muse" in "Traditions." Like Joyce's Bloom, Heaney must continue to endure the cultural fragmentation that inevitably resulted from British colonialism.

Heaney rarely relies on Joyce, however; rather, he assembles his own company of outcasts in *Wintering Out*. In poems such as "Servant Boy" and "The Last Mummer," his heightened sense of Ireland's tumultuous history compels him to identify with victims of poverty and dispossession. Following the death of Elizabeth Tudor, the English government proceeded in 1610 with its scheme for the plantation of the six Ulster counties. Original Irish owners of the land were driven out and Scottish Presbyterian grantees put in their place. Penal laws imposed on Catholics after the resounding defeat of the Irish Jacobites by William of Orange at the Boyne in July 1690 established a self-perpetuating Protestant elite, especially in Northern Ireland. Under these laws, Catholics were barred from service in the army and navy; moreover, they were forbidden to practice law or to occupy any civic position. Catholics could not vote, hold office under the Crown, or purchase land. They were denied the privilege of attending school either at home or abroad; to make matters worse, the Catholic Mass was officially proscribed.[34] "Servant Boy" is set in the eighteenth century, the halcyon years of the Protestant manor houses whose decline Yeats eulogizes in his later works:

> He is wintering out
> the back-end of a bad year,
> swinging a hurricane-lamp
> through some outhouse;

a jobber among shadows.
Old work-whore, slave-
blood, who stepped fair-hills
under each bidder's eye.

                                                            (*Poems* 95)

Heaney derives the volume's title from the first line, a phrase limned by
Michael Parker in *Seamus Heaney: The Making of the Poet*: "In Ulster, the
verb 'to winter out' means to see through and survive a crisis, and is derived from a farming custom which involved taking cattle to a sheltered
area, feeding them on a minimum diet throughout the winter, before fatten-
ing them in the spring and summer."[35] Heaney's protagonist, displaced
from the land by the plantation system, must muddle through the fallow
season as best he can. Unable to pay his rent during the winter, he hires out
as a menial on one of the large estates. Heaney turns the language of the
dominant class in the form of the Old English kenning to his advantage,
applying epithets like "work-whore" and "slave-blood" to an individual
who maintains a carefully nurtured composure in the face of adversity.
Indeed, Heaney admires the youth's ability to remain patient and keep his
own counsel:

                                    how
            you draw me into
            your trail. Your trail

            broken from haggard to stable,
            a straggle of fodder
            stiffened on snow,
            comes first-footing

            the back doors of the little
            barons: resentful
            and impenitent,
            carrying the warm eggs.

                                                            (*Poems* 95)

Despite the tenuous footing, the young man brings the eggs in his charge
safely to the back door. It is a fragile peace that he keeps. Warm, embryonic, symbolic of regeneration, the eggs belong to the "little barons," but
also represent a pastoral mode of existence essential to the disenfranchised
people of the region. Heaney intuits his own crisis of identity in that of the
"jobber among shadows." Overt polemics scarcely touch the poem, al-

though it serves as an appropriate analogue to the strained atmosphere in Northern Ireland during recent decades.

In "The Last Mummer," Heaney explores the fate of another outcast, one whose situation even more closely parallels his own. The word "mummer" is Danish in origin, and designates a person "wearing a mask." Typically, mummers in both England and Ireland belong to acting troupes, and their performances are confined to Christmas and the New Year:

> Another Christmas custom that has survived into our own time is the Mummers, known in Antrim and Derry as the Christmas Rhymers, or Christmas Boys. Young men used to take part in the plays, but in recent years the mummers have been little boys. The "play" concerns the mock-battle, "death," and resurrection of a hero, sometimes called St. George, sometimes St. Patrick. The words are traditional and the boys dress in old clothes and wear false faces. It is often supposed that this custom is a debased survival of the English miracle play, but E. R. R. Green suggests that it is a survival of an agricultural fertility ceremony of pagan times.[36]

In Hardy's *The Return of the Native*, a novel that profoundly influenced Heaney's literary aspirations, the connection between mummer and poet is underscored when the hump-backed Father Christmas opens the performance with these lines: "Make room, make room, my gallant boys, / And give us space to rhyme."[37] Heaney's mummer carries a herdsman's ashplant under his arm, an indication of his status as a celebrant of pastoral rites. He is elderly and dishevelled, the lone survivor of an itinerant trade. On an evening thick with fog and mist, he "pads up the terrace" of a slate-roofed Ascendancy manor, only to discover that "The luminous screen in the corner / has them charmed in a ring." The mummer cannot suppress his contempt for these people bathed in the cathode rays of a television set:

> St. George, Beelzebub, and Jack Straw
>
> can't be conjured from mist.
> He catches the stick in his fist
>
> and, shrouded, starts beating
> the bars of the gate.
>
> (Poems 96)

There is precious little music in those bars, and the first section ends as he stalks off down the lane: "His boots crack the road. The stone / clatters down off the slates." In section two, Heaney describes the mummer not only as the keeper of ritual, but also as a master of rhetoric and invention. A man obliged to improvise his honor from day to day, he has spent his life treading a narrow way between the factions of caste and creed: "He came trammelled / in the taboos of the country // picking a nice way through / the long toils of blood" (*Poems* 97). Like the poet, the mummer is a protean figure, embodying reality and illusion: "His straw mask and hunch were fabulous // disappearing beyond the lamplit / slabs of a yard." Section three begins with a cricket's treble piped from the hearth, as Heaney dreams a procession of mummers filing out the door. But the lamp flares in the draft, and the poet's reverie dissolves:

> Melted snow off their feet
>
> leaves you in peace.
> Again an old year dies
>
> on your hearthstone, for good luck.
> The moon's host elevated
>
> in a monstrance of holly trees,
> he makes dark tracks, who had
>
> untousled a first dewy path
> into the summer grazing.
>
> (*Poems* 97–98)

The eucharistic moon invokes both the ritual and communal significance of the mummer's visit. The metaphor is Dionysian, combining pagan and Christian elements; moreover, it conveys Heaney's nostalgia for the vatic role of the poet. For Heaney, the poet seems as much an anachronism in contemporary society as his solitary mummer. "The Last Mummer" dramatizes the artist's growing isolation from the larger culture.

In "The Other Side," Heaney deals on a personal level with the cultural crisis in Northern Ireland. Reminiscent of the poetry in *Death of a Naturalist*, his approach involves a return to his rural childhood where "a neighbour laid his shadow / on the stream, vouching // 'It's poor as Lazarus, that ground.'" An austere Protestant, the farmer ironically stands "thigh-deep in sedge and marigolds," and resorts to a religious aphorism to express an unsolicited critique of his Catholic neighbor's field. Heaney puns on the observation, calling it a "biblical dis*missal*, / that tongue of chosen people" (italics mine). Not without affection, he recalls how the brooding follower of Calvinist doctrine unconsciously flew his own colors: "*white*-haired, / swinging his *black*thorn" (italics mine). But a bitter truth underlies the old farmer's words: after the Battle of the Boyne, land settlements in Ireland invariably favored the Williamite Protestants.[38] In section two, only Heaney's wry sense of humor deflates a situation potentially taut as the Orange drums that annually celebrate the Protestant victory in 1690:

> For days we would rehearse
> each patriarchal dictum:
> Lazarus, the Pharoah, Solomon
>
> and David and Goliath rolled
> magnificently, like loads of hay
> too big for our small lanes,
>
> or faltered on a rut—
> "Your side of the house, I believe,
> hardly rule by the Book at all."
>
> (*Poems* 113)

He and his siblings view the old gentleman's patriarchal dicta as loads of hay too cumbersome for their memories. When the neighbor opines that Catholics place overmuch emphasis on salvation within the hierarchy of grace, the young Heaney privately wonders at his counterpart's ability to interpret scripture according to an infallible inner light: "His brain was a whitewashed kitchen / hung with texts, swept tidy / as the body o' the kirk." However jocular the repartee, antipathies do exist. But an abrupt turn occurs in section three. The Protestant neighbor, perhaps lonely in spite of his prosperous acres, stops by in the evening. Heaney confides that "the rosary was dragging / mournfully on in the kitchen," and yet the neighbor maintains a respectful silence throughout the seemingly interminable recitation: "not until after the litany / would the knock come to the door." The poet observes, while unobserved himself, the caller's awkwardness:

> Should I slip away, I wonder,
> or go up and touch his shoulder
> and talk about the weather
>
> or the price of grass-seed?
>
> (*Poems* 114)

Heaney's portrayal of the relations between Catholic and Protestant in a rural Derry setting is both sensitive and effective. Neither side dares to broach the myriad political issues that divide Northern Ireland along sectarian lines. A certain mutual respect appears evident, but conversation about the weather or grass-seed is clearly meant to hold in abeyance more volatile topics.

Although Heaney's rural Protestant in "The Other Side" is by no means as splenetive as his urban counterpart in "Docker," the tension that characterizes the fragmented Ulster province prevails throughout the poem. That Heaney chooses to vent his concern about sectarian divisions by focusing on a neighbor proves crucial to the question of identity. In an essay titled "Place, Pastness, Poems: A Triptych," published in a special issue of *Salmagundi*, he addresses religio-political conflict and his own crisis of identity in archaeological terms:

> The contemplation of such things emphasises the truth of that stunningly simple definition of our human neighbor offered by the old school catechism. "My neighbor," the catechism declared, "is all mankind." So I think of my mesolithic Ulster neighbor, and of his flint flakes, flint spears and arrowheads which were found in abundance at New Ferry on the River Bann during the drainage of the river in the early part of the century. Seeing these on display in the Ulster Museum in Belfast once gave me a vision of those first hunters among the reeds and bushes at the lower end of our parish and I thought of them not as having disappeared but as being at one with the farmers and clayworkers and fishermen and duck-shooters who were the geniuses of the place when I first got to know it. And that time scale, that double sense of great closeness and great distance, subtly called into question the factual and sectarian divisions which are and have long been pervasive in that part of the country. I do not say that a sense of the mesolithic ancestor could solve the religio-political conflicts of the Bann Valley but I do say that it could significantly widen the terms of the answer which each side could give to the question, "Who do you think you are?"[39]

The potential resolution to Heaney's crisis of identity, the answer to the question "Who do you think you are," once again evolves from the locus of the given world. Just beyond the bevelled glass set in the museum case, the flint arrowheads and meticulously flaked spear tips of the Mesolithic period point to a common ancestry for all the current inhabitants of Ulster. The poet envisions a Stone Age hunter chipping an arrowhead, and sparks leap as he discovers a new ballistics slumbering in the core of igneous rock. Of course, Heaney cannot say with impunity whether the shard of serrated stone will serve primarily as a tool for hunting or a weapon for tribal warfare. But he has a literal touchstone for imagining the original "geniuses of the place" as virtual contemporaries, people with the capacity for "neighbourly murder" who also faced a daily choice. The Tollund Man, however, would provide Heaney with his primary archaeological metaphor for sectarian violence in Northern Ireland.

P. V. Glob's narrative about an Iron Age bog corpse recovered in May 1950, as evening was gathering on Tollund Fen in the Bjaeldskov Valley of Denmark, struck resonances in Heaney's imagination similar to those he experienced in the Ulster Museum. Like the poet's grandfather in "Digging," the agricultural workers who happened on the Tollund Man were cutting turf for a tile stove and hearth. The body unearthed in the umber-brown peat was so perfectly preserved by the bog's tannic acids that the two slanesmen, fearing a recent murder, called the police at Silkeborg. The local museum contacted Glob at Aarhus University, and subsequent tests proved the dead man to be over two thousand years old. Though Heaney seems more inclined to ascribe his inspiration to the photographs in *The Bog People*, Glob's account of the Tollund Man's discovery affords an intimate portrait of a European ancestor who is both remote and immediate:

> He lay on his damp bed as though asleep, resting on his side, the head inclined a little forward, arms and legs bent. His face wore a gentle expression—the eyes lightly closed, the lips softly pursed, as if in silent prayer. It was as though the dead man's soul had for a moment returned from another world, through the gate in the western sky.[40]

The geological correspondences between Ireland and Denmark—clay-sogged river valleys and dense peat bogs—were phenomenal enough. But when Heaney learned that the Tollund Man had been the victim of a ritual sacrifice intended to appease an ancient earth goddess, he sensed a historical and cultural continuum encompassing all of northwest Europe: "Taken in relation to the tradition of Irish political martyrdom for that cause whose icon is Kathleen Ni Houlihan, this is more than an archaic barbarous rite: it is an archetypal pattern" (*Pr* 57). In section one of "The Tollund Man," he promises to make a solemn pilgrimage:

> Some day I will go to Aarhus
> To see his peat-brown head,
> The mild pods of his eye-lids,
> His pointed skin cap.
>
> In the flat country nearby
> Where they dug him out,
> His last gruel of winter seeds
> Caked in his stomach,
>
> Naked except for
> The cap, noose and girdle,

I will stand a long time.
Bridegroom to the goddess,

She tightened her torc on him
And opened her fen,
Those dark juices working
Him to a saint's kept body,

Trove of the turfcutters'
Honeycombed workings.
Now his stained face
Reposes at Aarhus.

(*Poems* 125)

Heaney reduces his earlier pentameter line to cadenced monosyllables in the opening stanza, relying on alliteration, assonance, and consonance for rhythmic integrity throughout the poem. Unlike Plath's "antique museum-cased lady" in "All the Dead Dears," something volatile persists in the Tol-lund Man's vegetable countenance, a faint crackling beneath the "mild pods of his eye-lids." But the ceremonial, even celebratory aspects of this death, the cruel and unnatural deliberation involved, are compressed into a single past participle: "Caked." Thus, within the larger context of the poem, the designation "Bridegroom" cannot mean anything other than victim. The genuine masterstroke follows in the sinewy syntax of line thirteen: "She tightened her torc." "Torc" not only recalls the constricting rope at the bridegroom's throat, but also denotes the tribal collar of twisted gold worn by Celt, Saxon, and Viking. Originally an ornamental neck-ring indicating allegiance to the goddess Nerthus, in Heaney's *oeuvre* it will expand to form a circle of violence that includes all the warlike inhabitants of the North.

In section two, the poet draws a direct parallel between the bog sacri-fices in Iron Age Jutland and victims of Irish sectarian strife. He contem-plates "risking blasphemy" in Christian terms, consecrating the bogs as holy ground and imploring the intercession of the martyred Tollund Man:

pray
Him to make germinate

The scattered, ambushed
Flesh of labourers,
Stockinged corpses
Laid out in the farmyards,
Tell-tale skin and teeth
Flecking the sleepers

> Of four young brothers, trailed
> For miles along the lines.
>
> (*Poems* 126)

According to Heaney, the second and third stanzas derive from "[p]art of the folk-lore of where I grew up," an incident in which four Catholic brothers were killed by Protestant paramilitaries, their bodies "trailed along the railway lines, over the sleepers as a kind of mutilation."[41] The lurching syntax of section two awakens the spectral image of heads burst like ripe gourds, broken teeth sown the length of the railbed. Compared to this hideous scenario, the Tollund Man's mien is singularly sedate. In section three, Heaney takes up the ancient cart-tracks that lead to a place of ritual execution:

> Something of his sad freedom
> As he rode the tumbril
> Should come to me, driving,
> Saying the names
>
> Tollund, Grabaulle, Nebelgard,
> Watching the pointing hands
> Of country people,
> Not knowing their tongue.
>
> Out there in Jutland
> In the old man-killing parishes
> I will feel lost,
> Unhappy and at home.
>
> (*Poems* 126)

A tipcart for farm use and also a vehicle for carrying condemned persons to their final destination, the "tumbril" is set in motion by long *e* sounds in "freedom." The deep ruts leading to the Germanic earth goddess's sacred bog and the killing fields of Northern Ireland intersect in the phrase "old man-killing parishes." Heaney's identification with the Tollund Man, his sense of being "lost, / Unhappy and at home" is virtually complete. His archaeological metaphor not only grants "the religious intensity of the violence [in Northern Ireland] its deplorable authenticity and complexity" (*Pr* 57), but also provides a vital Counter-Sublime to Yeats's Cathleen ni Houlihan.

But Heaney's *agon* with Yeats would take an odd turn at this point in his career. Having once established a vast analogue for Ireland's sectarian Troubles in "The Tollund Man," simultaneously allaying his personal crisis of identity by locating himself within a larger cultural milieu, Heaney unaccountably failed to consolidate his thematic and aesthetic gains. Searching for a more diverse and inclusive national myth than Yeats's Cuchulain, he erred too far in the direction of Joyce's example. In a collection of prose poems entitled *Stations* (1975), Heaney returns to his days at boarding school with the hope of capturing the mock-heroic elements of Stephen Dedalus's personality in *Portrait of the Artist as a Young Man*. Anne Stevenson describes *Stations* as "a series of psycho-autobiographical sketches,"[42] but the prose poem was not Heaney's forte. Moreover, Geoffrey Hill had already completed *Mercian Hymns*, a similar work that eclipsed Heaney's efforts. In Heaney's own words, "What I had regarded as stolen marches in a form new to me had been headed off by a work of complete authority."[43] Because *Mercian Hymns* (1971) would inform and partially influence Heaney's *North*, it is worth examining in some detail.

Mercian Hymns focuses on the sovereignty of Offa, supreme overlord of Mercia from A.D. 757 to 796 and the first of the Anglo-Saxon kings to style himself *Rex Totius Anglorum Patriae*. Describing Offa as a willing participant in the public evils of his day, Hill traces parallels between the rule of the Mercian king and his own boyhood in England's West Midlands during World War II. The collection comprises a cycle of thirty prose versets wherein archaeology and history are conflated with events and objects of the twentieth century.

With an irrepressible, childlike delight, Hill's Offa revels in the *scop*'s recitation of his feats, which range from builder of "the historic rampart and ditch" to architect of the citadel erected "at Tamworth." His list of titles embrace the quotidian ("saltmaster") as well as the exalted ("friend of Charlemagne"). The response at the end of the catalogue is straightforward and unabashed: "'I liked that,' said Offa, 'sing it again.'"[44] Although Hill's own childhood appears idyllic ("I drank from honeycombs of chill sandstone"), it retains little of the Wordsworthian aura. Here is section seven:

> Gasholders, russet among fields. Milldams, marlpools
> that lay unstirring. Eel-swarms. Coagulations of
> frogs; once, with branches and half-bricks, he
> battered a ditchful; then sidled away from the
> stillness and silence.

> Ceolred was his friend and remained so, even after
> the day of the lost fighter: a biplane, already
> obsolete and irreplaceable, two inches of heavy
> snub silver. Ceolred let it spin through a hole
> in the classroom-floorboards, softly, into the
> rat-droppings and coins.

> After school he lured Ceolred, who was sniggering
> with fright, down to the old quarries, and flayed
> him. Then, leaving Ceolred, he journeyed for hours,
> calm and alone, in his private derelict sandlorry
> named *Albion*.[45]

Unlike most practitioners of the prose poem, Hill continually arrests attention through dense nodes of language. The alliterative cadences recall the Old English sagas of Offa's mead-hall, vowels and consonants congealing in the thick ooze of "marlpools" and "Eel-swarms." Emphatic plosives—such as "half-bricks," "battered," and "ditchful"—mimic the boy's capricious pounding of the amphibian conclave into a clabbered mass. Far from trivializing Hitler's *blitzkrieg*, Hill relies on a grim particularity to hint that the frogs who complained to Zeus in the medieval version of Aesop's fable now have a king other than the benign log first sent them.

Offa fosters a yearning for coins splendidly wrought, for tapestries riddled into epic narratives by masters of the needle—and just as it is "safe to presume the king's anger" should anyone tamper with his possessions—Hill's young protagonist harrows his companion, Ceolred, for losing the precious replica of "snub silver." Lord of his private *Albion*, he sets his imprimatur on all things in his domain in section ten:

> He adored the desk, its brown-oak inlaid with ebony,
> assorted prize pens, the seals of gold and base
> metal into which he had sunk his name.[46]

Forging language into the living artifact of the poem will be the ultimate pleasure of the fledging poet. Heaney remarks of Hill in his essay "Englands of the Mind": "Words in his poetry fall slowly and singly, like molten solder, and accumulate to a dull glowing nub" *(Pr* 160). In section thirteen, we see Offa attain immortality, ensconced in the legend on a coin:

> Trim the lamp; polish the lens; draw, one by one, rare
> coins to the light. Ringed by its own lustre, the
> masterful head emerges, kempt and jutting, out of
> England's well. Far from his underkingdom of crin-
> oid and crayfish, the rune-stone's province, *Rex
> Totius Anglorum Patriae*, coiffured and ageless,
> portrays the self-possession of his possession,
> cushioned on a legend.[47]

Warden of the buried tower, "England's well," liege of specimen fern and crayfish, Offa returned to the unregenerate clay a millennium ago, and yet time has not effaced his lustre. Children in section nineteen "haul a sodden

log, hung with soft shields of fungus, and launch it upon the flames" like
the funeral ship of the Danish ring-lord Scyld Scefing. Hill's evocation of
Beowulf, an epic possibly composed by a Mercian *scop* and dedicated to
Offa's court, suggests that the ritual was familiar to the Anglo-Saxon
monarch, even as "he entered into the last dream of Offa the King."[48] Undoubtedly mock-heroic, the image nevertheless recalls the Viking ships
disinterred at Gokstad and Oseberg: archaeology and history intermingle
in layer after layer of *Mercian Hymns*.

In one of the earliest book-length studies on the poet's work, Blake
Morrison speculates as to why Heaney released *Stations* in a modest pam-
phlet numbering twenty-one poems, none of which he included in *Poems
1965–1975*: "some of the narrator's quasi-chivalric boastings ('I was
champion of the examination halls, scalding with lust inside my daunting
visor,' 'I have wandered far from that ring-giver and would not renegue on
this migrant solitude') sounded uncannily like those of Offa in Geoffrey
Hill's *Mercian Hymns*."[49] Hill ably captures the gleefully parodic tone of
Joyce's mock-heroic style, whereas Heaney's prose poems amount to little
more than a series of forced conceits. Nevertheless, Heaney quite skillfully
adopts his own version of Hill's dual narration in *North*. Few critics other
than David Lloyd have noticed the affinities between *Mercian Hymns* and
North:

> Heaney fuses ancient impulse and present reality in Part I of *North* primar-
> ily by merging his voice and sensibility with figures from mythology, liter-
> ary texts, or historical periods. His contemporary, English poet Geoffrey
> Hill, uses a similar technique in the poem sequence *Mercian Hymns*. Like
> Hill, Heaney analyzes and critiques his country's political and social life
> by showing how archaic elements of history and myth underpin and par-
> tially direct the consciousness of contemporary individuals. In *Mercian
> Hymns*, Hill undertakes a single fusion: he merges elements of his life and
> consciousness—mostly from his childhood years in the English mid-
> lands—with elements from the historical and imagined life of Offa, the
> eighth-century king of Mercia. Heaney, on the other hand, undertakes mul-
> tiple fusions with . . . historical figures such as the Vikings and the bog
> people of Denmark.[50]

Identity, cultural and personal, emerges as the ultimate concern of both
Mercian Hymns and *North*. Hill compares Offa's historical kingship to the
capricious and self-serving antics of his own childhood, thus presenting us
with a searing indictment of a particularly English inheritance. In *Mercian
Hymns*, the prince becomes the maker rather than the agent of the social
will. In *North*, however, Heaney refuses to confine himself to the "great

man" theory of history and myth; for him, narrations extolling the transcendent deeds of the individual, satirical or otherwise, necessarily disregard the broader matrix of bygone days that shape the present. His speaker in "Antaeus," a giant who husbands his strength through contact with the quotidian soil of his birth, declares a certain scorn for his "sky-born and royal" antagonist, Hercules: "He may well throw me and renew my birth / But let him not plan, lifting me off the earth, / My elevation, my fall." Apotheosis is anathema. Like the speaker of "Antaeus," the poem which opens Part I of *North*, Heaney contrives to stay close to the earth. Whether he writes about the Viking settlement excavated from Wood Quay in Dublin or the Iron Age corpses exhumed from layers of peat in Denmark, Heaney strives to recover a sense of cultural continuity beyond the scope of an Offa or a Cuchulain.

Heaney's Viking sequence—"North," "Viking Dublin: Trial Pieces," and "Funeral Rites"—centers on a period that the Saxon *scops* and Icelandic *skalds* invariably depict as heroic, albeit tainted by a lugubrious worldview. Norwegian and Danish piracy, fueled by trade, spread outward near the end of the eighth century to embrace England, Ireland, Scotland, and Wales. Scandinavian shipbuilders had perfected reliable raiding-ships that had no need of deep water, secure anchorages, or quaysides: "Their construction and shallow draught allowed them to use any sloping beach as their harbor and to manoeuvre in waters unsuitable for most European vessels of that time."[51] Norse bands were comprised of young warriors who attached themselves to men of mature strength—usually royals and aristocrats—in the spirit of the Germanic *comitatus*, with its reciprocal obligations of protection and reward on the one side, and loyalty and service on the other. In the last decade of the eighth century, Viking fleets not only plundered English monasteries at Lindisfarne and Jarrow, they also conducted lightning raids on Irish monastic strongholds at Rathlin, Inishmurray, and Inishboffin. All of northwest Europe came under their influence, as dragon-prowed vessels plied the Thames and the Shannon, the Elbe and the Seine, the Loire and the Rhone. Heaney posits a source of cultural identity in these Dark Age incursions by sea-brigands who soon became colonists and were eventually absorbed by the conquered territories. But if the poems in *North* have a certain skaldic ring, they also capture the less heroic tone of ecclesiastical chronicles that dubbed the Viking era "a sword age, a wolf age, a wind age." Indeed, the cultural custodians of the medieval period viewed the Viking wars as a series of ongoing conflicts essentially religious in nature. In a consoling letter to the community at Lindisfarne, Alcuin descanted bitterly on the heathen temperament of the Northmen:

> The pagans desecrated the sanctuaries of God, and poured out the blood of the saints about the altar, laid waste the house of our hope, trampled on the bodies of saints in the temple of God, like dung in the street. What can we say except lament in our soul with you before Christ's altar, and say: "Spare, O Lord, spare thy people . . . lest the pagans say, 'Where is the God of the Christians?'"[52]

Founder of a school of theology and literature in the court of Charlemagne, Alcuin objected less to the Viking's militancy than to the fact that they were pagans. After all, his own patron had offered the Franks the choice of Christianity or the sword, for which service Pope Leo III had crowned Charlemagne "Holy Roman Emperor" on Christmas Day, 800. In Ireland, some of the heads of the great monasteries took the field against the Northmen: "The abbot of Terryglass and Clonenagh and the deputy-abbot of Kildare were killed fighting the Vikings at Dunamase in 845."[53] Perhaps the tendency of Church chroniclers to interpret Iron Age strife in northwest Europe as a religious struggle prompted Heaney to choose the Viking legacy as a vast analogue to the contemporary Troubles in Northern Ireland. More likely, he sees the current violence as part of a timeless tribal impulse, an inherent yearning for the old blood-feud that manifests itself "in only slightly different ways across the millennia."[54]

Despite the apocalyptic strains of "North," Heaney makes definite strides toward clarifying his identity as an artist. He infuses the opening stanza with an expectant mood buttressed by sheer panorama:

> I returned to a long strand,
> the hammered shod of a bay,
> and found only the secular
> powers of the Atlantic thundering.
>
> (*Poems* 174)

The adjective-noun combinations "long strand" and "hammered shod" consist of words Germanic in origin, hard consonants pitched like cold, intractable metal. Both visually and aurally, the image recalls Ted Hughes's description of Viking oarsmen in "The Warriors of the North": "The snow's stupefied anvils in rows." But when Heaney tells us that the sea-cliffs echo only a "secular" thunder, the evocation of Thor's minions quickly fades. The speaker then faces "the unmagical / invitations of Iceland." Indeed, his aim appears to be a demystification of the Scandinavian epics: "If Auden succumbed to the pagan 'magic' of Iceland and its sagas, Heaney alludes to the sagas only to dismiss their deceptive romanticism. His apocalypse strives to purge the 'heroic' dross from the hard historical facts."[55] Nevertheless, the poet hearkens suddenly to the allure of ancestral voices:

those fabulous raiders,
those lying in Orkney and Dublin
measured against
their long swords rusting,

those in the solid
belly of stone ships,
those hacked and glinting
in the gravel of thawed streams

were ocean-deafened voices
warning me, lifted again
in violence and epiphany.

(Poems 174–75)

These voices are obviously closer to home than those emanating from Iceland and Greenland. In 841, Norwegian raiders built a longfort at Dublin, and while the site was of little significance to the rest of Ireland, it became an international trading center connected with continental Europe and other Viking settlements in Asia. But Heaney refuses to assess these "fabulous raiders," these marauding colonists, by either bardic or ecclesiastical standards. He rather resorts to archaeological scrutiny, measuring them against the image of their long swords rusting in blue clay. The locution "stone ships" refers to the most common form of boat burial in the North: a warrior was laid in a grave dug below the frost line, and the plot surrounded by massive stones arranged so as to resemble a ship's hull. Heaney then shows us ingots of fossilized bone "hacked and glinting" in the glacial melt of a streambed. Moreover, these lines bear a residue of linguistic ore, as *hacked*, *glinting*, and *thawed* derive from Old English or Old Norse. The voices of the dead and dismembered Vikings offer up a Joycean epiphany:

The longship's swimming tongue

was buoyant with hindsight—
it said Thor's hammer swung
to geography and trade,
thick-witted couplings and revenges,

the hatreds and behindbacks
of the althing, lies and women,
exhaustions nominated peace,
memory incubating the spilled blood.

(*Poems* 174–75)

The longship is the perfect metaphor for the Viking Age, its alluvial tongue imparting bitter truths. In its wake, the heroic values of the skaldic sagas become synonymous with the vices of kings and imperial governments from medieval Norway to twentieth-century Britain. The "hatreds and behindbacks" so prominent in *Njal's Saga* scarcely differ from the sectarian and political violence in Northern Ireland today. Heaney puns on "althing," which is archaic for "the whole thing," but also was the name of the notoriously ineffective judicial and legislative parliament of the Icelanders. Of course, the blow of "Thor's hammer" represents the coin of power; however, Heaney's parallel between the Viking blood-feuds and Ireland's current sectarian Troubles is perhaps subtler than we realize. According to James Graham-Campbell and Dafydd Kidd, the conversion of Scandinavians to Christianity was gradual, and fierce pagan beliefs often existed in close proximity to supposedly milder Christian ones. This dichotomy manifested itself even in the emblem of faith worn by each faction:

> Is, for example, that Icelandic silver pendant from Foss really a stylized hammer worn to invoke the protection of Thor? It is certainly made in the tradition of such pendants, with its animal-headed suspension-loop, as one can see by comparing it with that from Bredsatra, but it has been given a distinct cross-shape. . . . The jeweler whose mould was found at Trendgaarden in Denmark was a man of ingenuity and good business sense, as it was made for casting hammers and crosses at the same time.[56]

Heaney's own knowledge of Viking culture is extensive, and the implication that Thor's hammer and Christ's cross come from the same psychic crucible cannot be overlooked. He creates a mythic parallel based on archaeological evidence, a fusion between "ancient impulse and present reality" as cunning as any in Geoffrey Hill's *Mercian Hymns*. In the closing stanzas, the longship moves from hindsight to vatic utterance, instructing Heaney on the artist's role within a chaotic milieu:

> It said, "Lie down
> in the word-hoard, burrow
> the coil and gleam
> of your furrowed brain.
>
> Compose in darkness.
> Expect aurora borealis
> in the long foray
> but no cascade of light.
>
> Keep your eye clear
> as the bleb of the icicle,

> trust the feel of what nubbed treasure
> your hands have known."
>
> (*Poems* 175)

"Word-hoard" is the Old Norse kenning for language, wherein the poet must follow the labyrinthine toils of his wit like a winter serpent twining for warmth. For the illumination of his "long foray," Heaney can expect only distant tints on the far horizon. But why must his eye remain cold, clear as the "bleb" of an icicle? Such a lens is the very distillate of the Northern ethos; it can bend and refract, even distort. Moreover, his metaphor gainsays the arduous burrowing encouraged earlier, the admonition to "Compose in darkness." To achieve full identity as an artist, Heaney must ultimately live by the rough braille of his senses, and thus he returns in the last two lines to the "nubbed treasure" of the world at hand. Heaney abjures the violence but not the final epiphany of "North":

> For Heaney the ancient mythic principles—honor, fate, revenge, fame—that once sustained Iceland's and Ireland's "heroic" cultures have melted away. When he tells himself at the end, "trust the feel of what nubbed treasure / your hands have known," he is returning to his former persona, Incertus. He feels in the dark for what he cannot see for certain.[57]

Heaney continues his search for the artist's place within the larger design of history in "Viking Dublin: Trial Pieces." This time he identifies with an unknown Viking jeweler's apprentice, as he describes bone trial pieces taken from recent excavations at Wood Quay in Dublin. Viking art was presentational rather than representational; interlocking animal motifs were common, and the Ringerike style—interlacing serpents and foliage—was widely adopted in Ireland.[58] In section one, Heaney's trimeter line fuses with the deft incisions of his Norse precursor: "the line amazes itself // eluding the hand / that fed it." The poet emphasizes the sculptural intricacy of the carving as well as its improvisational nature. From this calligraphic tracery, the familiar longship, "a swimming nostril," gradually emerges. Here is section two entire:

> These are trial pieces,
> the craft's mystery
> improvised on bone:
> foliage, bestiaries,
>
> interlacings elaborate
> as the netted routes
> of ancestry and trade.
> That have to be

> magnified on display
> so that the nostril
> is a migrant prow
> sniffing the Liffey,
>
> swanning it up to the ford,
> dissembling itself
> in antler combs, bone pins,
> coins, weights, scale-pans.

(Poems 176–77)

Joyce's influence is doubly manifest, as the serpentine and foliate interlacings of the Ringerike style grow to resemble the Norseman's "netted routes / of ancestry and trade." This image not only alludes to the elaborate maze created by the master artisan of the Minoan world, it also evokes the nets of "nationality, language, and religion" that Stephen Dedalus vows to "fly by" in *A Portrait of the Artist as a Young Man*. In a sense, Heaney succeeds in eluding the snares of history, as his perceived affinity with the Viking artist intimates the possibility of a non-Celtic heritage. But can such an escape be anything more than an illusion? The longship "swanning it up to the ford" with a Spenserian majesty insists on impending colonialism. The participial phrase similarly recalls the rapacious Zeus in Yeats's "Leda and the Swan." Indeed, the Norse sea-raiders are seen as "dissembling," pirates trading in cultural artifacts actually exhumed from Wood Quay over a thousand years later. Thomas Heffernan comments on the dual role of the Vikings who originally settled Dublin:

> In Ireland as elsewhere the Viking has worn two faces. Many Irish schoolchildren in past generations were taught to see the Vikings as marauders and nothing else. A handful of politicians and others who were raised with this view were occasionally heard during the Wood Quay controversy asking, why save the remains of those pirates? The Viking's other face is that of the civilizer and artisan, the face seen by visitors to the recent traveling exhibition of Viking art or to the Gokstad ship in Oslo or to any of the major Viking restorations. Which is the real Viking? The answer, of course, is both.[59]

Heaney shows us both faces of the Dublin Vikings. Traders and artisans dealing in "antler combs" and "bone pins," these Ostmen also waged war and extorted gold from anyone willing to ransom the peace. However, Donnchad Midi, the overking of the Uí Néill, looted and pillaged more churches in Leinster than did the Ostmen.[60] With regard to ruthlessness, the Viking colonists were often outdone by Celtic tribes. In section five, Heaney deliberately conflates the Vikings of history with those of myth:

Come fly with me,
come sniff the wind
with the expertise
of the Vikings—

neighbourly, scoretaking
killers, haggers
and hagglers, gombeen-men,
hoarders of grudges and gain.

With a butcher's aplomb
they spread out your lungs
and made you warm wings
for your shoulders.

Old fathers, be with us.
Old cunning assessors
of feuds and of sites
for ambush or town.

(Poems 178–79)

Here the cultural parallel that Heaney terms an "archetypal pattern" issues primarily from the juxtaposition of "neighbourly" and "scoretaking / killers." He resorts to Gaelic slang when he describes the Vikings as loquacious bargainers ("hagglers") and usurers ("gombeen-men"). In the third quatrain, the poet dips into a myth that resulted from a mistranslation of skaldic verse:

> A misunderstanding has led historians from Saxo to the present day to believe that the Vikings practiced what is known as the blood-eagle sacrifice. The details vary, from simply cutting the shape of an eagle into the back of the victim to the more lurid practice of opening the rib cage to form "wings." The source is a verse describing an eagle, the carrion bird, slashing the backs of men killed in battle.[61]

Heaney appropriates this gruesome flight of fancy for his own purposes, inasmuch as it leads to an echo of Stephen Dedalus's invocation at the close of *A Portrait of the Artist*: "Old father, old artificer, stand me now and ever in good stead."[62] For Heaney, the cursive lines incised into bone trial pieces ("a rib or a portion cut / from something sturdier") reiterate a deep truth about the Vikings as bearers of culture. Because historians have traditionally represented the Vikings as cruel and enigmatic, their contributions to European civilization have been sorely underrated. According to Thomas Heffernan, the influence of Scandinavian artists appeared even in the medieval Church:

Some of the trial pieces, the practice work of the carvers, were especially significant from an artistic and historical point of view. Breandán O Ríordáin observed a number of similarities between designs found carved in bone on the site and designs familiar from old Irish metalwork and manuscript illumination. He compared one trial piece showing two semi-interlaced animals to one of the early panels of the shrine of the Cathach of Columcille made during the eleventh century in Kells.[63]

In "Viking Dublin: Trial Pieces," Heaney attempts to retrace a cultural and aesthetic identity through art. By identifying with the young carver of bone trial pieces, he neither excoriates nor celebrates the violent excesses attributed to the Northmen. He rather expresses his faith in art as a consolation for the chaos of history, and at the same time proposes an alternative to existing narratives. The phrase "Old fathers" not only provides a Joycean resonance, it also anticipates a time when the Lord's Prayer would be recited in a Germanic tongue. "Our Father" is much closer to the Old English *Faeder ure* than to the Latin *Pater noster*. For critics who complain that Heaney comes down too much on the Catholic side in *North*, this merits consideration.

In "Funeral Rites," Heaney expresses a fervent desire to transcend the constant sectarian strife that has so dramatically defined his own personal identity and that of his culture. Indeed, the poem enacts the tension he describes in *Preoccupations*, between the voices that pull "back through the political and cultural traumas of Ireland, and out towards the urgencies and experience of the world beyond it" (*Pr* 35). Moreover, it foreshadows the next phase in his career: his movement outward to a wider, more universal sense of identity, on a personal, spiritual, cultural and literary level. Heaney engages his crisis of identity in a communal setting reminiscent of "Mid-Term Break." Unlike the earlier elegy for his four-year-old brother, the poem is processional in tone, a veritable rite of passage: "I shouldered a kind of manhood / stepping in to lift the coffins / of dead relations." In painstaking detail, Heaney tallies one by one the images that attend a peaceful death in Northern Ireland. He remembers bodies prepared and laid out

> in tainted rooms,
> their eyelids glistening,
> their dough-white hands
> shackled in rosary beads.
>
> Their puffed knuckles
> had unwrinkled, the nails
> were darkened, the wrists
> obediently sloped.

The dulse-brown shroud,
the quilted satin cribs:
I knelt courteously
admiring it all

as wax melted down
and veined the candles,
the flames hovering
to the women hovering.

(Poems 170)

These stanzas from section one seem to extol the serene stupor, called by
Emily Dickinson "a formal feeling," which accompanies grief. In the first
quatrain quoted above, hands once capable of earnest grasping are now
"dough-white," delicately fettered by the accoutrements of prayer. The
passive tone carries over into the next stanza. Swollen knuckles might connote anger, but these are "puffed" and "unwrinkled," complacent if no
longer tractable. An ameliorating warmth fills the room, a gentle thaw pervasive as the liquid *l* sounds in "dulse-brown," "quilted," "knelt," and
"melted." Heaney kneels "courteously / admiring it all," entranced by his
own eye for minutiae, until an abrupt tonal shift fixes and fuses the imagery like silver filigree or gold inlay on the Viking sword-hilt found at
Hedeby:

And always, in a corner,
the coffin lid,
its nail-heads dressed

with little gleaming crosses.
Dear soapstone masks,
kissing their igloo brows
had to suffice

before the nails were sunk
and the black glacier
of each funeral
pushed away.

(Poems 171)

The intricately worked crosses adorning the coffin lid signal a biting cold,
an implacable Northern ambience. Faces become "soapstone masks,"
brows contract and glisten like wind-polished ice. Heaney describes the fu-

neral cortege as a "black glacier" that seems to launch itself across the chilly forenoon. Indeed, the image chimes with his own translation of the burial ship passage from *Beowulf*: "A ring-necked prow rode in the harbour, / clad with ice, its cables tightening."

Section two raises the spectre of "neighbourly murder," the sectarian violence in Ulster that recalls the age of the Norse blood-feud. The circle of violence and retribution causes the poet to mourn not only the deceased, but also "the vanished rituals of grief and consolation themselves."[64] Thus, Heaney's doleful comment: "we pine for ceremony, / customary rhythms." Heaney does not yearn for the "ceremony of innocence," as Yeats would have it in "The Second Coming," or even for the blandishments of satin-upholstered coffins with diminutive crosses engraved on the nail-heads. He rather longs for the sense of continuity between the individual and the larger culture that communal mourning provides. And he once again contrives a mythic scenario based on archaeological data. Heaney imagines the cortege slowly advancing toward "the great chambers of Boyne." These megalithic passage tombs with corbelled roofs and crypt-like side chambers connect Ireland and England to the spiritual memory of Bronze Age Europe:

> During the third and fourth millennia B.C., there spread from the Mediterranean area, along the Atlantic coasts of Europe, northwards into Scandinavia and the north European mainland the custom of building great tombs of stone intended for what is known as "collective burial," that is to say, each tomb contained many burials.[65]

The stone sepulchres of Ulster thus transcend their stubbornly local character, and restore Northern Ireland to a time before the current cycle of "neighbourly murder." Moreover, Heaney's imaginary funeral has distinctly non-sectarian undertones. As the ignitions of limousines arc and fire, "the whole country tunes / to the muffled drumming // of ten thousand engines." The procession does not move to the boisterous eructations of Orange drums celebrating victory along the River Boyne; its pace is solemn and modulated, a triumphant approach toward the burial mounds. The poet then revives the Norse motif, as he compares the gleaming black motorcade to the serpent-prowed longship of the *Poetic Edda*: "the procession drags its tail / out of the Gap of the North" (173).

In section three, Heaney appropiates an incident from the Icelandic epic *Njal's Saga* to suggest an analogue between the Viking code of blood vengeance and the ongoing cycle of retribution in Belfast. He imagines the stone rolled back into the mouth of the megalithic tomb, and the funeral procession heading homeward. Delving into the etymology of the countryside, he returns place-names such as Strangford and Carlingford to their roots in Old Norse: "we will drive north again / past Strang and Carling fjords." So intense is Heaney's desire for the suspension of hostilities that he invests this ritual mourning with the power to assuage all factions: "the cud of memory / allayed for once, arbitration / of the feud placated." He extends the analogy between past and present by comparing the victims interred at Newgrange to a murdered Icelandic thane:

> imagining those under the hill
>
> disposed like Gunnar
> who lay beautiful
> inside his burial mound,
> though dead by violence
>
> and unavenged.
> Men said that he was chanting
> verses about honour
> and that four lights burned
>
> in corners of the chamber:
> which opened then, as he turned
> with a joyful face
> to look at the moon.
>
> (*Poems* 172–73)

The past participle "disposed" initially links burial with abjection, creating a curious alloy of beauty and atrocity. But in light of the concluding stanzas, "disposed" must be read to mean "Inclined." Resplendent in his sepulchre, Gunnar's disposition or inclination goes beyond peace and contentment to a singular delight in cadences of his own making. As Elmer Andrews comments in *The Poetry of Seamus Heaney: All the Realms of Whisper*: "Heaney's project is the achievement of the momentary peace . . . in which all oppositions are reconciled in the self-contained, transcendent poetic symbol."[66] In *Njal's Saga*, Gunnar's beatific verses are a portent, inciting his son, Hogni, to revenge. In "Funeral Rites," however, the warrior-poet enjoins the culture to disavow the heroic code of blood vengeance. Heaney's mythic Northman would break the pattern of cruel retaliation that motivates epic heroes from Homer's Achilles to Milton's Satan. Unlike Cuchulain and the Men of Ulster, Gunnar prefers the balm and benediction of peace to incessant warfare. Neil Corcoran asserts that the poem "urgently desires an end to the terrible cycle, but it can imagine such a thing only in a mythologized visionary realm."[67]

Although some critics contend that Heaney indulges a Yeatsian romanticism in "Funeral Rites," the resurrected Gunnar does not represent the heroic or bardic ideal so much as the marvellous. If Heaney seems reluctant to exorcise the figure of the poet, he continues elsewhere to reclaim the linguistic heritage of the North. In "Bone Dreams," he foregrounds the fragmentation of both Irish and British culture in an attempt to exhume the precious relics of the Germanic oral tradition. Defining the Old English kenning for the body (*ban-hus*) as a skeleton in the tongue's metaphorical dungeon, Heaney uncovers layer after layer of cloying rhetoric urged by the exigencies of empire:

> I push back
> through dictions,
> Elizabethan canopies,
> Norman devices,
>
> the erotic mayflowers
> of Provence
> and the ivied latins
> of churchmen
>
> to the scop's
> twang, the iron
> flash of consonants
> cleaving the line.
>
> (*Poems* 183)

The "erotic mayflowers" and "ivied latins" evoke the ornate capitals of historical tracts and genealogies that sprang up during the period of Norman domination. Only by awakening the "scop's twang" can the poet cut through the floral dictions of Provençal and Latin to the iron consonants of Old English. For Heaney, the alliterative tradition of German oral literature is a vital source of cultural identity:

> In the coffered
> riches of grammar
> and declensions
> I found *ban-hus,*
>
> its fire, benches,
> wattle and rafters,
> where the soul
> fluttered a while

in the roofspace.
There was a small crock
for the brain,
and a cauldron

of generation
swung at the centre:
love-den, blood-holt,
dream-bower.

(*Poems* 183–84)

The phrase "cauldron / of generation" could apply not only to Old English and Old Norse, but also to the bogs of the Jutland peninsula. Like Joyce, Heaney has come to view English as "not so much an imperial humiliation as a native weapon."[68]

At this point, Heaney intensifies his search for identity along mythic and archaeological lines by extending the bog metaphor broached in "The Tollund Man." Usually accorded more grudging homage than the earlier poem, Heaney's "Bog Queen" is nevertheless a key figure in his reliquary assembled from the marshes and fens of northwest Europe. The Bog Queen of Moira, an aristocrat of the Viking culture occupying Ireland in the tenth century, was hacked from a peat floe south of Belfast in 1781. A Danish corpse extracted from Heaney's native turf, her presence validates his mythic connection between contemporary Northern Ireland and Iron Age Denmark. Indeed, Thomas Foster contends that "the poem could be construed as the cornerstone on which Heaney builds the book [*North*], allowing the connection between the two cultures to be more than metaphorical fancy."[69] Heaney adopts a first-person persona chillingly reminiscent of Plath's "Lady Lazarus." Steeped in fermenting juices "between turf-face and demesne wall," the jewel-bedecked corpse senses the earth moving in its diurnal rounds. Her flesh records the passage of geologic time, a metamorphosis like the slow mineral growth of a stalactite:

My body was braille
for the creeping influences:
dawn suns groped over my head
and cooled at my feet,

through my fabrics and skins
the seeps of winter
digested me.

(*Poems* 187)

Alive to the "creeping influences" of all creation, she cares nothing for the trappings of wealth: "My diadem grew carious, / gemstones dropped in the peat floe / like the bearings of history." A more significant element is the empathic surge that Heaney works into the language; barely perceptible at first, it gathers force line by line:

> My sash was a black glacier
> wrinkling, dyed weaves
> and phoenician stitchwork
> retted on my breasts'
>
> soft moraines.
> I knew winter cold
> like the nuzzle of fjords
> at my thighs.

(Poems 188)

The exquisite precision of these images counterpoints the gradual passing of the millennium. Indeed, the sash described as "a black glacier / wrinkling" recalls the triumphal procession in "Funeral Rites." Unlike the Tollund Man and Gunnar, however, she is not a victim of ritual sacrifice or factional murder. Still, her violation seems as inevitable as the currents of history: "I was barbered / and stripped / by a turfcutter's spade." Respectfully reinterred by the peat-laborer, "who veiled me again / and packed coomb softly / . . . at my head and my feet," the Viking aristocrat might have continued her journey unhindered, if not for the intervention of her eighteenth-century counterpart:

> Till a peer's wife bribed him.
> The plait of my hair,
> a slimy birth-cord
> of bog, had been cut
>
> and I rose from the dark,
> hacked bone, skull-ware,
> frayed stitches, tufts,
> small gleams on the bank.

(Poems 189)

The "slimy birth-cord / of bog," albeit metaphorical, suggests the voluptuous mingling of the Celtic strain with the Germanic tribes of the North. A spectral resurrection ensues, and it is no accident that the piecemeal images—"hacked bone, / skull-ware, / frayed stitches"—conjure "those fabulous raiders" of "North" who lie "hacked and glinting / in the gravel of thawed streams." Thomas Foster emphasizes the importance of this parallel:

> The bog poems, and "Bog Queen" more particularly, act as the pivotal point on which the volume turns. Most of part 1 to this juncture has concerned itself with Scandinavian history and instances of overlapping between that history and Ireland's. The remainder of the book concerns itself primarily with Irish history, especially the backgrounds and events of the Troubles in Ulster. The bog poems attempt to legitimize the bond between the two movements as something more than the poet's caprice or novel coincidence; rather, in demonstrating a common blood culture, the sequence insists on the historical nature of society's violence against its members, not as a way of sanctioning that violence but of comprehending it.[70]

Unlike Yeats's Leda, the Bog Queen leaves no question as to whether she puts on both the knowledge and power of inexorable forces. She belongs not to the realm of received myth, but rather to the "locus of the given world," to the vast sweep of natural and human history.

In his remaining bog poems—"The Grabaulle Man," "Punishment," and "Kinship"—Heaney consolidates his mythic North, deepening the parallels between recent sectarian killings in Ulster and victims of ritual violence in Iron Age Denmark. Once again, the dank tarns and rush-choked fens of the Jutland peninsula provide Heaney with "ruminant ground," a source of common identity between past and present. "The Grabaulle Man" focuses on a corpse wrested from a section of bracken and peat in Nebelgard Fen, eleven miles east of Tollund:

> As if he had been poured
> in tar, he lies
> on a pillow of turf
> and seems to weep
>
> the black river of himself.
> The grain of his wrists
> is like bog oak,
> the ball of his heel
>
> like a basalt egg.
> His instep has shrunk
> cold as a swan's foot
> or a wet swamp root.

His hips are the ridge
and purse of a mussel,
his spine an eel arrested
under a glisten of mud.

                                                    (*Poems* 190)

At first, Heaney's Grabaulle Man appears to be little more than a pot-
pourri of random metaphors, a dark amalgam of vegetable fibers, igneous
rock, mineral ooze, and rucked shell. Insentient except for his spine, a
barely restrained ripple, he seems to mingle utterly with the fecund earth.
But as Shakespeare averred by proxy of his Danish prince, "Foul deeds
will rise, / Though all the earth o'erwhelm them, to men's eyes."[71] Indeed,
we share the experience of discovery, as a head comes clear of the
morass. The ceremonial gash is a "cured wound," not healed but ironically preserved by the bog's tannic acids. Where the acolyte to Nerthus
dragged his dagger, the Grabaulle Man's throat "opens inwards to a dark
/ elderberry place." Mysterious and remote in time, the wound might well
have been inflicted yesterday: "Who will say 'corpse' / to his vivid cast?
/ Who will say 'body' / to his opaque repose?" Heaney emphasizes the
Grabaulle Man's consecration to an insatiable fertility goddess. Never directly mentioning Nerthus or her Irish incarnation, Cathleen ni Houlihan,
the poet relies on implied metaphor to describe the effects of the victim's
two thousand-year gestation. His hair is "a mat unlikely / as a foetus's,"
and his removal from the bog becomes a painful second birth: "a head
and shoulder / out of the peat, / bruised like a forceps baby." Although the
bog seems to glut and hold fast, Heaney brings a stark image to full
fruition:

                    now he lies
            perfected in my memory,
            down to the red horn
            of his nails,

            hung in the scales
            with beauty and atrocity:
            with the Dying Gaul
            too strictly compassed

            on his shield,
            with the actual weight
            of each hooded victim,
            slashed and dumped.

                                                    (*Poems* 191)

Specific anatomical detail, especially "the red horn / of his nails," shifts the mood of the poem to that of a post-mortem. Heaney compels himself to weigh the beauty of art against historical reality. *The Dying Gaul* was originally cast in bronze at Pergamon by an ally of Rome, King Attalos I, to commemorate his victory over Celts raiding in Asia Minor during the third century B.C.[72] He has the "moustached archaic face" that Heaney cites as common to the Irish countryside, and he also wears about his neck the torc of the goddess. As his lineaments were first kneaded into clay before the molten bronze was poured, *The Dying Gaul* underwent a rebirth not unlike the Grabaulle Man's. But Heaney sees his attitude as "too strictly compassed," too beautifully contrived. According to Glob's radiocarbon tests, the Grabaulle Man was a near-contemporary of the Celtic warrior who provided the inspiration for *The Dying Gaul*, but he manifests for Heaney "the actual weight / of each hooded victim, / slashed and dumped." Moreover, the poet draws a subtle parallel between victims of atrocities past and present. Sacrifices to Nerthus were often hooded, as have been recent victims of the Ulster Defence Association:

> Scores of young Catholics were found with hoods over their heads and bullets through their brains. Others were found in a condition better imagined than described, with mutilations, throat cuttings and every form of atrocity.[73]

Writing about the ritual slaughter of a pre-Christian inhabitant of Denmark enables Heaney to reinforce his theory regarding an "archetypal pattern" of violence in the North; more significantly, his richly allusive methodology prevents the poem from lapsing into blatant polemics. In "Ulysses, Order and Myth," Eliot asserted that Joyce's ability to "manipulate a continuous parallel between contemporaneity and antiquity" had "the importance of a scientific discovery."[74] Just as Hill managed to apply Joyce's mythic method to the historical Offa of Mercia, Heaney links Glob's archaeological discovery, the anonymous Grabaulle Man, with a centuries-old cycle of violence in northwest Europe. The Ulster poet momentarily resolves his crisis of identity by placing himself within a cultural and historical milieu that greatly exceeds the boundaries of the six northern counties. Heaney also continues to exploit his gift for etymological resonances: his Grabaulle Man "seems to weep // the black river of himself." Viking colonizers named the tidal pool created at the point where the River Poddle entered the Liffey *Dubh Linn*, "the black pool."[75]

In "Punishment," a disturbingly confessional poem, Heaney admits to his own participation in the ways of a fallen culture. His subject is a fourteen-year-old girl of the first century A.D., an adulteress drowned in

Windeby bog for her folly. Heaney's tendency to identify, even empathize, with the victim reveals itself in the opening lines: "I can feel the tug / of the halter at the nape / of her neck." But an ill wind springs up immediately, interceding between the poet and the pubescent girl: "It blows her nipples / to amber beads, / it shakes the frail rigging / of her ribs." A quasi-erotic image, the chill breeze plays on the girl's naked front, and its caress turns her nipples to fossilized resin. Telltale signs of humiliating cruelty appear, as Heaney likens her shaved head to "a stubble of black corn." He then opts for a mode of direct address oddly reminiscent of a Petrarchan love lyricist:

> Little adulteress,
> before they punished you
>
> you were flaxen-haired,
> undernourished, and your
> tar-black face was beautiful.
> My poor scapegoat,
>
> I almost love you
> but would have cast, I know,
> the stones of silence.
>
> (*Poems* 193)

As Henry Hart notes, Catholic girls in Northern Ireland have recently been "cauled in tar" for defying the taboos of the Provisional I.R.A.[76] Chief among these is the dating of British soldiers, particularly officers, and for Heaney the shorn skull of the Windeby Girl calls to mind recent reprisals in Ulster:

> I who have stood dumb
> when your betraying sisters,
> cauled in tar,
> wept by the railings,
>
> who would connive
> in civilized outrage
> yet understand the exact
> and tribal, intimate revenge.
>
> (*Poems* 193)

In "Punishment," Heaney accepts responsibility for the more reprehensible aspects of his culture. Earlier on, "The Tollund Man" expressed the disquieting continuum between modern Irish culture and ritual executions in Iron

Age Denmark, the familiar feeling of being "lost, / Unhappy and at home."
While "Punishment" indeed lacks the "dramatic tension" of "The Tollund
Man," as Andrews notes, it acknowledges Heaney's sense of guilt, or at
least of complicity, about certain aspects of the present cycle of violence in
Ulster. Though he identifies with the victims of violence, he soberly admits
the ability to comprehend "the exact / and tribal, intimate revenge." In the
poem's closure, the word "exact" retains both verbal and adjectival qualities, suggesting a vengeance exacted and exacting, brutally precise. The
sense of being drawn toward "the old vortex of racial and religious instinct" and alternately to "the mean of humane love and reason" (*Pr* 34)
finds its way, with grim specificity, into Heaney's poetry. In "Punishment,"
Heaney confronts the Troubles more directly than in "The Tollund Man,"
squarely facing both his own cultural identity and its effects on his identity
as an artist. Indeed, this desire to expiate a sense of guilt or complicity with
regard to the Troubles pervades the next phase of Heaney's crisis of identity, informing the poetry of *Field Work* (1979) and becoming the driving
force behind *Station Island*.

"Kinship," the culmination of the bog poems and the centerpiece of the
volume, both recapitulates and repudiates Heaney's mythic North. Composed of six parts, each containing six quatrains, the poem imitates "the
shifting, sucking movement of the bog itself."[77] As its title suggests, the
piece is a search for poetic and cultural identity in the face of a fragmented
culture; moreover, in "Kinship," Heaney confronts Yeats more intimately
than ever before. Once again, empathy for an ancient victim of ritual sacrifice draws Heaney into the past:

> Kinned by hieroglyphic
> peat on a spreadfield
> to the strangled victim,
> the love-nest in the bracken,
>
> I step through origins
> like a dog turning
> its memories of wilderness
> on the kitchen mat.

(Poems 195)

The turning represents an archetypal pattern, an instinctual, pre-conscious
memory: the canine circles as his feral ancestor did, nestling a covert lair
among reeds and tall grasses. If the image is a furtive jab at Yeats, a deliberate demystification of his interlocking cones and gyres, it is also self-par-
odic, demonstrating Heaney's wry knowledge of his own tendency to be

lured into "the old vortex." Indeed, a mood of self-deprecation and resig-
nation pervades the entire poem.

Like Antaeus in *North*, Heaney recognizes the source of his strength.
The first four parts of "Kinship" lovingly render the bog as a fecund source
of identity: it is "soft," "[r]uminant ground," the perfect storehouse of
memory, a symbol of the Gaelic language. Embracing its elusiveness, the
poet mixes Old English kennings and Latinate terms in a catalogue of
metaphors that acknowledges its terror and beauty: "Insatiable bride. /
Sword-swallower, / casket, midden, / floe of history."

Section 3 illuminates Heaney's own poetic "diggings" in the bog. The
emblematic "turf-spade" discovered by the poet and sunk into the bog implies a sexual union with the goddess Nerthus, a mingling of eros and
thanatos. A desire for order, a longing for unity fuels the sexual imagery of
this section. The spade becomes the "twinned . . . obelisk" of Nerthus's
hermaphrodite statue;[78] then, beneath the patriarchal "bearded cairn," it is
transformed to the "cloven oak-limb" that served as a crude effigy of the
goddess.[79] The images bring us back to the earlier bog poems of *North*: "I
stand at the edge of centuries / facing a goddess."

In section 4, Heaney invokes Yeats's "The Second Coming": "This
centre holds / and spreads." Here the crisis of identity seems temporarily
suspended; the bog serves as an apt metaphor for the paradox of life itself:
"sump and seedbed, / a bag of waters // and a melting grave." The concluding quatrain satirizes Heaney's own anguished obsession with the dead, describing the poet as a "weeping willow / inclined to / the appetites of
gravity," perhaps too profoundly influenced by the forces he has described.

Subsequent sections address the issues of identity and kinship most directly. If the hand-carved rims of the cart wheels in section 5 suggest the
ancient tumbril of "The Tollund Man," they also recall the wagons used to
carry the statue of Nerthus on her spring journeys and the turf-cart of
Heaney's great-uncle Hugh Scullion.[80] Indeed, Heaney conflates bog
victim and close relation, effacing the accidents of their respective historical periods, and placing himself, with a tinge of irony, in the role of "privileged / attendant, a bearer / of bread and drink, / the squire of his circuits."
Imagining the bog victim as a vital participant of a living rural culture,
Heaney claims him as a spiritual ancestor. The poet's unfeigned delight in
his intimate relationship with his uncle recalls the profound respect for his
grandfather in "Digging" and his father in "Follower." Indeed, Andrews
traces "the celebratory intensity"[81] of this passage back to early poems like
"Follower":

> When summer died
> and wives forsook the fields

> we were abroad,
> saluted, given right-of-way.
>
> Watch our progress
> down the hawlit hedges,
> my manly pride
> when he speaks to me.
>
> (*Poems* 199)

The image of "bread and drink" intimates a longing for communion, the same keen desire for ritual expressed in "Funeral Rites."

The poet appeals finally to Tacitus, the Roman historian whose *Germania* recounts the cult of the goddess Nerthus, thus invoking not a victim of violence but a fellow witness to the mores of a turbulent culture. Heaney here achieves a crucial link between Nerthus and Yeats's Cathleen ni Houlihan in the phrase "mother ground": "Our mother ground / is sour with the blood / of her faithful." Moreover, his identification with the historian yields an additional parallel, equally telling: "the legions" who "stare / from the ramparts" summon the specter of British forces in Ulster. Heaney implores Tacitus to return "to this / 'island of the ocean' / where nothing will suffice," alluding to Yeats's query in "Easter, 1916": "Too long a sacrifice / Can make a stone of the heart. / O when may it suffice?"[82] The younger poet asserts the brutal, timeless cycle of violence in northwest Europe: no sacrifice will ever be sufficient. He seeks in Tacitus a mutual observer who will understand and recount the complex forces that feed the seemingly endless cultural conflict. With the use of first-person plural pronouns, Heaney implicates himself in the violence of his culture, albeit in an ironic tone: "report us fairly, / how we slaughter / for the common good." Heaney's closure in "Kinship" appears less a refutation of Yeats's question than a woeful assent. The end of the poem amounts to a partial deconstructing of the mythic North forged earlier in the volume. The search for kinship has proven almost entirely futile, and the poet must still face the reality of sectarian violence in Ulster.

The poems that constitute the second part of *North* represent a more public poetry. Confronting the Troubles in Northern Ireland directly, they eschew the impulse to link the violence to cultural precedents; as a result, they often lack the subtlety and artifice of the bog sequence. Here Heaney returns to a longer line and more regular metric, though the diction at times seems colloquial and slack. For the most part, these poems are too didactic, often lapsing into strict reportage of events. Among the most notable exceptions are "Whatever You Say, Say Nothing" and "Singing School," both of which figure prominently in Heaney's *agon* with Yeats.

At this point in his career, Heaney's sense of identity is almost sub-sumed by the larger cultural crisis. The opening section of "Whatever You Say, Say Nothing" finds him in Ulster just returned from America: "back in winter / Quarters where bad news is no longer news." The lines betray a brisk impatience with British correspondents who seek "'views / on the Irish thing," having staked out the Irish conflict as their own territory and chronicled "the long campaign from gas / And protest to gelignite and sten." For Heaney, the glib dictions of those not directly involved or threat-ened are too detached, "remote from the psychology of the Irishmen and Ulstermen who do the killing" (*Pr* 57). Yet his diatribe extends to include his own hypocrisy and that of his community. The worn responses of Irish citizens cannot begin to adequately address, much less illuminate the situ-ation: "'Oh, it's disgraceful, surely, I agree,' / 'Where's it going to end?' 'It's getting worse.' / 'They're murderers.' 'Internment, understandably.'"

In section 2, Heaney juxtaposes the evocation of Yeats's "Meditations in a Time of Civil War" ("Men die at hand") with the detached, clichéd lan-guage of a journalistic account ("In blasted street and home / The gelig-nite's a common sound effect"). With an acerbic wit, the poet exposes clichés by engaging in them himself. Here strident rhythms deplore not so much a lack of emotional engagement as the absence of a sincere admis-sion of the emotional impact of the conflict:

> Long sucking the hind tit
> Cold as a witch's and as hard to swallow
> Still leaves us fork-tongued on the border bit:
> The liberal papist note sounds hollow
>
> When amplified and mixed in with the bangs
> That shake all hearts and windows day and night.
>
> (*Poems* 213)

Section 3 lapses into self-parody, as Heaney impishly puns on his own name, equating himself with James II, whose Catholic followers were dis-placed from a Williamite settlement after his defeat at the Battle of the Boyne.[83] In spite of his humor, the poet returns to his earlier persona of In-certus: "Yet for all this art and sedentary trade / I am incapable." He blames "[t]he famous // Northern reticence, the tight gag of place / And times." Centuries of occupation have left their mark. What Polly Devlin calls "the historical necessities of keeping your head down and your eyes averted so as not to attract notice or unwanted attention"[84] have become ingrained: self-effacement has become self-protection, "the deceit and duplicity of the Ulster consciousness which Heaney recognizes in himself."[85] The line

"And whatever you say, you say nothing" brings into play the subtle means of determining friend and foe in the "land of password, handgrip, wink and nod, / Of open minds as open as a trap." Both sides are carefully attuned to the intricate dimensions of identity in Northern Ireland. "Besieged within the siege, whispering morse," Irish Catholics are set apart by their names and schools; indeed, as Polly Devlin notes, the warring factions can be identified by their use of language: "the very pronouns in speech are used to widen gaps between people who have nothing different about them but whose common history has made them enemies."[86]

In section 4, the poet drives down "a dewy motorway" past Long Kesh prison, "the new camp for the internees." Introduced in August 1971 to stem I.R.A. harassment of British forces, internment without trial merely heightened the intensity of the conflict:

> Whole areas were sealed off, paratroopers smashing down doors and literally dragging men from their homes in front of hysterical wives and terrified children, the brutal knock in the middle of the night reeking of totalitarianism about its dirty work.[87]

The increased violence generated greater Catholic support for the "Provos," perpetuating a cycle of mutual hostilities that would eventually culminate in Bloody Sunday. A glimpse of the camp awakens for Heaney the horror of recent events. The "white mist" covering the ground adds a surreal quality to a landscape already scarred with bomb craters and machine-gun posts, images of terror all too familiar to Heaney: "it was déjà-vu, some film made / Of Stalag 17, a bad dream with no sound." The poem ends with a gesture of stoic endurance, as humiliation takes on a communal flavor: "Coherent miseries, a bite and sup, / We hug our little destiny again."

Of the poems in the second part of *North*, "Singing School" concerns itself most with identity, noting the difficulties of the artist who practices his craft in the midst of a cultural crisis. An autobiographical piece in six parts, the poem registers Heaney's growing alienation and inability to maintain a sense of composure in the face of constant conflict. Heaney records epiphanous moments and encounters with others that amount to formative experiences in his poetic development. As Charles J. Rzepka notes in his study of the poetic identity of Wordsworth, Coleridge, and Keats, "[i]t is through the encounters depicted in their poetry that . . . poets seek to test, reintegrate, and come to terms with their disparate and often temporarily confused selves and affirm the historical and social reality of the true self that persists behind the masks and throughout the vicissitudes of the search for recognition."[88] The first part, "The Ministry of Fear," dedicated to fellow Irish poet and critic Seamus Deane, traces their friendship from the days as students at St. Columb's College through their subsequent development as writers, their residence at Belfast and Berkeley, their eventual success. This section recalls Heaney's loneliness in his initial week at St. Columb's ("I was so homesick I couldn't even eat / The biscuits left to sweeten my exile"), as well as the exchange of poems in which "Vowels and ideas bandied free / As the seed-pods blowing off our sycamores" and "hobnailed boots from beyond the mountain" trod "all over the fine / Lawns of elocution." But it also records the stern discipline administered at school: "On my first day, the leather strap / Went epileptic in the Big Study" (*Poems* 219). Like British occupation, Irish Catholicism is a crucial element in the environment Heaney aptly terms "The Ministry of Fear": priests wield their authority no less severely than the British. Polly Devlin has remarked on the repressiveness of the Irish Catholic upbringing and education: "certainly there were many truly devout people . . . who gained comfort from religion, and not just disturbance of their spirit and terrorism and fear. But those two last stalked our childhood in a horrid linkage with righteousness and Christ, and they stalk Northern Ireland still."[89] Later in the poem, the sensual pleasures of summer freedom and sexual awakening are suddenly interrupted late one evening, when policemen detain the young Heaney at a roadblock. The official inspection of Heaney's letters, which contained Deane's poetic drafts, offers a veiled commentary on the problematic identity of poets in Northern Ireland, traditionally regarded as second-class citizens: "Ulster was British, but with no rights on / the English lyric." Yet Heaney here ironically implies that such a milieu played its part in their literary triumphs: like Wordsworth, they have been "[f]ostered alike by beauty and by fear."

Part 2, "A Constable Calls," records an incident of "Arithmetic and fear" from a child's perspective. Heaney's father must recount the crops he has planted, while the constable records the information in the "heavy ledger," later called "the domesday book." Though the constable neither threatens nor reassures, his trappings awe and terrify: the "fat black handlegrips" of his bicycle blaze in the sunlight, and empty pedals dangle "relieved / Of the boot of the law" (*Poems* 221).The young boy recognizes his father's omission of "a line / Of turnips." Convinced that it may prove compromising, he resigns himself to a bleak fate: "I assumed / Small guilts and sat / Imagining the black hole in the barracks." In this section, Heaney recognizes his participation in a tradition of subterfuge once essential for survival. The constable's departure without incident does not diminish the explosive potential of such an encounter: "His boot pushed off / And the bicycle ticked, ticked, ticked" (*Poems* 222).

Section 3 is little more than a grotesque caricature of Protestant drums that "preside, like giant tumours" every 12 July in Northern Ireland. In section 4, Heaney introduces a genuine note of exile, remembering his sojourn in Madrid during the summer of 1969: "as I sweated my way through / The life of Joyce, stinks from the fishmarket / Rose like the reek off a flax-dam" (*Poems* 224). A spate of surreal images—gules of wine, black-shawled crones, the patent leather of the Guardia Civil shining like the proverbial dead herring in moonlight—conjures the spirit of Federico Garcia Lorca, victim of a Falangist death squad whose strong-arm tactics anticipated the Provisional I.R.A. and the Ulster Defence Association by thirty years. Indeed, Heaney's tenuous identification with Lorca seems particularly ominous. Unlike Rafael Alberti, Lorca returned to his beloved Andalusia and was shot in a sweltering olive grove near the first rocky outcrops of the Sierra de Alfacar.[90] Should Heaney return to strife-torn Belfast? Retreating to "the cool of the Prado," he encounters the brutal vigor of Goya's works:

> Goya's "Shootings of the Third of May"
> Covered a wall—the thrown-up arms
> And spasm of the rebel, the helmeted
> And knapsacked military, the efficient
> Rake of the fusillade. In the next room
> His nightmares, grafted to the palace wall—
> Dark cyclones, hosting, breaking; Saturn
> Jewelled in the blood of his own children,
> Gigantic Chaos turning his brute hips
> Over the world. Also, that holmgang
> Where two berserks club each other to death
> For honour's sake, greaved in a bog, and sinking.
>
> (*Poems* 224–25)

The shooting of Spanish patriots on Principe Pio Mountain by Napoleon's troops is perhaps the most famous of Goya's paintings, and the parallel between the event depicted and the murder of Ulster citizens both Catholic and Protestant emphasizes the timeless nature of such atrocities. Heaney refers to the chasseurs' bullrush-tufted shakos as "helmets," a technically correct term that lends the nightmare scene a more contemporary ambience. The picture of Saturn devouring his own offspring alludes to Joyce's Dedalean maxim: "Ireland is the old sow that eats her farrow."[91] Heaney then compares Goya's *Duel with Cudgels*—in which two Galician herdsmen bludgeon each other senseless—to a Norse "holmgang," a duel to the death between berserkers. Both Lorca and Goya remind Heaney that the artist in the midst of cultural crisis, like the protagonist of "The Last Mummer," must tread "a nice way through / the long toils of blood // and feuding."

Sections 5 and 6 of "Singing School" foreground Heaney's desire for self-actualization as a poet; however, the larger cultural crisis inevitably impinges on his quest for artistic identity. "Fosterage" acknowledges his early debt to both Michael McLaverty and Gerard Manley Hopkins. Indeed, the closure could be a brief paean to either the Irish author and headmaster or the English poet: "He discerned / The lineaments of patience everywhere / And fostered me and sent me out, with words / Imposing on my tongue like obols." An ancient Greek coin struck in silver, the obol amounted to one-sixth of a drachma. Heaney rolls the long vowels on his tongue, savoring the currency and weight of language artfully rendered. In "Exposure," the last segment of "Singing School," Heaney engages Yeats for the last time in *North*, having already chosen partial exile in the Irish Republic: "It is December in Wicklow: / Alders dripping, birches / Inheriting the last light" (*Poems* 227). He now lives in Dublin, in a stone house overlooking Joyce's squat Martello tower from *Ulysses*. He wades through "Husks, the spent flukes of autumn," pondering what he terms "My responsible *tristia*." Is he writing "For the ear? For the people? / For what is said behind-backs?" As usual, the question of identity is foremost in his mind:

> I am neither internee nor informer;
> An inner émigré, grown long-haired
> And thoughtful; a wood-kerne
>
> Escaped from the massacre,
> Taking protective colouring
> From bole and bark, feeling
> Every wind that blows;
>
> Who, blowing up these sparks
> For their meagre heat, have missed
> The once-in-a-lifetime portent,
> The comet's pulsing rose.
>
> (*Poems* 228)

When Heaney mentions his "responsible *tristia*," he puns aurally on Trieste, Joyce's initial place of exile in the Mediterranean. Still, he has not quit his native sod: he describes himself as a "wood-kerne," a Gaelic outlaw fleeing the random and premeditated violence of Northern Ireland.

Like Yeats's Magi, he remains "unsatisfied," but rather than scan the heavens for a portent, he searches the embers heaped before him. Whether it is the comet's "pulsing rose" or an actual rose arching its slow meteor over the back fence, ultimately he must become the "inner émigré" who looks within for the true source of identity.

The linguistic and cultural excavations of *Wintering Out* and *North* reflect Heaney's desire to come to terms with the initial outbreak of violence and the continuing cultural crisis in Northern Ireland. Indeed, place-name poems such as "Anahorish," "Toome," and others represent a desire for continuity, an attempt to recover what Erikson calls a "surrendered identity"[92] of cultures that have been colonized or absorbed. "Servant Boy" and "The Last Mummer" express an admiration for individuals who retain a strong sense of identity even in the midst of crisis, surviving yet refusing to be absorbed. "Traditions" and "Bone Dreams" examine the connection between language and identity, exploring the marks that colonization leaves on a native language. Yet it is literal excavation that fuels Heaney's imagination: archaeological discoveries of the bog corpses in Denmark and the Viking settlement in Dublin provide Heaney with controlling metaphors from "the locus of the given world"—images and symbols that vividly capture the nightmare of history. Like Yeats, Joyce, and other twentieth-century Irish writers, Heaney seeks "to define and interpret the present by bringing it into significant relationship with the past" (*Pr* 60). His technique owes much to Joyce's "mythic method," though contemporary English poet Geoffrey Hill's fusion of the life of Mercian king Offa with his own childhood in the West Midlands afforded Heaney a much more recent example. By virtue of "The Tollund Man" in *Wintering Out*, Heaney traces contemporary sectarian strife in Ulster back to the cult of a pre-Christian earth goddess, Nerthus, who was worshipped throughout northwest Europe. With "The Tollund Man" and the subsequent bog sequence of *North*, Heaney concocts a Counter-Sublime to the heroic ideals of Yeats's Cathleen ni Houlihan and Cuchulain, presenting a grim and fitting analogue to contemporary violence in Ulster. Unlike Yeats, Heaney's longing to forge a national identity depends upon a return to a past that is more real than legendary, a Joycean particularity that offers "the actual weight / of each hooded victim, slashed and dumped." In much the same way, Heaney portrays the Vikings who settled Dublin as "neighbourly, scoretaking / killers," colonizers absorbed by Irish culture to which they contributed. Like the bog people, they serve as the racial and spiritual ancestors of those involved in the current cycle of violence in Northern Ireland.

With his bog poems and Viking sequence, Heaney seeks identity within a larger cultural milieu: his sense of familial and cultural identity extends to include Iron Age Denmark and other countries in northern Europe. But his empathy for the bog victims goes beyond mere identification to self-implication, as he recognizes the brutal nature of his own native culture: compassion is balanced by a realization that he too would insist on "the exact / and tribal, intimate revenge" ("Punishment"). Jahan Ramazani has observed that "Heaney takes the poetics of self-accusation and self-impli-cation further than Yeats does, seldom permitting himself the grand self-justifications of Yeats's bardic mode."[93] For the first time in his work, kinship takes on negative as well as positive aspects; he acknowledges the reprehensible behavior of both sides, including the extreme nature of Irish Catholicism. As Polly Devlin notes, "Its history of social ostracism, the legal persecution that drove it underground where it had to nourish itself on itself, has nurtured it into something more obsessive than the Catholic faiths of other countries."[94] Heaney deplores the warring factions' attacks on their own no less than their violence against each other. In the bog poems, Heaney's familial and religious identity seem to fuse, reflecting a clannish, tribal identity that recognizes its own atrocities but silently en-dorses the mores of the group. Yet Erikson sees the creative individual's acceptance of negative identity as "the very base line of recovery," for it can still "contribute something akin to a collective recovery."[95]

In his anguish over the Troubles, Heaney ponders the role of the artist in a cultural crisis. Thus in *Wintering Out* and *North* he seeks kinship with a mummer whose art is displaced by modern technology and with a Viking jeweler's apprentice who etches a sample pattern into a piece of bone. Sub-sequent poems call upon Goya and Lorca as well as fellow Irish poets, who all remind him that the artist must be equally true to his artistic gift in times of war and social upheaval. Not surprisingly, the later poems of *North* seem beset with guilt and despair. The evocations of Yeats suggest that Heaney now senses firsthand both the difficulty of forging a national iden-tity and the trials of living through civil war. While Heaney's journeys, both literal and imagined, through northwest Europe may explain the prob-lem of contemporary sectarian strife in Ulster, they do nothing to alter it; the awareness of an "archetypal pattern" does not dispel the violence. Though the earlier "Funeral Rites" sought to transcend cultural fragmenta-tion and reach a common ground, such an achievement no longer seems possible. Neither the vast excavations of Heaney's early mid-career nor the move south to County Wicklow have assuaged his personal crisis of iden-tity. After the "long foray" of *North*, he finds himself seeking a "door into the light."

3

Field Work and *Station Island:*
"A Door into the Light"

H<small>EANEY'S TIMELY OBSERVATIONS ABOUT THE</small> "<small>DAUNTING PRESSURES AND</small> responsibilities" of the poet who would "forge the uncreated conscience of the race" (*Pr* 60) seem almost to foreshadow the critical reception to *North*. Blake Morrison archly remarked on the "necrophiliac" tendencies of the bog sequence; Morrison, among others, suggested that Heaney had granted the sectarian violence a "historical respectability" it had not received elsewhere.[1] To be sure, as Thomas Foster has noted, some of the most vocal critics of *North* "are tied up with the Irish Question" and "seem to lack a perspective on the matter of violence in the poems." Moreover, Foster adds, "[A]rtistic 'seeing' is not the same thing as sanction."[2] Most troubling to Heaney, it seems, were the implications that the bog poems were not deeply felt, that he had seized on the bog as an emblem for Irish experience solely as a result of reading P. V. Glob's *The Bog People*. Michael Parker, at least, acknowledges that the bogs were an early and important part of Heaney's personal history: "[F]rom childhood, bogland had been 'a genuine obsession,' since it covered such a large area of his home territory."[3]

Critics' comments and the volume's aesthetic and commercial success aside, *North* did not really solve the crisis of identity for Seamus Heaney on a personal level. In "Exposure," the sixth and final sequence of "Singing School," he sees himself as "An inner émigré, grown long-haired / And thoughtful; a wood-kerne // Escaped from the massacre." Heaney discusses his dilemma in a 1979 interview with James Randall: "I remember writing a letter to [Irish playwright] Brian Friel just after *North* was published, saying I no longer wanted a door into the dark—I want a door

into the light."[4] For Heaney, the "door into the light" may well hold both a
literal and historical meaning. According to E. Estyn Evans in *Irish Folk
Ways*, traditional Irish houses often date back to a time when window glass
was a luxury or when residents were taxed on the number of windows per
house. Thus the house typically had few windows, and those few were
small, placed away from the prevailing winds. As a result, "The ever-open
door . . . admitted most of the light."[5] In this context, the "door into the
light" literally serves as a pathway into the heart of the living community.

Heaney had already achieved national stature as a poet when he moved
from Northern Ireland to Glanmore, County Wicklow, in July 1972;
indeed, the Belfast *Protestant Telegraph* devoted a half-page to his departure for the Republic, describing him as "the well-known Papish propagan-
dist."[6] Despite the carping of those critics and polemicists obsessed with
sectarian divisions in Ulster, *North* signalled Heaney's arrival on the international scene. However, his prodigious attempt to fashion a viable mythos
embodying the cultural identity of northwest Europe culminated in a vision
almost hermetic in its remoteness, and awakened in him an urgent need to
dispel the cold grandeur hammered into every line of *North*. In the interview with Randall, Heaney emphasized a yearning "to come back to
be[ing] able to use the first person singular to mean *me* and my lifetime."[7]
Freed from the last vestiges of the pseudonym Incertus by the recognized
level of his poetic achievement, he now faced an impasse familiar only to
the most accomplished contemporaries. Lawrence Lipking offers a striking
synopsis of this dilemma in his recent study, *The Life of the Poet*:

> For much of this century intelligent critics have made a point of not read-
> ing the lives of the poets. The poem itself, they have said, must acquire a
> life of its own. And in recent years this reaction has gone still further: we
> have begun to hear about the *death* of the poet. The lives of the poets must
> be sacrificed, ruthlessly expunged from our consciousness, according to
> critics like Roland Barthes, in order to make a place for the reader, or the
> imperatives of structure. . . . Hence a great deal of modem criticism may be
> viewed as an attempt to render poems anonymous, to free them from the
> lives of the poets.[8]

From Heaney's perspective, the New Critical concept of the persona no
longer served as an adequate mode of expression; nor could he blithely
accept the nihilistic postulates of poststructuralist theorists such as Barthes.
At this point in his career, the example of Robert Lowell proved seminal.
Between 1973 and 1977, Heaney hosted a program called *Imprint* for
Radio Eirann, and his discussion of Lowell's later volumes—*History*
(1973), *For Lizzie and Harriet* (1973), and *The Dolphin* (1973)—earned

him the respect and friendship of the older poet. Lowell's *Life Studies* (1959) had already transformed the American literary scene, introducing an intensely personal style termed "Confessional" by M. L. Rosenthal, although some recent critics have described it as "the poetry of personal extremity."[9] Notwithstanding the suicides of other Confessionalists such as John Berryman and Sylvia Plath, Heaney recognized that Lowell was ultimately a survivor: "They [Berryman and Plath] swam away powerfully into the dark swirls of the unconscious and the drift towards death, but Lowell resisted that, held fast to conscience and pushed deliberately toward self-mastery" *(Pr* 223). But even more crucial to Heaney at this juncture was Lowell's unswerving "fidelity to his personal intuitions and experiences" (221). Lowell's confident self-awareness as a poet, as an artist with an intimate life uniquely his own, would provide Heaney with a salient model for his fifth volume, *Field Work* (1979). Here Heaney's voice becomes more direct and engaging, evincing a greater concern for the bonds of familial and spiritual kinship. The third sonnet in the Glanmore sequence amply illustrates his newly acquired impulse toward spontaneous utterance:

> This evening the cuckoo and the corncrake
> (So much, too much) consorted at twilight.
> It was all crepuscular and iambic.
> . . . .
> I had said earlier, "I won't relapse
> From this strange loneliness I've brought us to.
> Dorothy and William—" She interrupts:
> "You're not going to compare us two . . .?"
> Outside a rustling and twig-combing breeze
> Refreshes and relents. Is cadences.
>
> *(FW* 35)

Heaney equates the cuckoo's song and the ratchet-cry of the sedge-warbling corncrake with the roughed-up syntax and diction of his sonnet, a music at once "crepuscular and iambic." More significant is his implied comparison between the Glanmore house and Wordsworth's Dove Cottage, even though he allows his wife Marie to cut him short in the process: "You're not going to compare us two . . . ?" The dialogic exchange enables Heaney for the first time to affirm his own status as a poet; and if he declines to place himself, as Dante did, in company with Homer, Virgil, Horace, Ovid, and Lucan, we may now view him as less humbly aspiring. According to Michael Parker, Heaney found Lowell's interest in and support of his work "fortifying," thus prompting the younger poet to speak with the autobiographical assurance of one who had already earned his place "on the minor slopes of Parnassus."[10] Lowell's encouragement and example validated Heaney's sense of identity as a poet, leading him to trust his impulse toward a more personal and domestic voice. Not that Heaney became a praiser of his own past or present: indeed, many careers would falter under the relentless self-scrutiny that Heaney brings to bear on himself and his art. In the words of Henry Hart, his poetry "seems to gain force and immediacy" because of it.[11]

In "Oysters," the opening poem of *Field Work*, Heaney's "door into the light" turns on the gritty hinges of shucked bivalves. Initially, his mood is puckishly hedonistic, opting for delight in sheer indulgence:

> Our shells clacked on the plates.
> My tongue was a filling estuary,
> My palate hung with starlight:
> As I tasted the salty Pleiades
> Orion dipped his foot into the water.
>
> (*FW* 11)

A consonantal staccato like castanets suggests a festive air in the very first line, as does the briny tang of celestial membrane burst on palate and tongue. However, Heaney couples opulence with rapine in the second stanza: "Alive and violated / They lay on their beds of ice." Safely ensconced in a restaurant in the Republic, partaking of the "Glut of privilege," he experiences a sudden guilt: "Over the Alps, packed deep in hay and snow, / The Romans hauled their oysters south to Rome." He imagines "damp panniers" disgorging a heap of edible mollusks, a living trove that symbolizes the prerogatives of empire. Immediately he becomes angry

> that my trust could not repose
> In the clear light, like poetry or freedom
> Leaning in from sea. I ate the day
> Deliberately, that its tang
> Might quicken me all into verb, pure verb.
>
> (*FW* 11)

Here "verb" cannot in its purest signification be other than a noun, and rendered thus inert it gathers effluence only from the transubstantial power of the poetic imagination. Henceforth, poetry must arise from a lyric impulse, an active confrontation with life not quite broached in *North*. At least one scholar has described "Oysters" as "a sort of prologue for the volume as a whole, an attempt at creation by fiat, at turning the unresolved conflicts and turmoil of one's life into something realized, artistic, whole."[12]

In "After a Killing," the first part of "Triptych," Heaney observes "Two young men with rifles on the hill, / Profane and bracing as their instruments" (*FW* 12). The poem embodies a direct encounter with the threat of sectarian violence involving no attempt to explain it in terms of tribal blood-feuds or trace it back to the dubious compensations of the *wergild*, the Germanic "man-price" that reckoned spilled entrails at the rate of so many coins. Years spent listening to "thick rotations" of British army helicopters have exacted a toll no longer explainable from any save a personal perspective. As a result, Heaney begins to long for half-forgotten moments denoting the unique and the particular, those images somehow self-defining in their sudden clarity:

> I see a stone house by a pier.
> Elbow room. Broad window light.
> The heart lifts. You walk twenty yards
> To the boats and buy mackerel.
>
> And to-day a girl walks in home to us
> Carrying a basket full of new potatoes,
> Three tight green cabbages, and carrots
> With the tops and mould still fresh on them.
>
> (*FW* 12)

The "cascade of light" for which Heaney indulged little hope throughout *North* seems near at hand. We can almost see the sun startling rainbow tints from the bellies of fresh mackerel, scent the ripe "mould" on piled vegetables. But the poet cannot sustain this degree of pastoral integrity throughout the volume; inevitably, he reverts to memories of British occupation in the North. "The Toome Road" recalls a disorienting encounter near Mossbawn:

> One morning early I met armoured cars
> In convoy, warbling along on powerful tyres,
> All camouflaged with broken alder branches,
> And headphoned soldiers standing up in turrets.
>
> (*FW* 15)

No invasion was ever so shocking or abrupt since the third apparition summoned by the Weird Sisters in Act 4, Scene 1 of *Macbeth* augured true: "Macbeth shall never vanquished be until / Great Birnam Wood to high Dunsinane Hill / Shall come against him." The tires of the armor-plated vehicles "warble" like birds in an early morning thicket, and conspire to make the invaders' forced attempt at mimesis—the hacking of alder

branches for camouflage—all the more sinister. The unspoken rebuke that
follows stems from Heaney's current sense of identity with the land: "How
long were they approaching down my roads / As if they owned them? The
whole country was sleeping." The historical perspective of *North* is held in
momentary abeyance, as the poet vigorously asserts the rights of a property
owner: "I had rights-of-way, fields, cattle in my keeping, / Tractors hitched
to buckrakes in open sheds, / Silos, chill gates, wet slates, the greens and
reds / Of outhouse roofs" (*FW* 15). Unlike the overreaching Thane of
Cawdor in Shakespeare's play, he is content with his small demesne. But
occupying armies, even when benign, are an old story in Ireland; indeed,
Heaney's earliest memories hark back to American maneuvers in County
Derry:

> I would begin with the Greek word, *omphalos*, meaning the navel, and
> hence the stone that marked the centre of the world, and repeat it, *ompha-*
> *los, omphalos, omphalos*, until its blunt and falling music becomes the
> music of somebody pumping water at the pump outside our back door. It is
> Co. Derry in the early 1940s. The American bombers groan towards the
> aerodrome at Toomebridge, the American troops manoeuvre in the fields
> along the road, but all of that great historical action does not disturb the
> rhythms of the yard. There the pump stands, a slender, iron idol, snouted,
> helmeted, dressed down with a sweeping handle, painted a dark green and
> set on a concrete plinth, marking the centre of another world. Five house-
> holds drew water from it. (*Pr* 17)

Years later, the pump still stands like a helmeted sentry in the yard. From
subterranean depths, it draws life-sustaining water to light; moreover, it is
the guardian of secret origins, of a redemptive source that remains inviolable even as the British juggernaut breaks the dawn silence: "O chario-
teers, above your dormant guns, / It stands here still, stands vibrant as you
pass, / The invisible, untoppled omphalos." In "The Toome Road," Heaney
seems to betray an outraged sense of propriety almost completely absent
from his previous verse. His anger at the military presence on the Mossbawn acres underscores a personal sense of connectedness to the soil. The
poet's crisis of identity is temporarily suspended when he refuses to express his ire through the historical analogues so prevalent in *North*.

Unlike the earlier "Funeral Rites," the elegies in *Field Work* reveal a
personal and immediate engagement with the lingering specter of sectarian
murder. "The Strand at Lough Beg" envisions the final moments of
Heaney's second cousin, Colum McCartney, an Armagh carpenter waylaid
and shot as he drove home from a football match in Dublin.[13] The poem
opens with the image of McCartney "Leaving the white glow of filling sta-

tions" on Dublin's outskirts, and beginning the long ascent "towards New-townhamilton / Past the Fews Forest, out beneath the stars" (*FW* 17). As soon as the protagonist quits the familiar haunts of men, Heaney imagines him retracing unawares the path of mad Sweeney, the legendary medieval king who fled before the myriad hobgoblins conjured by a cleric's curse in the *Buile Suibhne*: "[T]hat road, a high, bare pilgrim's track / Where Sweeney fled before the bloodied heads, / Goat-beards and dogs' eyes in a demon pack." The poet then juxtaposes against these fantastic images a plausible scenario for the ambush: "What blazed ahead of you? A faked road block? / The red lamp swung, the sudden brakes and stalling / Engine, voices, heads hooded and the cold-nosed gun?" Prosaic enough in the light of day, the hooded men become headless torsos on the dark road; more-over, the gun is "cold-nosed," feral as the phantom pack that pursued Sweeney over the upland Fews. The implied metaphor lends the small-cal-iber pistol's sudden yap a terrible clarity. Heaney points up the random and gratuitous nature of the killing, emphasizing that his cousin was flagged down "Where you weren't known and far from what you knew: / The low-land clays and waters of Lough Beg, / Church Island's spire, its soft tree-line of yew." Whether he was detained by members of the Provisional I.R.A. or Protestant paramilitaries, McCartney lost the identity that com-munity confers when he ventured out along the starlit roads. In the se-cond stanza, Heaney not only claims kinship with the victim, he also at-tempts to restore him to his proper element. He recalls their youth in rural Ulster:

> There you used hear guns fired behind the house
> Long before rising time, when duck shooters
> Haunted the marigolds and bulrushes,
> But still were scared to find spent cartridges,
> Acrid, brassy, genital, ejected,
> On your way across the strand to fetch the cows.
> For you and yours and yours and mine fought shy,
> Spoke an old language of conspirators
> And could not crack the whip or seize the day:
> Big-voiced scullions, herders, feelers round
> Haycocks and hindquarters, talkers in byres,
> Slow arbitrators of the burial ground.
>
> (*FW* 17)

Heaney's setting scarcely resembles that of the traditional pastoral elegy. The "bulrushes" at the margins of the lough suggest Stygian waters, a foreshadowing of death. Moreover, his cousin fears the duck hunters'

brass-gleaming and red-jacketed cartridges; recently discharged and scattered about, they are redolent of a violence both alien and mechanical:
"Acrid, brassy, genital, ejected." The initial trochees in the fifth line capture the emphatic recoil of a pump-action shotgun. The poet then descants
on the old Northern reticence, recounting how he and his kinsman were
conspirators only in the art of animal husbandry, unschooled in factional
disputes. Uninvolved "in anything at all political,"[14] McCartney has run
afoul of those who know only too well how to "crack the whip or seize the
day."

Having returned the victim to his own milieu, in the third stanza
Heaney recalls cattle grazing "Up to their bellies in an early mist" and
Lough Beg shining "like a dull blade with its edge / Honed bright." He
suddenly misses McCartney's slow footing behind him in the sedge: "I
turn because the sweeping of your feet / Has stopped behind me, to find
you on your knees / With blood and roadside muck in your hair and eyes."
Heaney's ritual cleansing of the body not only mollifies the fatal wound
but also restores identity to one disfigured by a brutal death:

> Then [I] kneel in front of you in brimming grass
> And gather up cold handfuls of the dew
> To wash you, cousin. I dab you clean with moss
> Fine as the drizzle out of a low cloud.
> I lift you under the arms and lay you flat.
> With rushes that shoot green again, I plait
> Green scapulars to wear over your shroud.

(*FW*18)

The face that emerges beneath the damp moss in Heaney's sedulous hand
is not the Tollund Man's, or even the moustached archaic countenance of
a rural ancestor. It is his second cousin's. Moreover, the act of purification
is non-transcendental: "he cleanses the dead man not with fire but with
dew and with earthly 'moss / Fine as the drizzle of a low cloud.' Instead
of sending the dead man up into the clouds, the clouds come down to the
earth."[15] Thus Heaney curtails any tendency toward the sort of apotheosis
that could estrange the poet from his subject. If the scapulars he plaits
"shoot green again," implying renewal, the gesture identifies McCartney
as distinctly Catholic, and therefore a member of the religious community that nurtured Heaney in his youth. "The Strand at Lough Beg"
marks Heaney's first effort to internalize the current Troubles within an
elegiac frame, to deal with sectarian death on a personal level. Indeed,
Elmer Andrews insists that the issue of psychic identity permeates *Field
Work*:

Field Work constructs an Irish landscape at once politically-charged, communal, relevant: but it is a kind of cultural landscape moulded out of Heaney's own psychic disposition. He deals with the contemporary crisis, not by accepting the formulation it is given in the public world, but by making his own domesticated imagery, his own terrain, take the colour of it. Hence, the countryside which had once meant bulls and blackberry-picking, forges and furrows, is now constantly under threat.[16]

The issue of identity proves far more complex in "Casualty," an elegy for a Lough Neagh fisherman named Louis O'Neill. A regular at the Ardboe public house owned by Heaney's father-in-law, he is a master of the articulate gesture, adept at extinguishing glass after glass:

> He would drink by himself
> And raise a weathered thumb
> Towards the high shelf,
> Calling another rum
> And blackcurrant, without
> Having to raise his voice,
> Or order a quick stout
> By a lifting of the eyes
> And a discreet dumb-show
> Of pulling off the top.
>
> (*FW* 21)

Heaney's taut trimeter line, as well as his alternating rhyme scheme, echoes Yeats's "The Fisherman"; however, Heaney's protagonist is a long-time acquaintance with a distinctive personality rather than the archetypal figure for whom the Sligo laureate would write a poem "As cold / and passionate as the dawn." Obviously, O'Neill's taciturn eloquence extends beyond the expert "down-turn of wrist / When the flies drop in the stream" that Yeats so admired. O'Neill belongs to a generation of eel poachers whose livelihood depended on successfully eluding the water bailiff on Lough Neagh. During O'Neill's youth, fishing rights on the Lough—originally acquired by chicanery and corruption in the sixteenth century—were owned by a London-based company that issued licenses grudgingly and also applied "restrictions and stipulations, including one that the licensee must sell his catch to the consortium at prices lower than those on the open market."[17] Like the speaker of "Whatever You Say, Say Nothing," the fisherman in "Casualty" inhabits the "land of password, handgrip, wink and nod, / Of open minds as open as a trap." Heaney expresses fondness for the old man's peculiar brand of subtlety and candor:

> I loved his whole manner,
> Sure-footed but too sly,
> His deadpan sidling tact,
> His fisherman's quick eye
> And turned observant back.
>
> (*FW* 21)

The interrogative turn of O'Neill's "observant back" will return to haunt Heaney again and again. "[A]lways politic / And shy of condescension," the poet resorts to evasions of his own when the eel-fisher questions him about his art: "I would manage by some trick / To switch the talk to eels / Or lore of the horse and cart" (*FW* 21–22). Both Heaney and his protagonist fight shy of what might be a baited hook. Ironically, O'Neill subsequently dies in a bombing incident:

> He was blown to bits
> Out drinking in a curfew
> Others obeyed, three nights
> After they shot dead
> The thirteen men in Derry.
> PARAS THIRTEEN, the walls said,
> BOGSIDE NIL.
>
> (*FW* 22)

Why did the fisherman refuse to obey the curfew imposed by the I.R.A. for the Wednesday night following Bloody Sunday? For the moment, Heaney offers no definitive explanation; in part 2, he describes the funeral for the thirteen Catholic victims killed by British troops on 30 January 1972, and relates how O'Neill defied the sanctions of his own community:

> The common funeral
> Unrolled its swaddling band,
> Lapping, tightening
> Till we were braced and bound
> Like brothers in a ring.
>
> But he would not be held
> At home by his own crowd.
>
> (*FW* 22)

Here Heaney's meticulous use of participles—"swaddling," "Lapping," "tightening," "bound"—suggests a familiar constriction, as if the torc of the goddess invoked in "The Tollund Man" were slowly asserting its lethal magic; moreover, the cadence of these lines implies a hypnotic lock-step, a funeral tread moving away from personal grief and toward communal outrage. Both Morrison and Corcoran view the passage as a negative depiction of tribal solidarity; in fact, Tim Pat Coogan stresses the potency of public funerals in generating support for the I.R.A.[18] Although Heaney admits that O'Neill "drank like a fish," the old man was apparently more the victim of an unquenchable spirit than a raging thirst. He could not resist "the lure / of warm lit-up places," the quiet conviviality of "gregarious smoke" hovering through the pubs. Nevertheless, Heaney must ask the essential question, "How culpable was he / That last night when he broke / Our tribe's complicity," and the old angler responds almost mockingly:

> "Now you're supposed to be
> An educated man,"
> I hear him say. "Puzzle me
> The right answer to that one."
>
> (FW 23)

In section 3, Heaney represents the mourners at O'Neill's funeral as "quiet walkers / And sideways talkers," people who "move in equal pace / With the habitual / Slow consolation / Of a dawdling engine." The engine's rhythm dissolves into the wake of O'Neill's fishing boat:

> I was taken in his boat,
> The screw purling, turning
> Indolent fathoms white,
> I tasted freedom with him.
> To get out early, haul
> Steadily off the bottom,
> Dispraise the catch, and smile
> As you find a rhythm
> Working you, slow mile by mile,
> Into your proper haunt
> Somewhere, well out, beyond.
>
> (FW 23–24)

The fisherman allows the gleam and drag of the current to move through him like an unbidden joy, to carry him as he works the line "well out, beyond" into his own vast and solitary element. Heaney immediately intuits the affinity between their respective crafts, and implores O'Neill's further tutelage: "Dawn-sniffing revenant, / Plodder through midnight rain, / Question me again" (24). Indeed, Corcoran considers "Casualty" crucial to Heaney's search for personal and aesthetic identity:

The apparently confident analogies between poetry and rural crafts in the earlier work, which "bound" the poet to the community, have been replaced, in the analogy of "Casualty," by something much edgier, more uncertain, more "tentative": one of the community's skills, as it is practised by the strong-willed O'Neill, offers a lesson in questioning the community's own values and presumptions. Heaney's invitation to O'Neill to "Question me again" may be regarded as initiating the elaborate self-questioning of "Station Island."[19]

"Casualty" is the harbinger of a change in Heaney's attitude toward those things that poetry can legitimately encompass. It celebrates the untrammeled spirit of the individual, the subversive yet life-affirming potential of the lyric moment. In an essay titled "The Interesting Case of Nero, Chekhov's Cognac and a Knocker," Heaney cites "Jung's thesis that an insoluble conflict is overcome by outgrowing it, developing in the process a 'new level of consciousness'" (*GT* xxii). Although Heaney's "new level of consciousness" does not come to full fruition until he undertakes the arduous pilgrimage at the heart of *Station Island*, the personal tone of "Casualty," as opposed to "The Forge" or "Thatcher," presages his growing commitment to artistic freedom and the necessities of the imagination.

"Elegy," a memorial poem for Robert Lowell, reprises Heaney's burgeoning desire for a poetry of personal utterance: "The way we are living, / timorous or bold, / will have been our life" (*FW* 31). Several factors may have influenced Heaney's tendency to identify with the American poet. Like Heaney after his relocation from Northern Ireland to the Republic, Lowell often found himself at odds with the political climate of his day. In his twenties, Lowell converted to Roman Catholicism, and as a result, the confrontation between Boston's stodgy Protestant ethos and the Irish Catholic community became a recurring theme in his early poetry. Lowell also deplored the civilian casualties that resulted from the bombings of London, Dresden, and Hiroshima during World War II, suffering brief internment himself as "a fire-breathing Catholic C.O." More likely, Lowell's refusal to allow history to impinge on his self-awareness as an artist attracted Heaney to "the master elegist / and welder of English." His recollection of Lowell's final visit to Glanmore in September 1977 bears a remarkable resemblance to afternoons spent on Lough Neagh with Louis O'Neill:

> As you swayed the talk
> and rode on the swaying tiller
> of yourself, ribbing me
> about my fear of water,

what was not within your empery?
You drank America
like the heart's
iron vodka,

promulgating art's
deliberate, peremptory
love and arrogance.

(*FW* 31)

As Elmer Andrews asserts, "'Elegy' registers Heaney's tender feelings towards the life of anguish and crisis that lies behind Lowell's poetry, his gratitude for the art that Lowell could not or would not separate from life."[20] Moreover, the poem is not the mawkish homage that some critics claim. Heaney alludes in the second of the above stanzas to a practical joke "Cal" once played on him. In 1976, he called to see Lowell in a small private hospital, and the elder poet prompted him to indulge in "a restorative nip from his Imperial After Shave bottle, which he had assured me contained Benedictine."[21] Thus Heaney envisions Lowell taking a bitter dram of his own, imbibing the hard and tempestuous spirits of Jonathan Edwards, Cotton Mather, and Melville's Captain Ahab. Nevertheless, Heaney expresses personal affection and gratitude for Lowell's exemplary devotion to their mutual craft, "the course set wilfully across / the ungovernable and dangerous" (*FW* 32).

"In Memoriam Francis Ledwidge" returns Heaney to the cultural and historical perspective that dominated *North*. Born in Slane, County Meath, in 1887, Ledwidge joined the Fifth Battalion of the Royal Iniskilling Fusiliers during October 1914; after surviving the Gallipoli landings and the Serbian front, he was killed, as Heaney's note reminds us, near the Ypres Salient on 31 July 1917.[22] Reared in the valley of the Boyne, the site of Catholic Ireland's "last stand" against Williamite forces in the late seventeenth century, Ledwidge did not fully experience Ireland's divided heritage until the outbreak of World War I. Heaney's poem opens with the speaker standing before a piece of stock commemorative statuary, a bronze Tommy similar to hundreds of others that dot the Four Kingdoms:

The bronze soldier hitches a bronze cape
That crumples stiffly in imagined wind
No matter how the real winds buff and sweep
His sudden hunkering run, forever craned

Over Flanders. Helmet and haversack,

The gun's firm slope from butt to bayonet,
The loyal, fallen names on the embossed plaque.

(*FW* 59)

Heaney deftly captures the romantic nostalgia often associated with World War I by simply describing the cape more appropriate to a statue of Sir Walter Raleigh than a British rifleman up to his bootstraps in Flanders mud. The sculptor ironically chose the perfect medium for his subject: what better substance than bronze to recreate the stiff corrugations visited by an imaginary wind? Heaney's rhythms give us a genuine sense of young infantrymen slogging through shell-pitted terrain in the repetition of *u* sounds in "sudden hunkering run." His rendering of the rifle's "firm slope from butt to bayonet" recalls the absurd close order drill employed during the suicidal "walkovers" on the Western Front. A generation of souls disappears into the gleaming column of names inscribed on a plaque. Having first exposed some of the discrepancies between patriotic sympathy and the terrible cost of World War I, Heaney suddenly switches the setting and tone: "It all meant little to the worried pet // I was in nineteen forty-six or seven, / Gripping my aunt Mary by the hand." Strolling the Portstewart promenade hand in hand with his beloved aunt, the eight-year-old Heaney encounters idyllic scenes reminiscent of the Georgian era: "Courting couples rose out of the scooped dunes. / A farmer stripped to his studs and shiny waistcoat / Rolled the trousers down on his timid shins." We see the familiar penchant for imagistic clarity in the young farmer's sunstruck studs; moreover, the swain's unwonted modesty is engagingly humorous. Heaney then alludes to rural Irish rituals that recur throughout his *oeuvre*: "Country voices rose from a cliff-top shelter / With news of a great litter— 'We'll pet the runt!'— / And barbed wire that had torn a friesian's elder." But the barbed wire strikes a sinister note, conjuring a vision of soldiers caught up in miles of bristling steel strung across the Somme and Ypres countrysides. Only at the beginning of the sixth quatrain does Heaney address the fallen poet: "Francis Ledwidge, you courted at the seaside / Beyond Drogheda one Sunday afternoon. / Literary, sweet-talking, countrified." The point of identification is obvious, although strained and specious; indeed, Heaney seldom achieves the level of thought and language we have come to expect of him:

I think of you in your Tommy's uniform,
A haunted Catholic face, pallid and brave,
Ghosting the trenches with a bloom of hawthorn
Or silence cored from a Boyne passage-grave.

(*FW* 60)

The pathos of the "Catholic face, pallid and brave" amounts to special pleading and diffuses the irony implicit in the fact that Ledwidge wears a "Tommy's uniform." On the other hand, the silence "cored from a Boyne passage-grave" reminds us of Ledwidge's birthplace near the megalithic tombs at Newgrange, and recalls Wilfred Owen's haunting description of trench warfare in "Strange Meeting": "It seemed that out of battle I escaped / Down some profound dull tunnel, long since scooped / Through granites which titanic wars had groined."[23] But for the most part, Heaney's elegy is too elliptical to sustain a consistent tone; moreover, it appears that he seeks to establish a tenuous connection between his aunt and the dead soldier-poet:

> It's summer, nineteen-fifteen. I see the girl
> My aunt was then, herding on the long acre.
> Behind a low bush in the Dardanelles
> You suck stones to make your dry mouth water.
>
> It's nineteen-seventeen. She still herds cows
> But a big strafe puts the candles out in Ypres.
>
> (FW 60)

Doubtless Heaney refers to the many young men and women whose prospects of marriage and children were dramatically reduced by the staggering toll of World War I, but a rural upbringing forms the sole affinity between his Aunt Mary and Ledwidge. Heaney strives to see his own crisis of identity in Ledwidge's plight, and goes so far as to quote his fellow poet and countryman directly in the twelfth quatrain:

> "To be called a British soldier while my country
> Has no place among nations. . . ." You were rent
> By shrapnel six weeks later. "I am sorry
> That party politics should divide our tents."
>
> (FW 60)

Here it becomes evident that Heaney is disingenuous in his choice of poets to eulogize. Ledwidge had been a labor organizer in County Meath prior to the war, and claimed to believe in the old adage that "England's misfortune is Ireland's chance." Notwithstanding his reservations, he did not hesitate to join the Tenth Irish Division, mainly because his Anglo-Irish patron, Lord Dunsany, was serving as an officer in the expeditionary force. Dunsany was on leave during the week of the Easter Rebellion, and in spite of being wounded by the insurgents, never faltered in his friendship toward Ledwidge. Returning home a few days later, Ledwidge mooned about the ruins of the General Post Office, and subsequently wrote an elegy for Thomas MacDonagh, but aside from a quarrel with a British duty officer who refused his request for extended leave, he contributed nothing to the Rebellion. The lines Heaney chooses to quote derive from a letter that Ledwidge wrote to an American professor seeking biographical information for a series of lectures on contemporary poets:

> I am sorry that party politics should ever divide our own tents but am not without hope that a new Ireland will arise from her ashes in the ruins of Dublin, like the Phoenix, with one purpose, one aim, and one ambition. I tell you this in order that you may know what it is to me to be called a British soldier while my own country has no place amongst the nations but the place of Cinderella.[24]

One would hope that these sentiments had been expressed directly to Lord Dunsany, but they were not. In short, Ledwidge was a literary opportunist who lacked the courage of his political convictions. Unlike Wilfred Owen, he made no effort to accurately portray the horrors of modern warfare, and even Curtayne concedes that "he contributed nothing to war poetry as such, [and] he cannot be accurately described as a war poet."[25] Perhaps Heaney offers a more revealing portrait of Ledwidge in his article "The Labourer and the Lord":

> His tensions might be represented in his sporting interests—he played Gaelic football for the local team but liked to be in on the cricket which Dunsany arranged each summer; or in his literary affiliations—he was friendly with Thomas MacDonagh, executed in 1916, and wrote his best-known poem to his memory, yet his first volume was introduced to the world by a Unionist peer and published while he was serving with the British Army. (*Pr* 203)

We can readily discern in Ledwidge's personality a crisis of identity that superficially resembles Heaney's, but the difference lies in the frankness with which Heaney replied to Penguin Books when the publisher included his poems in an anthology of contemporary British poetry:

> be advised
> My passport's green.
> No glass of ours was ever raised
> To toast *The Queen*.[26]

Heaney concludes "In Memoriam Francis Ledwidge" with a return to the British Tommy cast in bronze; again, he addresses the fallen Irishman directly:

> And as the wind tunes through this vigilant bronze
> I hear again the sure confusing drum
>
> You followed from Boyne water to the Balkans
> But miss the twilit note your flute should sound.
> You were not keyed or pitched like these true-blue ones
> Though all of you consort now underground.
>
> (*FW* 60)

An impromptu note rises through the "vigilant bronze," metamorphosing into "the twilit note your flute should sound." This pastoral image suggests that Ledwidge should have remained in the Boyne valley, and responded to the war with a Joycean *non serviam*. Indeed, Heaney earlier imagined the young man "peddl[ing] out the leafy road from Slane // Where you belonged, among the dolorous / And lovely." As an elegy for pre-war Georgian innocence, "In Memoriam Francis Ledwidge" is an effective poem. But Heaney's implied analogy between himself and Ledwidge ultimately does not hold. Obliged to carry the weight of Heaney's own crisis of identity, his sense of divided origins and responsibilities, Ledwidge inevitably becomes a minor player in a theater of conflict too vast for his modest gifts to encompass.

"In Memoriam Francis Ledwidge" almost certainly represents an attempt to emulate Lowell's "For the Union Dead." But Heaney's commemorative bronze too closely parallels St. Gaudin's bas-relief of Colonel Robert Shaw and his "bell-cheeked Negro infantry."[27] In 1863, Shaw led the all-black Massachusetts 54th Regiment in a fatal assault on Battery Wagner, a fortress guarding Charleston Harbor. The young officer's body was subsequently thrown into a ditch "and lost with his 'niggers,'" a mass burial not unlike the one that overtakes Ledwidge and his British comrades in Flanders. Unfortunately, Heaney's poem lacks the startling transitions, the almost pre-rational cohesion of "For the Union Dead." "In Memoriam Francis Ledwidge" never achieves the magisterial tone of Lowell's public ode, and contains more pathos than tragedy.

Although Heaney recovers in the "Glanmore Sonnets" the intensely personal voice made accessible by Lowell's example, he significantly avoids the solipsism endemic to the Confessional mode. According to Robert Langbaum, "[t]he solipsist-narcissist syndrome defines the main problem of identity treated by literature since the Romantics."[28] Most Confessional poets, including Lowell, Berryman, and Plath, harbored the need for a strong individuality that could reject old values and generate new ones, but their utter self-absorption often led to isolation from both nature and the empirical truths that inform day-to-day existence. In the "Glanmore Sonnets," Heaney continues to trust the personal voice that enabled him to slough off the hermetic grandeur of *North*, but he also returns to the domestic "spots of time" that invest the earlier poems in *Death of a Naturalist*—"Digging," "An Advancement of Learning," "Blackberry-Picking," and "Follower"—with striking immediacy. Again, Langbaum's analysis of the Romantics, especially Wordsworth, offers helpful insight into Heaney's evolving identity:

> The pleasurable tranquility that is soul exists outside us as well as inside; it exists in those places hallowed by significant experiences. Place, in Wordsworth, is the spatial projection of psyche, because it is the repository of memory. We can understand the relation in Wordsworth between mind and nature, once we understand that Wordsworth evolves his soul or sense of identity as he identifies more and more such hallowed places. We can understand the relation in Wordsworth between the themes of memory and growing up, once we understand that for Wordsworth you advance in life by traveling back again to the beginning, by reassessing your life, by binding your days together anew.[29]

Heaney has referred to the "Glanmore Sonnets" as his "marriage poems,"[30] but the ten-poem cycle also reassesses the initial encounter between "world and word" broached early in his career. The "creatural existence" that Heaney celebrated in *Death of a Naturalist* is refurnished from the perspective of an adult: in short, the poet puts aside childish things, no longer relying on the mediation of a speaker whose perceptions of the world remain essentially nascent in the face of accumulated experience. Nevertheless, a distinct continuity between past and present informs the "Glanmore Sonnets," inasmuch as the Glanmore cottage in County Wicklow serves as a Southern counterpart to the rural environs of Mossbawn. In his November 1988 interview with Bel Mooney, Heaney reveals that the roles of husband and parent figured prominently in his decision to move to Wicklow, but it is clear that he also sought to refresh his own sensibilities during the Glanmore sojourn:

> I wanted the kids to have that sort of wild animal life that I had. They were like little rodents through the hedges. . . . I wanted that eye-level life with the backs of ditches, the ferns and the smell of cow-dung, and I suppose I didn't want to lose that in myself.[31]

The first line of Sonnet I echoes the poet's intention in "Digging" to delve with a pen rather than a spade: "Vowels ploughed into other: opened ground." But it would seem that Heaney's tool of choice is no longer the cumbersome slane. The *V* in "Vowels" becomes an ideogram for the well-honed ploughsock, and the successive *o* sounds in the line lead aurally to "opened ground." However, in the process of effacing the boundaries between world and word, Heaney refuses to lapse into a self-reflexive system of signs:

> Our road is steaming, the turned-up acres breathe.
> Now the good life could be to cross a field
> And art a paradigm of earth new from the lathe
> Of ploughs. My lea is deeply tilled.
>
> (*FW* 33)

The earth is fecund, almost sentient, a rich presence that breathes frost into the unseasonably mild February air. Heaney equates "the good life" with pacing off his own acres, simultaneously comparing his art to "earth new from the lathe" or moldboard of a plough. Here the idea of shaping anew proves paramount: as the ploughman moves the field tier by tier toward the bounteous yield of autumn, so the poet realigns his inner resources and moves toward a more profound awareness of himself and others. The "paradigm" or pattern is deeply familiar, arousing old memories and absorbing individual perceptions into an intuited whole: "Old ploughsocks gorge the subsoil of each sense / And I am quickened with a redolence / Of the fundamental dark unblown rose." The pristine rose, intricate as a knot, seems the embodiment of sensuality, and yet it more readily evokes the Dantean symbol of the Host of the Blessed[32] than the carnal rose of the *carpe diem* motif. The metaphorical "dark unblown rose" intimates a new beginning for Heaney, and suggests that the poet must return to his origins if he wishes to evolve a singular identity. Sonnet I closes with a haunting recognition: "Wait then . . . Breasting the mist, in sowers' aprons, / My ghosts come striding into their spring stations. / The dream grain whirls like freakish Easter snows" (*FW* 33). Like figures in a tapestry, the apparitions recede into the warp and woof of the "dream grain" broadcast from their own hands.

Sonnet II recapitulates and reinforces the aesthetic premise set forth in the previous poem. Once again, proximity to nature is essential, as words acquire a scurrying life of their own: "Sensings, mountings from the hiding places, / Words entering almost the sense of touch / Ferreting themselves out of their dark hutch" (*FW* 34). Irrepressible as Heaney's own children ("like little rodents through the hedges"), words must embody the pre-articulate and instinctual before the poet brings them to light. Heaney then relates an amusingly sophisticated analogue to this proposition:

> "These things are not secrets but mysteries,"
> Oisin Kelly told me years ago
> In Belfast, hankering after stone
> That connived with the chisel, as if the grain
> Remembered what the mallet tapped to know.
>
> (*FW* 34)

We can easily imagine Kelly in an apron not unlike those worn by the sowers in Sonnet I; covered with the dust of pulverized stone, he simply re-iterates Michelangelo's near-mystical theory of art: the sculptor's challenge consists of locating the form that slumbers in the material. Heaney brings the theory to life in deft cadences, as glyptic *t* sounds mimic the mallet's tapping, throwing into sharp relief the contour of vowels in words such as "stone," "connived," and "know." Moreover, Heaney strives in language for what Rilke called "penetration into the confidence of things": "Those things that are outside us in daily life are absorbed into the artist's mind, where, without surrendering their material reality, they acquire a spiritual one as well."[33] But the poet must forsake what he has learned in both academic and artistic circles; simply put, he must get back to the source of his inspiration:

> Then I landed in the hedge-school of Glanmore
> And from the backs of ditches hoped to raise
> A voice caught back off slug-horn and slow chanter
> That might continue, hold, dispel, appease.
>
> (*FW* 34)

Hedge-schools were conducted by and for Irish Catholic peasants during the years of the Penal Laws, when no government provision for their education existed. According to Blake Morrison, these grass-roots institutions were often "[b]ased in barns, cow-sheds, and even the open air."[34] For Heaney, it is the literal hedge of Glanmore that presents possibilities of renewal: he seeks an attunement to nature minute as the horn of a slug negotiating its way through bramble and gorse. His closing couplet repeats the first line of Sonnet I, but the difference is more than syntactical: "Vowels ploughed into other, opened ground, / Each verse returning like the plough turned round." In "The Makings of a Music," Heaney emphasizes the Latin origins of "verse," extending its meaning to include Wordsworth's peculiar methodology:

"Verse" comes from the Latin *versus* which could mean a line of poetry but could also mean the turn that a ploughman made at the head of a field as he finished one furrow and faced back into another. Wordsworth on the gravel path, to-ing and fro-ing like a ploughman up and down a field, his voice rising and falling between the measure of his pentameters, unites the old walking meaning of *versus* with the newer, talking sense of verse. (*Pr* 65)

No longer the awkward neophyte stumbling along in his father's "hob-nailed wake" ("Follower"), Heaney maps each furrow with the precision of an expert. He acknowledges directly his debt to Wordsworth's sure-footed turn and counter-turn, but his growing sense of the polytropic potential of language also hints at the influence of Joyce, who, like Odysseus, was "a man of many turns."

In Sonnet III, Heaney tacitly compares the Glanmore dwelling to Wordsworth's Dove Cottage, and although his wife abruptly dismisses the analogy, the poet obviously brings time past to bear on time present. Not only does he claim spiritual kinship with Wordsworth, he also recognizes the aesthetic and philosophical obligation owed his English predecessor. Heaney would seem to agree with Langbaum's assertion that Wordsworth transformed the modern creative consciousness: "he caused us to be born anew by leading us back to nature and helping us to find in our roots there a new source of vitality and spirituality, by showing us how to start again from the beginning."[35] Indeed, Langbaum credits Wordsworth with establishing the model "of the modern self-creating, self-regarding identity, which draws its vital force from organic connection with nature."[36] In Sonnet V, Heaney seeks both personal and etymological roots in the natural world:

> Soft corrugations in the boortree's trunk,
> Its green young shoots, its rods like freckled solder:
> It was our bower as children, a greenish, dank
> And snapping memory as I get older.

> (*FW* 37)

As in *Wintering Out*, the poet looks to linguistic origins. The root of "boortree," "boor," is akin to the Old English *gebúr* meaning "dweller, husbandman, farmer," which derives in turn from *búr*: "dwelling, cottage, bower."[37] Dark as the hutch from which words ferret themselves in Sonnet II, the tree's bole and branches sheltered Heaney and his siblings as children. Heaney's imagery is highly tactile, concerned with surface and texture, from the "Soft corrugations" of the tree's trunk to its "rods like freckled solder." An alloy of lead and tin, solder in its molten form accumulates in glowing nubs and fuses metallic joints together; in an organic context, the image suggests the uniting of scion and stock to form a graft. But time and mutability have wrought a dramatic change. Like Wordsworth, whose "genial spirits . . . decay" as memory fades, so Heaney feels the branches of his childhood bower become "a greenish, dank / And snapping memory as I get older." Moreover, the years Heaney spent on "the fine / Lawns of elocution" ("The Ministry of Fear") have taught him a different name for his sheltering boortree:

> And elderberry I have learned to call it.
> I love its blooms like saucers brimmed with meal,
> Its berries a swart caviar of shot,
> A bouyant spawn, a light bruised out of purple.
> Elderberry? It is shires dreaming wine.
>
> (FW 37)

"Elderberry" seems a misnomer to Heaney, and his recollections focus on the brimming white blossoms that eventually yield tart berry clusters. These he describes in a series of metaphors beginning with "a swart caviar of shot." "Swart," from the Old English *sweart*, can be traced back to the Old High German *swarz*, meaning black. "Shot" ultimately derives from the Old Norse *skot*, and lends a volatile cast to the fruit that loads each branch. "Caviar," the roe of the sturgeon, alludes to the cold, fish-breeding waters of the North. But these highly impressionistic images and weighty etymologies give way to a "bouyant spawn," which in turn becomes a luminescence "bruised" out of darker hues. Heaney rejects the locution "elderberry" as peculiarly British, as "shires dreaming wine." He then reiterates his original premise: "Boortree is bower tree, where I played 'touching tongues' / And felt another's texture quick on mine." The boortree is also a place of sexual awakening; unlike the "shires dreaming wine," the image of "touching tongues" proves more tactile than gustatory, a subtle delectation more intoxicating than fermenting fruit. Heaney rolls the word "boortree" like a ripe berry on his tongue, and experiences more than the simple pleasures of the text. The return to nature, to personal and etymological origins, provides an awakening almost spiritual in its intensity. But in order to find this "door into the light," to discover a self-regarding identity uniquely his own, the poet must retrace his connection to nature through language: "So, etymologist of roots and graftings, / I fall back to my tree-house and would crouch / Where small buds shoot and flourish in the hush" (*FW* 37).

Throughout the "Glanmore Sonnets," Heaney revisits in a County Wicklow setting the themes that dominate *Death of a Naturalist*. Unlike

Shakespeare's Neoplatonic spirit Ariel, who "howled away twelve winters"[38] imprisoned in the cleft of a pine by the witch Sycorax, the poet
draws strength and sustenance from the corporeal world and the sensual
pleasures of his native boortree. In Sonnet VIII, he strives to realize a current sense of identity with his wife. The horizon is clairvoyant with lightning as his ax-bit heats up in the splintering grain of a log. By the time the
first plush drop plummets home, Heaney has sought shelter from the
storm: "Thunderlight on the split logs: big raindrops / At body heat and
lush with omen / Spattering dark on the hatchet iron." The subdued eroti-
cism of these lines quickly yields to portentous imaginings reminiscent of
the Scots border ballads or *Macbeth*:

> This morning when a magpie with jerky steps
> Inspected a horse asleep beside the wood
> I thought of dew on armour and carrion.
> What would I meet, blood-boltered, on the road?
>
> (*FW* 40)

Heaney's arcane phrasing in line seven, "blood-boltered," unmistakably
alludes to *Macbeth* and the scene wherein the usurper sees the royal lineage of Banquo reaffirmed in a vision: "Now I see 'tis true; / For the
blood-boltered Banquo smiles upon me / And points at them for his."[39]
The poet also strikes a subtle resonance between Sonnet VIII and "The
Toome Road": he imagines "dew on armor and carrion," and we recall immediately the branch-laden armored cars that disrupted the sylvan calm of
early morning in County Derry. Indeed, Heaney implies that violence and
foreboding are his own inheritance; the guilt he accrued for fleeing the
Troubles in the North still lacerates his conscience. The ensuing questions
evoke not only the familiar spirit of the second Weird Sister, but also the
volatile "slime kings" gathered for vengeance in "Death of a Naturalist":
"How deep in the woodpile sat the toad? / What welters through this dark
hush on the crops?" Remembering how song assuages even the most aber-
rant sorrows, he addresses his wife directly: "Do you remember that pen-
sion in *Les Landes* / Where the old one rocked and rocked and rocked / A
mongol in her lap, to little songs?" Divining his wife's presence in the
darkened house, Heaney silently entreats her to join him: "Come to me
quick, I am upstairs shaking. / My all of you birchwood in lightning"
(*FW* 40). Only the connubial embrace and sexual catharsis can release the
poet from what Michael Parker terms "the pangs of conscience and consciousness."[40] That Heaney employs elements of Shakespearean drama to
endow the domestic setting of the Glanmore sequence with intertextual
richness should not be too surprising at this juncture; along with Mar-

lowe's *Faustus*, *Macbeth* is the supreme example of the *psychomachia* or soul-battle.

Sonnet IX briefly externalizes the fears that plagued Heaney as a child: "Outside the kitchen window a black rat / Sways on the briar like infected fruit." The loathsome simile conjures the "rat-grey fungus, glutting on our cache" from "Blackberry-Picking." Indeed, the fire-eyed rodent he managed to face down in "An Advancement of Learning" rekindles its feral gaze, turning it in his wife's direction: "'It looked me through, it stared me out, I'm not / Imagining things. Go you out to it'" (*FW* 41). Vaguely resenting the intrusion, he goes out to confirm or allay his wife's fears:

> Did we come to the wilderness for this?
> We have our burnished bay tree at the gate,
> Classical, hung with the reek of silage
> From the next farm, tart-leafed as inwit.
>
> (*FW* 41)

The bay tree, a classic emblem of pastoral poetry, seems blighted by the specter that haunted the Mossbawn homestead. Moreover, Heaney never became inured to the almost casual violence required of the husbandman intent on his labors. He remembers with a shudder "Blood on a pitch-fork, blood on chaff and hay, / Rats speared in the sweat and dust of threshing." When Heaney arrives on the spot, the "empty briar is swishing" like a vague afterthought. Having once again banished the palpable evil, he looks back toward the cottage window: "and beyond, your face / Haunts like a new moon glimpsed through tangled glass." A symbol of cosmic harmony, the moon also connotes divinity and purity, but Heaney glimpses his image of transcendence through a glass at once distorted and capable of distortion. The equilibrium between inner and outer realms proves tenuous indeed: domestic rewards cannot utterly dispel the terrors of the psyche, whether these arise from the natural world or the political mayhem of the North. In *The Poetry of Resistance*, Sidney Burris comments on the parallels between "the radical pastorals of *North*" and "the more conservative pastoral elements of *Field Work*":

> A new feeling of intimacy governs these poems, and the etymology of the word *intimacy*—the Latin adjectival root "intimus" means innermost—implicates the values of the inner life. Nourished by the pastoral seclusion in Wicklow, the inner life yields for Heaney a peculiar wisdom, one that seems, when buffeted by the parade of public images found in much of his poetry—the tanks, the cars, the soldiers, the guns—pared down and perhaps unequal to the grand tasks often expected of his work. Yet, as the sequence indicates, the small world of personal affairs, with its compromises,

questions, and gratifications, is structurally analogous to the large world of political affairs, with its treaties, interrogations, and rewards.[41]

For Heaney, Glanmore is a microcosm of his previous experience; as an adult, he recognizes the larger implications of particularized forebodings prevalent in *Death of a Naturalist*. He now perceives that the rat—the plunderer of granaries, the infecter of fruit, the malign intelligence glaring forth from dank cisterns and the dark corners of barn and byre—is the symbol of an inchoate turbulence abroad in the world. Heaney sees at the heart of the Glanmore sequence "the makings of my adult self."[42] Like Wordsworth in the *Prelude*, he views the formation of identity "as a process of composing and transforming disparate and turbulent elements into an all-encompassing tranquility."[43] The closing lines of Sonnet X recall the first night Heaney and his wife spent together in a hotel:

> When you came with your deliberate kiss
> To raise us towards the lovely and painful
> Covenants of flesh; our separateness;
> The respite in our dewy dreaming faces.

> (*FW* 42)

The inevitable "separateness" that follows their sexual union does not diminish the "respite" they experience. Indeed, the separateness affirms their individual identities, which are not entirely subsumed in the ripening maturity of married love. The respite achieved, though temporary, lingers in the image of the couple's "dewy, dreaming faces." Sexual communion remains a vital element of their love and life, a source of physical and spiritual renewal. Of course, full realization of his identity as a poet occasionally forces Heaney to choose between perfection of the life or perfection of the work. In "An Afterwards," the poet's wife would plunge him and his literary compatriots "in the ninth circle" of Dante's hell. Indeed, her reproach seems to shatter the hard-won domestic idylls of Glanmore: "Why could you not have, oftener, in our years // Unclenched, and come down laughing from your room / And walked the twilight with me and your children" (*FW* 44).

On the whole, the poetry of *Field Work* displays a new sense of confidence, a trust in a more domestic voice and in the poet's personal identity as subject for poetry. In spite of Heaney's ability to bring his life and work together in *Field Work*, he has not yet resolved his roles and responsibilities as an artist during the Troubles. *Sweeney Astray* (1984), his subsequent translation or "version" of the medieval Irish epic *Buile Suibhne*, relates the story of Sweeney, king of Dal-Arie, a pagan Celt who becomes a birdman after the battle of Moira, when the curse of a cleric named St. Ronan is fulfilled. The poems composed by the mad king during his peregrinations express a poignant anguish unparalleled in Irish literature.

In his introduction to the volume, Heaney notes that his "primary relation with Sweeney . . . is topographical" (vi), arising from his move to County Wicklow, near Sweeney's burial ground. But his affinities with Sweeney run much deeper. Like the place-name poems of *Wintering Out*, *Sweeney Astray* provided a way to be simultaneously faithful to the English language and to Irish origins. In an interview with Seamus Deane in 1977, Heaney remarked that "the quest for such a repetition" motivated his translation of *Buile Suibhne*: "Maybe here there was a presence, a fable which could lead to the discovery of feelings in myself which I could not otherwise find words for, and which would cast a dream or possibility or myth across the swirl of private feelings: an objective correlative."[44] Indeed, on a number of levels, Sweeney splendidly dramatized Heaney's own crisis of identity, his sense of conflicting allegiances:

> [I]nsofar as Sweeney is also a figure of the artist, displaced, guilty, assuaging himself by his utterance, it is possible to read the work as an aspect of the quarrel between free creative imagination and the constraints of religious, political, and domestic obligation. (*SA* vi)

To be sure, Heaney is not the first to recognize the epic's embodiment of the artist's plight; in *The White Goddess* (1948), Robert Graves had called *Buile Suibhne* "the most ruthless and bitter description in all European literature of an obsessed poet's predicament."[45] In addition, with his Irish nationality, his former prominence and responsibility, his ambivalence about Christianity, and his exile, Sweeney proves a fitting protagonist for Heaney. As Henry Hart observes,

> Donning the tattered costume of the madman, Heaney externalizes the *hysterica passio* pent up in the politically beleaguered, exiled poet he identifies with and moves toward catharsis. If his confessionalism is histrionic it is also therapeutic, and perhaps more successively so than those brands practiced by Lowell, John Berryman, Plath, Anne Sexton, and Roethke, whose demons were not so easily exorcised.[46]

If the protagonist of *Buile Suibhne* served Heaney well, so did its style: "the bareness and durability of the writing" (vi) likely influenced his own desire "to be able to write a bare wire."[47] Moreover, the Sweeney saga provided him with a welcome sense of tradition: "Like Kinsella's Táin cycle and Montague's interest in Gaelic lore, it allowed Heaney to affirm a specifically Irish tradition that went beyond Yeats and Kavanagh."[48] Not surprisingly, Sweeney emerges again in *Station Island*, serving as Heaney's mask in the "Sweeney Redivivus" sequence.

Heaney's relentless effort to conspire toward a common bond with others appears momentarily suspended in *Sweeney Astray*, yet his identification with Sweeney evolves into a first-person celebration of nature as well as a tome of exile and lament. Indeed, the work's "double note of relish and penitence" initially aroused Heaney's interest in doing a translation (*SA* iii). Bereft of his original identity, Sweeney forges a new one, alternately mourning the loss of his place in the community, embracing his natural surroundings, and imploring God's mercy: "Blend me forever in your sweetness" (*SA* 20). In his efforts to bring him back to Rasharkin and cure him of his madness, Sweeney's half-brother Lynchseachan robs him of his familial identity, reciting a "litany" of false deaths: his brother, father, mother, wife, sister, daughter, and nephew, respectively. It is the news of his only son's death, however, that finally undoes Sweeney; he falls from the tree. Under Lynchseachan's care, he begins to regain his sanity, until a hag engages him in a leaping contest, and he goes mad again (55).

Despite the occasional return to the spare lines and lofty tone of *North*, Heaney's speaker rejoices in the infinite variety of the untamed countryside: clusters of hazel-nuts, stickle-backed briars, the cataract at Alternan, the mist-shrouded belling of mountain stags. Moreover, the trimeters of *Sweeney Astray* embrace the parochial as well as the universal, attaching a regional identity to the "many-tined" sovereigns of the steeps and glens. "Imagine them," Heaney implores us by proxy of his speaker:

> the stag of high Slieve Felim,
> the stag of the steep Fews,
> the stag of Duhallow, the stag of Orrery,
> the fierce stag of Killarney.
>
> (*SA* 18)

The above quatrain resonates with an ecstasy not unlike Gunnar's in "Funeral Rites," although here the mediator of Heaney's consciousness belongs to a cultural heritage closer to home. His protagonist's reconciliation to the Church ("To you, Christ, I give thanks / for your Body in communion") precedes the short prose interlude that points the way to the next stage in the poet's quest for identity: "Then Sweeney's death-swoon came over him and Moling, attended by his clerics, rose up and each of them placed a stone on Sweeney's grave."

The title-poem and centerpiece of Heaney's eighth book, *Station Island* (1984), is set on beds of stones believed to be the foundations of early monastic buildings at the site of St. Patrick's Purgatory, also known as Station Island, in Lough Derg, County Donegal. If the notion of a penitential journey seems distinctly medieval, recalling both Dante and Chaucer, Heaney borrows the structural interior for his long-poem from the banished Florentine rather than the London wayfarer who stopped overnight at Harry Bailly's Tabard Inn. Not surprisingly, the wraiths who people Heaney's purgatory are projections of his own psyche, familiar ghosts translated by the dreamlight of memory and troubled conscience. According to Sammye Crawford Greer in "'Station Island' and the Poet's Progress," the issue of identity continues to be Heaney's central concern:

> As the sequence progresses, the pilgrim-poet remembers experiences from his youth that reveal the quality of life in Ulster and encounters, in the manner of Dante, "shades," as Heaney says, "from my own dream life who had also been inhabitants of the actual Irish world," whose testimonies, reproaches, and advice define the condition in which he finds himself as he tries to affirm his identity as both Irishman and poet.[49]

Even in Dante's day, St. Patrick's Purgatory was famous throughout Europe, and on most Italian navigational maps the entire province of Ulster was designated "as nothing else but the cave" purported to be the entrance to the netherworld of Christian cosmology.[50] In Ireland, the regimen of St. Patrick's, which consists of the Fast, the Vigil, and the Station, still looms as the ultimate penance.

Some critics and scholars insist that *The Divine Comedy* merely serves as a literary model that enables Heaney to control his subject throughout "Station Island." To some extent, this proves to be the case; for example, Heaney's recognition scenes occasionally recall those in Homer's *Odyssey*, and his sense of phantasmagoria owes more to Joyce's Stephen Dedalus than to Dante's narrator. Moreover, St. Patrick's Purgatory, unlike Dante's place of atonement, is less a central dramatic event than a frame for Heaney's interior narrative. Indeed, the poet comes to Station Island as one fallen away from faith, and the competing claims of orthodoxy and individual identity lie at the heart of his ordeal. According to Michael Parker, Heaney endeavors at Joyce's behest to achieve "an antithetical, individualistic view of the poet's role and responsibilities, stressing self-assertion and the dream of lyric fulfillment instead of the orthodox Catholic 'virtues' of self-abasement, collective solidarity, and self-denial."[51]

Heaney divides "Station Island" into twelve sections, carefully measuring lines and stanzaic patterns to fit a variety of dramatic tableaux. In the first part, he encounters his alter-ego, Simon Sweeney, addressing him as "'an old Sabbath-breaker / who has been dead for years'" (61). The image of the roguish woodcutter "with a bow-saw, held / stiffly up like a lyre" strikes a distinctly rustic note, reminding us of the affinity between poet and rural laborer in both "Digging" and "Thatcher." This is the same rude harp that Heaney once used to cut a swath through the neat hedgerows of the English pastoral, but now he feels himself compelled along a different path. "Fallen into step" with other pilgrims "before the smokes were up," he hears the old pariah shout a belated warning: "'Stay clear of all processions!'" (63). Heaney employs the taut trimeter line of *North* and *Buile Suibhne* in section one: "A hurry of bell-notes / flew over morning hush / and water-blistered cornfields." The repetition of aspirates in "hurry" and "hush" lends an air of urgency to the plosive bell tones, and the image of cornfields broken out in a welter of dew conveys the arduous nature of the barefoot pilgrimage. The spectral Sweeney is not a figment of Heaney's imagination; indeed, the poet's introduction to *Sweeney Astray* offers the following revelation: "the green spirit of the hedges embodied in Sweeney had first been embodied for me in the persons of a family of tinkers, also called Sweeney, who used to camp in the ditchbacks along the road to the first school I attended" (viii). Like the Gaelic king of the medieval epic, the Sabbath-breaking Sweeney represents the *agon* "between free creative imagination and the constraints of religious, political, and domestic obligation" (vi). When Heaney confronts old Simon Sweeney for his religious lapses, the Dionysian figure reminds him of a childhood debt: "'I was your mystery man / and am again this morning.'" Apparently the tinker provided an early sounding board for Heaney's listing imagination:

> "When they bade you listen
> in the bedroom dark
> to wind and rain in the trees
> and think of tinkers camped
> under a heeled-up cart
>
> you shut your eyes and saw
> a wet axle and spokes
> in moonlight, and me
> streaming from the shower,
> headed for your door."
>
> (*SA* 62)

Come fresh from the rain-soaked ditchbacks in the guise of a bogey-man, Sweeney has always been the poet's breathing double in his unwillingness to bow before conventional wisdom and the doctrinal values of the larger culture. Moreover, even in the flesh, he was part will-o'-the-wisp, a living affirmation of the youthful Heaney's power to create. By proxy of Stephen Dedalus in *Ulysses*, Joyce underscores the affinity between the artist and the myriad self-recognitions that the creative intelligence compels: "We walk through ourselves, meeting robbers, ghosts, giants, old men, young men, wives, widows, brothers-in-love, but always meeting ourselves."[52] Although Heaney encounters himself in the person of Simon Sweeney, he does not heed the old man's warning; rather, he remains intent on "fac[ing] into my station":

> I trailed those early-risers
> who had fallen into step
> before the smokes were up.
> The quick bell rang again.
>
> (*SA* 63)

If Heaney finds himself momentarily drawn into the "drugged path" of ritual devotion, the customary drone of *paters* and *aves* cannot lull his senses indefinitely. As section II begins, he hears another voice in the press "raving on" about listening each night for "gun butts to come cracking on the door, / yeomen on the rampage, and his neighbour // among them, hammering home the shape of things" (*SA* 64). Here Heaney shifts to a *terza rima* as syntactically concise as Dante's, but he couples enjambment with a more varied rhyme scheme, thus lending this passage a rhythm appropriate to brisk colloquy. The poet encounters the first tutelary spirit, who happens also to be an Irish author, one with whom he can immediately identify: "'Round about here you overtook the women,' / I said, as the thing came clear. 'Your *Lough Derg Pilgrim* // haunts me every time I cross this mountain.'" The shade is William Carleton, a nineteenth-century novelist from County Tyrone, whose personal history, like Heaney's, was fraught with religious and cultural displacement:

> In 1818 some Ribbonmen (themselves of course Catholics) were hanged for burning to death a Catholic family in their own home, the 'reason' for the burning being that the family had refused to join the Ribbon Society. In Carleton's mind the incident stood for the worst kind of intercommunal feuding, violence inflicted on one's own "side," and it held a vivid place in his imagination because, while out walking in County Louth, he had accidentally seen the bodies of the Ribbonmen, which had been put in tar sacks and set up on gibbets to act as a warning.[53]

Indeed, his bitterness about the feuding between and among Catholics and Protestants prompted his eventual conversion to the Established Church.

Carleton's *Lough Derg Pilgrim* (1829) recounts his only pilgrimage to St. Patrick's Purgatory at the age of eighteen, and bitterly denounces all forms of pious devotion, dismissing the pilgrimage as a "great and destructive superstition."[54] In Heaney's poem, Carleton refers to his artistic life in terms of religious and political outrage: "hard-mouthed Ribbonmen and Orange bigots / made me into the old fork-tongued turncoat / who mucked the byre of their politics" (*SA* 65). Heaney remonstrates with his precursor, describing a band of Ribbonmen as playing hymns to Mary within earshot of his County Derry homestead: "By then the brotherhood was a frail procession / staggering home drunk on Patrick's Day." Heaney stresses the importance of this early experience, and then urges several key points of identity shared by both authors:

> "Obedient strains like theirs tuned me first
> and not that harp of unforgiving iron
>
> the Fenians strung. A lot of what you wrote
> I heard and did: this Lough Derg station,
> flax-pullings, dances, summer crossroads chat
>
> and the shaky local voice of education.
> All that. And always, Orange drums.
> And neighbours on the roads at night with guns."
>
> (*SA* 65–66)

In the ensuing debate, Heaney desperately pleads his responsibility to a vision of the "world become word" as opposed to the polemics of national and religious conflict: "'The alders in the hedge,' I said, 'mushrooms, / dark-clumped grass where cows or horses dunged, / the cluck when pith-lined chestnut shells split open.'" The words suggest a homespun albeit voluptuous indolence, a life of sensations as familiar to Carleton as to Kavanagh or Heaney. However, Carleton's rebuttal indicates that an appreciation of such things is no more a vocation than good health: "'All this is like a trout kept in a spring / or maggots sown in wounds— / another life that cleans our element'" (*SA* 66). Here Carleton's choice of metaphors is revealing: the image of the trout culling bugs and algae from a spring gives way to maggots feeding on putrefaction in the trench of a wound. Even the beauty of the native landscape cannot dispel his anger at the encroachments of sectarian violence on the emerging self, and having chastened the "optimistic" Heaney, he extends his analogy to encompass an abiding *contemptus mundi*: "We are earthworms of the earth, and all that / has gone through us is what will be our trace" (*SA* 66). Yet Heaney embeds in the term "trace" a tinge of its secondary meaning: to form, as letters or figures, with painstaking care. Heaney thus ventriloquizes through Carleton his own theory that we must first assimilate our personal experience before it can crystallize in language. According to Elmer Andrews, "Heaney knows—what Carleton did not—that until the quarrel is internalized we make rhetoric and not art."[55]

The most useful admonition of Carleton's shade stems from his first-hand knowledge of the Irish writer's lot as one of exposure and alienation: "It is a road you travel on your own." As his advice reflects, Heaney's precursor suffered his own crisis of identity, at least with regard to his literary pursuits: "Carleton is a conspicuous example of an Irish writer trying to make his way without the vital sustaining force of an available tradition. With nothing in his inheritance to help him towards an identity, he must improvise one for himself."[56] Like Heaney's encounters with subsequent literary "shades" in "Station Island," his meeting with Carleton enacts his own crisis of identity: "For Heaney, Carleton represents the plight of the artist in Ireland, his difficulty in clearing an imaginative space for himself."[57]

As if to suppress within himself any innate impulse toward the hard cynicism of Carleton, Heaney turns in section III to the soothingly ritual habits of devotion: "I knelt. Hiatus. Habit's afterlife." He fixes on a candle beading its wax rosary, and another image swims into his consciousness: "A seaside trinket floated then and idled / in vision" (*SA* 67). The object is a veritable *memento mori*, a remembrance of his father's younger sister Agnes, afflicted with tuberculosis in "pre-inoculation rural Ireland."[58] An invalid who died very young, the aunt appears symbolically as a delicate sea-trove, "a toy grotto with seedling mussel shells / and cockles glued in patterns over it." Slipped stealthfully from the lower compartment of an oak sideboard where it lay wrapped in tissue paper, the memento looms as an object of veneration: "pearls condensed from a child invalid's breath / into a shimmering ark, my house of gold / that housed the snowdrop weather of her death / long ago." Yet something innately sexual also attaches to the miniature shrine, a heartbreaking intimation of natal fires quelled by death: "It was like touching birds' eggs, robbing the nest / of the word *wreath*, as kept and dry and secret // as her name which they hardly ever spoke." Heaney can identify with his aunt only through this trinket, "a whitish gleaming secret deposited in the family sideboard like grave-goods in the tomb of a princess."[59] But the mood of veneration quickly vanishes:

> I thought of walking round
> and round a space utterly empty,
> utterly a source, like the idea of sound;

> like an absence stationed in the swamp-fed air
> above a ring of walked-down grass and rushes
> where we once found the bad carcass and scrags of hair
> of our dog that had disappeared weeks before.
>
> (*SA* 68)

The cold draught portends more than a sudden shift in the weather. The juxtaposition of his aunt's toy wreath with the "ring of walked-down grass and rushes" wherein the youthful Heaney discovered the dessicated remains of the family dog is calculated to raise one's hair at the nape. Death loses its prettified aspect when the poet remembers his first encounter with stark reality. Bereft of the lovely talisman that recalls the Litany of the Blessed Virgin ("a shimmering ark, my house of gold"), Heaney feels himself drawn into "the old vortex" characteristic of the bog poems. The power of religious ritual to console falters before the familiar and estranging phenomenon of death; meanwhile, the other pilgrims continue their blind circuits around the stone beds of the Purgatory.

In section IV, Heaney resorts once again to *terza rima*, as he attempts to reconcile his poetic identity with the daunting strictures of the Catholic Church. With his back to "the stone pillar and the iron cross," symbols of an immutable faith based on hieratic values, he is about to renounce "the World, the Flesh and the Devil," when another shade appears before him:

> I met a young priest, glossy as a blackbird,
> as if he had stepped from his anointing
> a moment ago: his purple stole and cord
>
> or cincture tied loosely, his polished shoes
> unexpectedly secular beneath
> a pleated, lace-hemmed alb of linen cloth.
>
> (*SA* 69)

The subtle disaffection of the young priest, Terry Keenan, is implicit in Heaney's description. If the image "glossy as a blackbird" fails to conjure the raven banners of the Danish pirates in *North*, it has distinctly pagan connotations. Moreover, the youthful cleric appears sleek and plausive: his cincture—which represents the power of the Church "to bind or loose"—is casually knotted, his shoes buffed to an "unexpectedly secular" sheen beneath the intricate lace hem of his vestment. Indeed, Heaney had almost forgotten him: "His name had lain undisturbed for years / like an old bicycle wheel in a ditch / ripped at last from under jungling briars, // wet and perished." The recollection awakens old discords, as the priest begins his recitation:

> "The rain forest," he said,
> "you've never seen the like of it. I lasted
>
> only a couple of years. Bare-breasted
> women and rat-ribbed men. Everything wasted.
> I rotted like a pear. I sweated masses."
>
> (*SI* 69–70)

Wracked with malarial tremors, disillusioned with the outward forms and arcane rituals of the Church, the priest perished in the foreign missions. For him, the Latin Mass lapsed into formula and prescribed emotion. His vocation dissipated in the face of poverty and privation that would have left true emissaries such as Saint Patrick undismayed. Heaney identifies with his plight, but foregoes sympathy: "'I'm older now than you were when you went away,' // I ventured, feeling a strange reversal. / 'I never could see you on the foreign missions.'" In fact, his tone becomes gently derisive:

> I could only see you on a bicycle,
>
> a clerical student home for the summer
> doomed to the decent thing. Visiting neighbours,
> Drinking tea and praising home-made bread.
>
> (*SI* 70)

Always cognizant of the similarities between priest and poet, Heaney also intuits the enormous disparity between the two roles. He knows that Stephen Dedalus's conception of the artist as "priest of the eternal imagination" is absurdly Byronic, but he also realizes that "the World, the Flesh and the Devil should not be renounced, but rather accepted, relished and confronted."[60] As a poet, he must fight shy of tribal complicity, and for this reason, iconoclasts such as the fisherman O'Neill and the sabbath-breaking Simon Sweeney are instructive presences for the shaping of his identity. Nettled by Heaney's observations, the priest replies defensively:

> "And you," he faltered, "what are you doing here
> but the same thing? What possessed you?
> . . . .
> Unless . . . Unless . . ." Again he was short of breath
> and his whole fevered body yellowed and shook.
>
> "Unless you are here taking the last look."
>
> (*SI* 70–71)

According to Elmer Andrews, Heaney is most emphatically "taking 'the last look' on the personal and cultural implications of his Catholic origins."[61] But if a last look were all the poet required to confirm his own vocation, why would he suffer the pain of reenactment by journeying to St. Patrick's Purgatory? Heaney sees in the young priest the very portraiture of what might have become his own predicament. As the vignette closes, he remembers shadowing the priest on his rounds as he once did his own father in "Follower": "steam rose like the first breath of spring, / a knee-deep mist I waded silently // behind him, on his circuits, visiting" (*SI* 71).

In section V, Heaney meets the shades of several "old fathers" who nurtured his love of language, literature, and learning early in his life: Barney Murphy, his Latin master at Anahorish School; Michael McLaverty, a novelist and short story writer who served as headmaster at St. Thomas Intermediate School in Ballymurphy, where Heaney began his teaching career; and the poet Patrick Kavanagh, whose rendering of Irish rural life validated Heaney's own experiences and poetic impulses. Significantly, Heaney designates them as "fosterers," invoking the tradition of "fosterage," an ancient custom among Norse, Saxon, and Celtic nobility of sending a son to spend his childhood with another family.[62] The former masters represent "geniuses of the place" no less than the "mound-dwellers" of "Anahorish" who wade "waist-deep in mist / to break the light ice at wells" and the farmers, clayworkers, fishermen, and duck hunters of the Bann Valley: "[T]hough they may be distinguished from the communal life of their place by their position and their Latin learning, [they] are nevertheless the bearers and keepers of native tradition."[63] Indeed, Heaney's literary and spiritual guides blend with the agrarian landscape, suggesting that his education marks not so much a departure as a shift to a more intellectual community.

Though he suffers from the infirmities of old age, the Latin teacher moves with the rhythms of the seasons: his Adam's apple works "like the plunger of a pump," his breath rushes "softly as scythes in his lost meadows." Moreover, Heaney juxtaposes the rituals of rural life with the discipline of school; he falls in behind Murphy vigilantly, "my eyes fixed on his heels / like a man lifting swathes at a mower's heels." The old man's voice husks and scrapes a greeting before returning to "the dry urn of the larynx." A vessel shaping and shaped by words, the metaphorical urn becomes the ultimate verbal icon, a sacred repository of language. After the shade relates that the site of the school has returned to its former landscape, the poet finds himself "faced wrong way / into more pilgrims absorbed in this exercise." Yet the power of memory and the love of language fostered by Murphy assuage the poet's profound sense of loss:

> As I stood among their whispers and bare feet
> the mists of all the mornings I set out
> for Latin classes with him, face to face,
> refreshed me. *Mensa, mensa, mensam*
> sang in the air like a busy whetstone.
>
> > (*SI* 73)

Heaney returns to the most elementary aspect of Latin grammar, the First Declension. He likens the singsong of young voices reciting their Latin to "a busy whetstone," and thus asserts a honing and refining, a growing attunement to the nuances of sound and meaning. Indeed, a sense of word becoming world pervades this segment. As the poet recognizes, his education expanded his identity beyond the realm of rural and family origins, into a literary tradition that included both English and Latin. Paradoxically, his early schooling contains both the seeds of his estrangement and his apprehension of the comforting, rejuvenating powers of language.

The poet next meets the shade of Michael McLaverty, another "old father" whose influence he celebrated at greater length in "Fosterage," part V of "Singing School" in *North*. Like Barney Murphy, McLaverty emerges as part of the landscape, "his cocked bird's eye / dabbing for detail" (*SI* 73). Slightly older than Heaney's own father, with his best-known novel appearing the same year Heaney was born, the headmaster from County Monaghan served as a literary and spiritual guide early in Heaney's poetic career. Indeed, Michael Parker numbers McLaverty among the "confirmatory presences and supportive voices . . . who assisted Heaney in the process of establishing a firm sense of his own identity from which he could create, and freeing himself from his *Incertus* past."[64] Though McLaverty's advice in "Fosterage" resembles that of the other literary shades ("Go your own way. / Do your own work"), he apparently helped the young poet find his way, introducing him to works and writers he had not yet encountered—most notably, to the work of Patrick Kavanagh, another writer from County Monaghan. Naturally, Kavanagh succeeds McLaverty in this section, his caustic wit a ready counterpoint to the gentle shades just before him. Kavanagh's mockeries of Heaney's earnest pilgrimage and inescapable attachment to Ireland imply his own conviction that the artist does not belong among the pilgrims at St. Patrick's Purgatory, as he declares in "Lough Derg": "They come to Lough Derg to fast and pray and beg / With all the bitterness of nonentities, and the envy / Of the inarticulate when dealing with the artist."[65] The elder poet cannot resist a last jab: "In my own day / the odd one came here on the hunt for women" (*SI* 74).

Like an apparition answerable to Kavanagh's summons, the object of Heaney's first infatuation suddenly materializes in section VI: "Freckle-face, fox-head, pod of the broom / Catkin-pixie, little fern-swish: / Where did she arrive from?" (*SI* 75). The rhythmic interplay of alliteration, assonance, and consonance with images connoting a winsome, childlike nubility lends startling clarity to the poet's remembrance: "her I chose at 'secrets' / and whispered to." The game "secrets" provides an aural approximation to "touching tongues" beneath the boortree in the fifth Glanmore Sonnet. Heaney shuts his ears to the basilica's tolling bell, and makes for "the bottle-green, still / Shade of an oak. / Shades of the Sabine farm / On the beds of Saint Patrick's Purgatory." But even allusions to Horace and the hedonistic delights of a jar of Massic wine—"Loosen the toga for wine and poetry / *Till Phoebus returning routs the morning star*"—cannot forestall Heaney's confrontation with his own sexual awakening, its boyhood ardors and mystifications: "my own long virgin / Fasts and thirsts, my nightly shadow feasts, / Haunting the granaries of words like *breasts*" (*SI* 75). Some scholars view section VI of "Station Island" as little more than a playful interlude reminiscent of Stephen Dedalus's adolescent reveries in *A Portrait of the Artist*. However, Heaney associates the Old English "*breasts*" with abundance, burnished grain secure in the word-hoard of memory. Even his sexuality, a crucial component of his identity, evolves not only through awareness of his native agrarian landscape but also through his growing acquisition of language. Indeed, the description of his pubescent sweetheart progresses from such fumbling endearments as "freckle-face" to the more dextrous kennings, "catkin-pixie" and "fern-swish." In stanza 1, he whispers "secrets" into the intricate portals of a girl's ear, but the image narrows abruptly in the third stanza: "As if I knelt for years at a keyhole / Mad for it, and all that ever opened / Was the breathed-on grille of a confessional" (*SI* 76). Overcome with desire for an experience he can only articulate in terms of a neuter pronoun ("Mad for it"), Heaney's progress toward a self-actualized identity has reached a critical stage for one raised within the Irish Catholic community. His sister-in-law Polly Devlin urges the personal fate of those who cannot transcend the moral strictures of the Church as a warning:

> "There is no harm in them," is what is always said of these old or prematurely old men and women, wistful and sad, who have long since abandoned or forfeited thoughts of marriage and children. Their upbringing and conditioning, the constraints of religion, the lack of a feasible future, seem profoundly to have damaged the courage and sense of self necessary to contemplate such a step; many have eked out their lives

without ever having had a romantic or sexual relationship with another person.[66]

Apparently, Kavanagh had not far to look in selecting a model for his sex-starved and spiritually thwarted Paddy McGuire. Fortunately, the epiphany comes for Heaney "that night I saw her honey-skinned / Shoulder-blades and the wheatlands of her back / Through the wide keyhole of her keyhole dress." He celebrates the benefice of fleshly communion by translating five lines from Canto Two of *The Divine Comedy*, a passage wherein Dante likens himself to flowers revived by Lucy's radiance:

> *As little flowers that were all bowed and shut*
> *By the night chills rise on their stems and open*
> *As soon as they have felt the touch of sunlight,*
> *So I revived in my own wilting powers*
> *And my heart flushed, like somebody set free.*
> Translated, given, under the oak tree.
>
> (*SI* 76)

In sections VII and VIII, Heaney encounters the shades of three men who were near contemporaries at the time death intervened; inevitably, sectarian violence figured in the demise of two. Section VII focuses on the testimony of a shopkeeper, a college acquaintance remembered as a "rangy midfielder in a blue jersey / and starched pants, the one stylist on the team," who was shot when he opened his door to a pair of off-duty British policemen in the middle of the night. Heaney's identification with the victim becomes manifest the moment the shade appears. As Heaney gazes into the waters of Lough Derg, he intuits the presence of another even before he glimpses his own reflection: "his reflection / did not appear but I sensed a presence / entering into my concentration." The shock of recognition is immediate:

> His brow
> was blown open above the eye and blood
> had dried on his neck and cheek. "Easy now,"
>
> he said, "it's only me. You've seen men as raw
> after a football match . . ."
>
> (*SI* 77)

The shade, William Strathearn, refuses to exchange greetings, but goes on to relate how the assassins knocked at his shop door after hours on the pretext of purchasing patent medicines for a sick child: "Open up and see what you have got—pills / or a powder or something in a bottle" (*SI* 78). Heaney skillfully adapts colloquial speech to the narrative flow of his *terza rima*; indeed, he comes nearest to capturing Dante's easy vernacular style in section VII. We never hear the enfranchised thugs bang off a half clip, but Strathearn's description of the murder is calculated to unnerve: "I remember the stale smell / of cooked meat or something coming through / as I went to open up. From then on / you know as much about it as I do" (*SI* 79). Heaney manages a blurted avowal of shame, as if his unwillingness to commit unequivocally to either Unionist or Loyalist factions had implicated him in the murder:

> "Forgive the way I have lived indifferent—
> forgive my timid circumspect involvement,"
>
> I surprised myself by saying. "Forgive
> my eye," he said, "all that's above my head."
> And then a stun of pain seemed to go through him
>
> And he trembled like a heat wave and faded.
>
> (*SI* 80)

In the earlier "Mid-Term Break," a growing sensitivity to the nuances of language set the youthful Heaney apart from his father and Big Jim Evans. Now the mature poet's practiced eloquence estranges him from his former friend and schoolfellow. Within the context of strife-torn Ulster, he feels most acutely the division between his artistic identity and the demand for political involvement:

> The central conflict in *Station Island* between the artist's devotion to his craft and the political demands of his conscience struggles toward resolution . . . Content to remain in the safe confines of his home where he can mull over poems, at the same time Heaney feels torn away by obligations to the community. His temperamental disaffection with "the angry role" does not preclude a militant desire to right the wrongs around him.[67]

In an article titled "Envies and Identifications: Dante and the Modern Poet," Heaney confirms the crucial role of identity in "Station Island": "The main tension is between two often contradictory commands: to be faithful to the collective historical experience and to be true to the recognitions of the emerging self."[68]

In section VIII, Heaney is kneeling "at the hard mouth of St. Brigid's Bed," when the ghost of his friend Tom Delaney appears at the station's limestone hub. Assistant Keeper of Medieval Antiquities at the Ulster

Museum, Delaney died prematurely of a chest ailment in 1979. As one whose unwavering enthusiasm for archaeology promoted the integration of Irish medieval studies into the European mainstream, Delaney's contribution to the Iron Age mythos Heaney forged in *North* would be impossible to overestimate.[69] Indeed, Heaney stresses the affinity between their pursuits. Deliberately conflating the roles of poet and archaeologist, he offers a vivid description of Delaney, "his scribe's face smiling," and then notices "the wing / of woodkerne's hair fanned down over his brow." The allusion recalls the poet's depiction of himself in "Exposure" ("a woodkerne / Escaped from the massacre"), as Heaney posits a shared identity that goes deeper than their respective vocations. Both men sought the life of the spirit by delving into the earth's marrow. Thus Heaney's memory of Delaney's last days is singularly disquieting: "'Those dreamy stars that pulsed across the screen / beside you in the ward—your heartbeats, Tom, I mean—/ scared me the way they stripped things naked'" (*SI* 81). The blips that winced and fluttered across the screen of the heart monitor signified a presence already too phantasmal for Heaney's hard-core empiricism. His usual banter faltered, and he left straight away for Dublin: "feeling I had said nothing / and that, as usual, I had somehow broken / covenants, and failed an obligation." Now he pauses to ask whether the parting handclasp did anything to assuage the mutual recognition that he and Delaney would never meet again. The shade replies unequivocally:

> "Nothing at all. But familiar stone
> had me half-numbed to face the thing alone.
> I loved my still-faced archaeology.
> The small crab-apple physiognomies
> on high crosses, carved heads in abbeys . . .
> Why else dig in for years in that hard place
> in a muck of bigotry under the walls
> picking through shards and Williamite cannon balls?"
>
> (*SI* 82)

Notwithstanding his ardor for field work, even Delaney occasionally felt the historical divisions inherent in Irish culture. His shade yields to that of Heaney's second cousin, Colum McCartney, who confronts the poet bitterly for aestheticizing sectarian murder in "The Strand at Lough Beg":

> "You confused evasion and artistic tact.
> The Protestant who shot me through the head
> I accuse directly, but indirectly, you
> who now atone perhaps upon this bed
> for the way you whitewashed ugliness and drew

the lovely blinds of the *Purgatorio*
and saccharined my death with morning dew."

(*SI* 83)

McCartney dismisses Heaney's verses as a betrayal, but clearly does not comprehend the artist's obligation to his craft and to himself. Ironically, the poet has more in common with the archaeologist than with his kinsman. Both he and Delaney dig for the hard facts of Irish and European history; for them, however, art becomes the means of transcending the polemics of time and place. The patient craftsmanship of the medieval artisan, his loving rendition of "small crab-apple physiognomies / on high crosses, carved heads in abbeys," inspires Delaney to sift through the "muck" of atrocity and bigotry; thus, both poet and archaeologist triumph over the life-belittling dead weight of iron shot cast in Birmingham.

In section IX, the voice of a hunger striker haunts the dormitory where the pilgrims sleep. In this regard, *Station Island* undoubtedly reflects its historical milieu: the volume appeared just three years after Irish Republicans in the H-Blocks of Maze Prison sought to recover their status as "political prisoners" by launching a hunger strike in March 1981. The protest gained international attention, and united Catholics in a smoldering fury against the British. Heaney's identification with the hunger striker is more a matter of personal than collective identity; the shade who speaks is Francis Hughes, a neighbour from Bellaghy, County Derry, whose life displayed the resolve Heaney finds lacking in his own. Best known as the second of ten to die in the 1981 protest, Hughes possessed plenty of mettle "for the angry role." He joined the I.R.A. while still a teenager, soon after being beaten at a roadblock, and embarked on a notorious career. Together with Dominic McGlinchey and Ian Milne, also of South Derry, he wreaked havoc on the British Army, the R.U.C., and the U.D.R. alike, acquiring the dubious distinction of appearing on "wanted" posters issued by the R.U.C.[70]

The striker's surreal monologue connects him to Heaney's Tollund Man: his stomach shrunken, "tightened and cracked," he also resembles "a white-faced groom, / A hit-man on the brink" (*SI* 84). Indeed, Padraig O'Malley characterizes the hunger strikes as "a reaching back to tribal allegiances" and "the myth of redemptive sacrifice."[71] Heaney neither glamorizes nor indicts the striker's life of violence. He imagines the young man's funeral. In his subsequent dream, the poet reaches his nadir, overwhelmed with "blanching self-disgust." His subconscious presents the image of a trumpet he once discovered in a loft—a symbol of poetry and art. The poet wakes to find it "Still there for the taking!"— thus expressing an exuberant joy about art as well as life. The memory of his refusal to try the instrument ("I thought such trove beyond me") provokes a bitter repudiation: "'I hate how quick I was to know my place. / I hate where I was born, hate everything // that made me biddable and unforthcoming'" (*SI* 85). The poet's realization of his inextricable attachment to his native land seemingly undercuts the desire to outgrow the impulse of "knowing his place": "As if the cairnstone could defy the cairn." Yet for Heaney, the awareness marks an initiation, a knowledge that he must free himself from his sense of obligation to his community. His image of "the tribe whose dances never fail / For they keep dancing till they sight the deer" (*SI* 86) illuminates the deadly resolve of Hughes and his fellow strikers. The blanket protest begun in 1976 had failed; the hunger strikes of 1980 had lost their effectiveness when a participant changed his mind. In 1981, the prospective participants were all carefully screened before beginning the protest, to assure its effect as a political instrument: "there could be no oscillation between determination and despair."[72] The ensuing strike proved a powerful native weapon against the English; yet Heaney's tribal dance suggests a fierce communal persistence that precludes the needs of the individual, much less the necessities of the imagination. If Heaney is too hesitant, his countryman was too easily drawn into "the old vortex of race and religious instinct." Hughes's answer to the crisis of identity represents a dangerous extreme. As Erikson notes in his prologue, the creative individual accepts the negative identity as the base line of recovery and begins to work through the crisis, but others are not so fortunate: "in young people not inclined toward literary reflection, such deepseated negative identities can be reabsorbed only by a turn to militancy, if not transient violence."[73]

In section X, Heaney wakes to the tangible, mutable world of the Station Island hostel at first light. He emphasizes the gradual return to an ordinary day through a series of sentence fragments: "Morning stir in the hostel. A pot / hooked on forged links. Soot flakes. Plumping water. / The open door letting in the sunlight" (*SI* 87). Objects are solid, even obdurate, each word deliberate as the forged links from which a cauldron is suspended. Moreover, it would seem that Heaney's coveted "door into the light" looms near at hand. He remembers an earthenware mug in his boyhood home "beyond my reach on its high shelf, the one / patterned with cornflowers, blue sprig after sprig / repeating round it." Clay spun on a potter's wheel, its smooth contours molded by an unknown artisan's knowing touch, the vessel is unpretentious as the cracked glaze fired into its surface or the cornflower motif "repeating" around its rim. Like Keats's Grecian Urn, the mug seems to exist outside of time, although young Heaney gleaned scant numinosity from its mere presence on the shelf:

"When had it not been there?" A symbol of cultural origins, as an artifact that bestows identity on a particular household the mug remains dormant until appropriated one night by mummers for a play: "the fit-up actors used it for a prop / and I sat in a dark hall estranged from it / as a couple vowed and called it their loving cup." The cup sheds its mundane aspect when the youth sees it transformed into the centerpiece of secular ritual. The mummers' incantations provoke a lyric epiphany: "Dipped and glamoured from this translation, / it was restored with all its cornflower haze // still dozing, its parchment glazes fast." Heaney becomes aware of the transfiguring power of ceremonial enactment outside the realm of the Church. He sees the miraculous arise from the ordinary, and immediately compares the safe return of the mug to Ronan's psalter retrieved unharmed from lough waters by an otter in *Buile Suibhne*. Thus Heaney remembers the first stirrings of his poetic identity, intimations of a world beyond the snug turf fires of County Derry: "The dazzle of the impossible suddenly / blazed across the threshold, a sun-glare / to put out the small hearths of constancy" (*SI* 88).

Section XI draws initially on a childhood memory that had surfaced in *Stations* and *Among Schoolchildren: A John Malone Memorial Lecture* (1983). Envious of the battleship his young Protestant friend was given as a Christmas gift, the young Heaney plunged the kaleidoscope he had received into a water cask, with unfortunate results: "Its bright prisms that offered incomprehensible satisfactions were messed and silted: instead of a marvelous lightship, I salvaged a dirty hulk."[74] The kaleidoscope, with its brilliant, shifting reflections, becomes an apt metaphor for the power of the imagination; the shade of a former confessor returns to remind the poet of "the need and chance // to salvage everything, to re-envisage / the zenith and glimpsed jewels of any gift / mistakenly abased" (*SI* 89). The attendant guilt and concern about sectarian matters and the poet's role in such a crisis have clouded the prismatic clarity of his vision. But the monk again counsels Heaney to recognize the nature of his poetic gift and cultivate it lovingly: "'Read poems as prayers,' he said, 'and for your penance / translate me something by Juan de la Cruz.'" The absolution renews the poet's faith in his own vocation: "he had made me feel there was nothing to confess." In the passage chosen for translation, "The Song of the Soul that Rejoices in Knowing God through Faith," the "eternal fountain" symbolizes not only the Holy Spirit but also Helicon, the source of poetic inspiration: "So pellucid it never can be muddied, / and I know that all light radiates from it / although it is the night" (*SI* 90). For the poet, these are clarifying waters. As Thomas Foster notes, sections X and XI may not offer a *Paradiso*, but they do provide "a way out of purgatory, a sustaining vision of the poet's role."[75]

Like Dante seeking guidance and instruction from Virgil, Heaney turns to Joyce in section XII. The spectral master proffers a hand "fish-cold and bony," but his intentions remain unclear:

> whether to guide
> or to be guided I could not be certain
>
> for the tall man in step at my side
> seemed blind, though he walked straight as a rush
> upon his ash plant, his eyes fixed straight ahead.
>
> (*SI* 92)

Leading and led by a blind man, Heaney seems to find his own voice in the old artificer's sure intonations: "a voice like a prosecutor's or a singer's, // cunning, narcotic, mimic, definite / as a steel nib's downstroke, quick and clean." Unlike Heaney, Joyce's darkness is physical rather than spiritual. Not only the most aesthetically accomplished but also the most worldly of the shades encountered by Heaney, he badgers the young poet for the lack of conviction implicit in undertaking a penitential journey: "Your obliga-tion / is not discharged by any common rite. / What you must do must be done on your own // so get back in harness" (*SI* 92–93). Heaney feels the rain lash his face, and confesses an identification with Joyce more in-tensely personal than we might have guessed:

> "Old father, mother's son,
> there is a moment in Stephen's diary
> for April the thirteenth, a revelation
>
> set among my stars—that one entry
> has been a sort of password in my ears,
> the collect of a new epiphany,
>
> the Feast of the Holy Tundish."
>
> (*SI* 93)

The poet's birthday—"a revelation / set among my stars"—coincides with a note from Stephen Dedalus's private journal in *A Portrait of the Artist*. In a diary entry dated 13 April, Stephen recalls with anger the Jesuit dean's ig-norance of both Gaelic and English etymology: "That tundish has been on my mind for a long time. I looked it up and find it English and good old blunt English too. Damn the dean of studies and his funnel! What did he come here for to teach us his own language or to learn it from us?"[76] Joyce reacts with irritation to Heaney's having enshrined young Dedalus's real-

ization that the language of empire has always been available for appropri-
ation: "'Who cares,' / he jeered, 'any more? The English language / belongs to us.'" Here Joyce states the obvious: the struggle for primacy in
English literature was won earlier in the twentieth century by Wilde, Yeats,
O'Casey, Synge, Kavanagh, and Joyce himself. He enjoins Heaney to slip
the snares of national and sectarian strife, to cease pondering the obligations of religious and tribal loyalty:

> "That subject people stuff is a cod's game,
> infantile, like your peasant pilgrimage.
>
> You lose more of yourself than you redeem
> doing the decent thing. Keep at a tangent.
> When they make the circle wide, it's time to swim
>
> out on your own and fill the element
> with signatures on your own frequency,
> echo soundings, searches, probes, allurements,
>
> elver-gleams in the dark of the whole sea."
>
> (*SI* 93–94)

Joyce ratifies the iconoclastic stance of the "dawn-sniffing revenant" Louis
O'Neill, the fisherman in "Casualty" who values the untrammelled spirit of
the lyric moment more than "our tribe's complicity." Religious abasement
and communal restraint are forms of enclosure that the artist must avoid at
all costs, thus the novelist's advice to "Keep at a tangent." If only for a
brief moment, the rapt inflections of the Joycean harangue enable Heaney
to forget his crisis of identity. Abruptly, the spell breaks off, as the old expatriate vanishes into curtains of mist raised by rain on sweltering asphalt:
"the tarmac / fumed and sizzled. As he moved off quickly // the downpour
loosed its screens round his straight walk" (*SI* 94). As Sammye Crawford
Greer notes, "the final continuation of his [Heaney's] artistic identity
comes in the words of release spoken by the shade of James Joyce in the
last section" of "Station Island."[77]

The poetry of "Station Island," while ambitious, is not always entirely
successful; its intensity almost invariably resides in the dramatic nature of
Heaney's encounters rather than in his language; briefly put, the poet
breaks faith with his essential lyric bent. Yet the sequence is one that
Heaney felt compelled to write. Indeed, he once described the poem as "a
kind of penance, like a big wheel I felt I had to turn myself on for a
while."[78] His journey of atonement reflects an inner anguish that some-
times leads to self-abasement, but also anticipates and deflates the criti-

cism of others. As Declan Kiberd remarks, "the worst that can be said against Heaney always turns out to have been said already of himself by the artist within the poems,"[79] and this is especially true of "Station Island." But Heaney's relentless self-scrutiny reaches its peak in the long poem: through the set of stations he concocts for himself, he justifies his artistic role, absolves himself for his retreat to the South, and banishes his misgivings, at least temporarily. Corcoran notes that the poem "defines a painful realignment between himself [Heaney] and his culture, and brings him to the point of newly steadied illumination."[80] The poet has achieved a sense of resolution; he stands poised on the threshold of his "door into the light," ready to set out with a renewed sense of confidence and purpose. With the culmination of "Station Island," Heaney finally accepts his literary identity, embracing what Thomas Foster calls "the gift that is unexpected, undeserved, out of all proportion to merit."[81] Heaney acknowledges, too, the full implications and responsibilities of his vocation. Understandably, he finds it difficult to endure the deaths of kinsmen, former teammates, and various acquaintances who became victims of sectarian strife after his migration to the Republic, but he also realizes that his staying at home could not have altered these events. His most productive efforts toward mitigating the Troubles will occur when he subjects his concerns and experiences to the rigors of art: indeed, the poet faces the unenviable challenge of probing the roots and authenticity of sectarian violence and eventually writing poems that are politically engaged yet aesthetically vital.[82] Henceforth, Heaney will insist on the poet's responsibility to his art and the necessities of the imagination, adopting a stance less apologetic and more aspiring than earlier in his career. In "Station Island," Heaney aligns himself with the most gifted members of both the modern Irish literary tradition and the European canon. Moreover, as Corcoran emphasizes, the volume is a new and unexpected departure for the poet:

> *Station Island* gives notice that Heaney's poetry, in its dissatisfied revision of earlier attitudes and presumptions, and in its exploratory inventiveness as it feels out new directions for itself, is now in the process of successfully negotiating what is, for any poet, the most difficult phase of a career—the transition from the mores and manners which have created the reputation, to the genuinely new and unexpected thing . . . a poetry . . . bristling with the risks and the dangers of such self-transformation but, at its high points, triumphantly self-vindicating too.[83]

The poetry of Heaney's early mid-career records vividly his attempt to come to terms with his literary identity and to resolve for himself the role of the artist in the midst of cultural crisis. By the end of "Station Island,"

Heaney has indeed found the "door into the light" he so earnestly sought after *North*. His penitential journey proves a virtual reenactment of his visit to Gallarus Oratory in 1967, described in a 1978 broadcast for Radio Eireann:

> Inside, in the dark of the stone, it feels as if you are sustaining a great pressure, bowing under like the generations of monks who must have bowed down in meditation and reparation on that floor. I felt the weight of Christianity in all its rebuking aspects, its calls to self-denial and self-abnegation, its humbling of the proud flesh and insolent spirit. But coming out of the cold heart of the stone, into the sunlight and the dazzle of grass and sea, I felt a lift in my heart, a surge towards happiness that must have been experienced over and over again by those monks as they crossed that same threshold centuries ago. This surge towards praise, this sudden apprehension of the world as light, as illumination. (*Pr* 189)

Beginning with *Field Work*, the poet derives a greater sense of identity from the community. With the poetry of Robert Lowell serving as a catalyst, Heaney develops a more domestic voice and subject matter. The poetry is direct and engaging; with "The Glanmore Sonnets," Heaney brings his life and work together, establishing a current sense of identity with his wife and others, and achieving a lush, redemptive sensuality. But *Field Work* is beset with fits and starts; in "Oysters" and other poems, the poet succumbs to sudden bouts of guilt for retreating South. Here Heaney reaches a crucial turning point: from *Field Work* on, he confronts the Troubles directly, briefly assuaging his crisis of identity when he refuses to channel his anger through the vast historical analogues that formed the foundation of *North*. Naturally, Heaney's poetry becomes even more elegaic, as he commemorates kinsmen and others whose deaths result from sectarian strife.

In "Casualty" and "Station Island," however, the nature of kinship proves far more complex than earlier in his work; as he realizes, he cannot sacrifice his artistic gift to the rigid strictures of any collective identity. Indeed, even as he seeks a deeper bond of kinship with the living, *Sweeney Astray* and *Station Island* evince an equal desire to belong to a literary tradition. Like Austin Clarke's "The Frenzy of Sweeney" and Thomas Kinsella's *Táin*, Heaney's translation of *Buile Suibhne* enabled him to see himself as part of the Irish literary tradition. It also afforded a means of confronting his own demons, a way of clarifying his own crisis by taking on the voice of another. The persona of Sweeney later proved a viable mask, uniting the parts of *Station Island* and serving as a much-needed alter-ego for Heaney. In much the same way, the multiple voices of "Station Island" provided the poet with a way of subduing his own crisis of identity. Moreover, Heaney's translation of Dante's Ugolino canto that closes *Field Work* and the first four cantos of the *Inferno* initially suggested the possibility of an Irish pantheon that could guide him in his struggle to break free of the claims of orthodoxy: "With Dante's example . . . I was encouraged to make an advantage of what could otherwise be regarded as a disadvantage, namely, that other writers had been to Lough Derg before me—William Carleton, Sean O'Faolain, Patrick Kavanagh, Denis Devlin, to mention only the English language forerunners."[84] Thus the poet emerges renewed, his vocation affirmed by the agonistic encounters with the shades of his literary ancestors.

Ironically, just as Heaney seemed to have reconciled the personal and literary aspects of his identity and opened a "door into the light," the deaths of his parents forced him to renegotiate his identity. When Margaret and Patrick Heaney died, in the autumn of 1984 and 1986, respectively, the poet experienced a profound sense of loss that would transform his subsequent poetry. In *The Haw Lantern* (1987), *Seeing Things* (1991), and *The Spirit Level* (1996), Heaney confronts death on a level more intensely personal than ever before; as he himself has observed, the poetry of his middle career bears the distinct imprint of "somebody who has been at two deathbeds, and who remains unchanged and completely changed by that."[85] In the presence of death the door into the light opens wider, as Heaney eschews the ritual aspects of mourning, and couples a poetics of loss with a Dantesque striving toward spiritual enlightenment.

4

A Poetics of Transcendence

IN HIS MIDDLE CAREER, SEAMUS HEANEY REDEFINES HIS PERSONAL AND poetic identity, achieving a more mature, assured lyric voice and a visionary quality unprecedented in his work. If a tone of release and confidence pervades the poetry of this phase, it has been hard-won. The "door into the light" that appears in *The Haw Lantern* and *Seeing Things* derives from the poet's troubling cultural legacy and his earlier wrestlings with conscience, as Elmer Andrews observes: "It is the very sense of imminent loss, dissolution and crisis that energises the visionary power."[1] Heaney's new departure affirms his consistent refusal to write the same book twice, an aspect of Yeats's poetic versatility that he admires in *Preoccupations*: "if you have managed to do one kind of poem in your own way, you should cast off that way and face into another area of your experience until you have learned a new voice to say that area properly" (110). But the mature style of his middle phase also grows out of new perspectives provided by constant travel across the Atlantic and relationships with poets of other nationalities. And, as Heaney notes in an interview with Thomas Foster, a writer approaching his fifth decade typically experiences "a certain rethinking of yourself, a certain distance from your first self."[2] For Heaney, however, the deaths of his parents intensified that period of reassessment, giving new meaning to his ongoing crisis of identity. *The Haw Lantern* and *Seeing Things* emerge from his encounters with death, which Heaney describes as "immensely mysterious and mercilessly ordinary" in a later interview with Steven Ratiner:

> Now in one moment there is life, now there is not life. And what has parted? It gives you a lack of shyness opposite words like "spirit," "soul," "life," whatever. So that is the turn, the crisis and the emboldening of language towards the ineffable areas.[3]

While his poetry remains elegiac, commemorating the deaths of his parents, his mother-in-law, translator Robert Fitzgerald, and others, it equally conveys a sense of redemption and renewal. In "Clearances," a sonnet cycle for his mother in *The Haw Lantern*, Heaney concentrates on moments of quiet interaction between his mother and himself. He thus returns to what Erikson calls "the earliest and most undifferentiated 'sense of identity.'"[4] The initial bond of mutual trust and recognition, as the poet becomes intensely aware, is a child's first sense of "hallowed presence," enabling him to develop other relationships and to enter adulthood.[5] Within his sonnet sequence, Heaney's skillful bridging of the temporal and the eternal suggests that memories cannot be eclipsed by time. Indeed, throughout the poetry of his middle career, Heaney reimagines and realigns his past in light of the present, thus clarifying his identity and achieving striking and subtle resonances that enliven his long lyric sequences as well as the shorter lyrics.

Ironically, the presence of death perhaps frees Heaney in some respects, as Parker observes:

> Critics have noted, and Heaney himself has commented on, a greater sense of ease and release within these last two volumes, a "freeing up" which may not be unconnected with bereavement. No longer constrained perhaps by his feeling for parental feelings, he appears less tentative, more candid in his observations on Catholic and Nationalist tradition.[6]

A number of the poems in *Seeing Things* ("The Ash Plant," "1.1.87," and "An August Night," among others) deal with the death of his father. Having witnessed the death of his parents, he thus faces his own mortality, or as Erikson phrases it, the realization that "I am what survives of me."[7] Heaney's response is not despair, but exhilaration. Especially in *Seeing Things*, he couples a poetics of loss with a Dantesque striving toward enlightenment. He views the "Shifting brilliancies" of this life with expectation, seeking and celebrating mutability rather than deploring it. The desire to see things in new ways, which surfaced in *The Haw Lantern*, recurs throughout *Seeing Things*. Taken together, the volumes preclude the belief that there is only one way of seeing anything, thus implying an eventual transcendence of the burdensome cultural legacy that troubled Heaney in previous collections. Indeed, as the sequence "Squarings" illustrates, Heaney remains intent on overcoming obstacles, even to the extent of arbitrarily imposing limits and boundaries himself.

According to Henry Hart, "Critics who expected from Seamus Heaney a rhetoric as consistently dense and pungent as his peat bogs and potato drills were startled by the lighter feel of *The Haw Lantern*."[8] The deftly wrought poems of Heaney's ninth volume do not always ratify Joyce's advice at the end of "Station Island," to "let go, let fly." Indeed, Heaney returns to basics in the first poem, "Alphabets," as he experiences anew the painstaking process of learning to write. Remembering his father's ability to project shadow images on the wall, he realizes that the negation of light offers only the most primitive articulation of the soul: "A shadow his father makes with joined hands / And thumbs and fingers nibbles on the wall / Like a rabbit's head" (*HL* 1). Soon the fledgling poet will scratch white symbols on a slate, marvelling at how he can trace the world of objects into a mysterious code: "There he draws smoke with chalk the whole first week / Then draws the forked stick that they call a Y. / This is writing." Heaney patiently rehearses the steps to illumination and self-affirmation, even as he suffuses the old emblems of agrarian life with a newly minted aura: "First it is 'copying out,' and then 'English' / Marked correct with a little leaning hoe." Moreover, his apprehension of the "world become word" increases in sophistication when he moves from the "[m]arbled and minatory" characters of the Latin alphabet to the florid loops and swirls of a calligraphic script: "The letters of this alphabet were trees. / The capitals were orchards in full bloom, / The lines of script like briars coiled in ditches" (*HL* 2). Having once established dominion over acres of "orchards" and "briars," he is ready to receive the Muse. A cross between the Blessed Virgin and Dante's Beatrice, she brings the page to life like a musical score:

> Here in her snooded garment and bare feet,
> All ringleted in assonance and woodnotes,
> The poet's dream stole over him like sunlight
> And passed into the tenebrous thickets.

> (*HL* 2)

In his first book, *Death of a Naturalist*, Heaney dramatized his development as a vessel of poetic consciousness, an impressionable child overwhelmed by the natural universe. "Alphabets," on the other hand, depicts a world scaled down to a miniaturist's fairy-tale dimensions. Far from being reductive, it is the poem of an adult who continues to perceive magic in the ageless ciphers. Helen Vendler locates in "Alphabets" a clever inversion of Heaney's early Wordsworthian approach: "Against Wordsworth's myth of a childhood radiance lost, the poem sets a counter-myth of an imaginative power that becomes fuller and freer with the child's expanding linguistic and literary power."[9] In the third and final section, Heaney equates the acquisition of writing and the sense of identity that this sacred technology bestows with the wonder experienced by a space explorer when a planet at once familiar and strange swims into his ken:

> As from his small window
> The astronaut sees all he has sprung from,
> The risen, aqueous, singular, lucent O
> Like a magnified and buoyant ovum—
>
> Or like my own wide pre-reflective stare
> All agog at the plasterer on his ladder
> Skimming our gable and writing our name there
> With his trowel point, letter by strange letter.
>
> (*HL* 3)

The astronaut's view of his native element—"a buoyant ovum" emblematic of imaginative fecundity—is perceptual as opposed to merely conceptual. Just so, the poet remembers his own "pre-reflective stare" as he saw for the first time the sequence of letters signifying his familial identity inscribed in damp plaster. The evanescent moment before the name congeals implies for Heaney the wonderful plasticity of the creative intelligence.

Heaney's new visionary impulse does not typically embrace, after the manner of William Blake, things that are utterly fantastic to the casual observer. Reacting against the imagistic vagueness of late Romantic and Pre-Raphaelite poetry, Pound encouraged his contemporaries to shun abstractions and to focus primarily on objects. Indeed, William Carlos Williams's dictum, "No ideas but in things," became the credo of the Imagist movement. However, early proponents of Imagism, Pound and Eliot included, astutely observed that the methodology tended to limit the imagination. According to Henry Hart, they were aware that "language mediates both things and ideas, transforming both into an artificial medium that is simultaneously abstract and concrete. In the word the world is both idea and object."[10] In the brief title poem of *The Haw Lantern*, Heaney yearns for a dynamic synthesis of the real and the imaginary:

> The wintry haw is burning out of season,
> crab of the thorn, a small light for small people,
> wanting no more from them but that they keep
> the wick of self-respect from dying out,
> not having to blind them with illumination.
>
> But sometimes when your breath plumes in the frost
> it takes the roaming shape of Diogenes
> with his lantern, seeking one just man;

so you end up scrutinized from behind the haw
he holds up at eye-level on its twig,
and you flinch before its bonded pith and stone,
its blood-prick that you wish would test and clear you,
its pecked-at ripeness that scans you, then moves on.

(*HL* 7)

The multiple tropes so typical of Heaney's early poetry are totally absent from the first stanza. The poet focuses on a single hawthorn berry burning against the white winter landscape. Like Wallace Stevens's blackbird, whose eye holds dominion over twenty snowy alps by virtue of its movement and implied sentience, the red berry is a lonely sentinel on a bleak frontier, a guardian of "the wick of self-respect." In the second stanza, Heaney transforms the hawthorn to the gnarled shape of the Stoic philosopher Diogenes scouring the Hellenic world with a lantern as he searches for "one just man." Suddenly, idea converts to object, as the diminutive "bonded pith and stone" becomes one bright drop pricked from the colorless terrain, its ripeness "pecked-at" but inviolable. The haw seems to scrutinize the poet even as he scrutinizes it, thus effacing and transcending the boundary between subjective and objective realms. Vendler contends that the berry represents "an almost apologetic flame, indirectly suggesting his [Heaney's] own quelled hopes as a spokesman for his fellow men."[11] But to read "The Haw Lantern" in such blatantly allegorical terms is perhaps misleading. In an interview with Rand Brandes, Heaney intimates that the poem serves as a mid-career *ars poetica*, a further ratification of his personal and literary identity:

"Haw" has always had a strange fascination for me. I like it as a little thing, as one of the little fruits or stones of the earth. Also I liked the phrase in the poem, "a small light for a small people." That's a true middle-years vision of the function of poetry. And yet I shouldn't really say that. . . . The function of *poetry* is to have a bigger blaze than that, but *people* should not expect more from themselves than adequacy. They should not confuse the action of poetry, which is at its highest, visionary action, with the actuality of our lives, which at their best are adequate to our smaller size. In "The Haw Lantern" poem, there's a sense of being tested and earning the right to proceed.[12]

But the ultimate "test" in *The Haw Lantern* evolves from a situation so common to the Ulster Catholic experience that the hawthorn berry seems a numinous phenomenon even before the poet engages its lyric potential. In "From the Frontier of Writing," British soldiers detain Heaney at a military roadblock, and he feels once again the "tightness and the nilness round that space / when the car stops in the road, the troops inspect / its make and number" (*HL* 6). The sense of "nilness" derives from having one's identity gauged in terms of the "make and number" of an automobile, and the situation worsens as the poet proceeds to the next checkpoint:

> So you drive on to the frontier of writing
> where it happens again. The guns on tripods;
> the sergeant with his on-off mike repeating
>
> data about you, waiting for the squawk
> of clearance; the marksman training down
> out of the sun upon you like a hawk.
>
> (*HL* 6)

Feeling oneself drawn up into the crosshairs of a rifle scope can make being itself an onerous experience, but Heaney's discomfort doubtless escalates as he hears his personal identity reduced to "data" filtered through the static on a two-way radio. However, the moment is not without its humor: likening the British marksman to a hawk would prove a hopeless cliché, were the image not aurally buttressed by the "squawk / of clearance" emitted by the radio's microphone. The moment of transcendence comes when Heaney reassumes the common wayfarer's anonymity, and thus paradoxically retrieves a sense of self that enables him to move on:

> And suddenly you're through, arraigned yet freed,
> as if you'd passed from behind a waterfall
> on the black current of a tarmac road
>
> past armour-plated vehicles, out between
> the posted soldiers flowing and receding
> like tree shadows into the polished windscreen.
>
> (*HL* 6)

At once literal and parabolic, Heaney's "frontier of writing" signifies the moment of release in the creative act wherein the poet slips the snares of religion and nationality. Indeed, "the black current of a tarmac road" evokes not only the meeting with Joyce in section twelve of "Station Island," but also the old artificer's subsequent exit into a tarmac that fumed and sizzled in a gentle downpour. The armored vehicles so prevalent in *Field Work* recede, and the soldiers become mere shadow images on a windscreen that first tenses, then flows. "The Haw Lantern" and "From the

Frontier of Writing" illustrate Heaney's continuing reconciliation to art as his chosen and proper sphere. As he states in the interview with Rand Brandes, by this point in his career he has arrived at a more realistic view of the function of poetry and the role of the individual artist. Moreover, he has reached an understanding of what to expect from himself in his poetry and his life. While he recognizes his own desire to stem the conflict in the North, he comprehends that his role is finally to deal with the Troubles as his own creative imagination dictates; yet he must not confine his art by assuming the position of spokesman for the North. If Heaney's symbolic acts of transgressing and transcending boundaries do not offer an end to the Northern crisis, they at least suggest the individual's potential for eventually getting beyond it.

While *The Haw Lantern* is ostensibly elegiac, its underlying mood tends toward the celebratory. Oddly, some scholars have deplored Heaney's return to "first things," the myriad objects of delight that inform the childhood vision of *Death of a Naturalist* and Geoffrey Hill's *Mercian Hymns*. However, in their introduction to *Seamus Heaney: The Shaping Spirit*, Catharine Malloy and Phyllis Carey correctly posit the poet's desire to locate the touchstones of personal and cultural identity in the defining images of his own past: "the search for origins as influences looks toward the small and minute—'The Haw Lantern,' 'The Spoonbait,' 'Alphabets'—emphasizing that the smallest entity or shape may be capable of far-reaching importance in achieving self-definition."[13] In "The Spoonbait," Heaney couples the sublime and the quotidian through dextrous control of an elaborate conceit:

> So a new similitude is given us
> And we say: The soul may be compared
>
> Unto a spoonbait that a child discovers
> Beneath the sliding lid of a pencil case,
>
> Glimpsed once and imagined for a lifetime
> Risen and free and spooling out of nowhere—
>
> A shooting star going back up the darkness.
>
> (*HL* 21)

In the homiletic tone of the first three lines, we hear echoes of Anglo-Saxon vernacular poetry after Saint Augustine began his slow conversion of the English petty kingdoms to Christianity in the early seventh century; however, the sliding tropes, each one subsuming its predecessor, more nearly recall the structural intricacy of the riddles and gnomic verse with which the *scop* so diverted the members of the pagan *comitatus*. The glittering spoonbait becomes a shooting star, then turns into the elusive drop that Dives implored from the depths of Hell in Luke 16:24: "It flees him and it burns him all at once // Like the single drop that Dives implored / Falling and falling into a great gulf." Heaney employs cinematic technique in his closure, offering first one ending, and then an alternative or coda:

> Then exit, the polished helmet of a hero
> Laid out amidships above scudding water.
>
> Exit, alternatively, a toy of light
> Reeled through him upstream, snagging on nothing.
>
> (*HL* 21)

The multiple tropes align Heaney with Joyce as a master of artifice who explores the full creative potential inherent not only in language but also in the things of this world. By linking the "toy of light" with the "polished helmet of a hero," Heaney endows the simplest of objects with an epic splendor. It is no accident that "The Spoonbait" appears *en face* with "A Ship of Death," Heaney's translation of the burial ship passage from *Beowulf* (2:26–52):

> They stretched their beloved lord in the boat,
> laid out amidships by the mast
> the great ring-giver. Far-fetched treasures
> were piled upon him, and precious gear.
>
> (*HL* 20)

The intertextual resonances between "The Spoonbait" and "A Ship of Death" are unmistakable, and demonstrate, moreover, that Heaney remains bent on tapping the Western literary tradition of Homer, Virgil, and Dante through the mundane particulars of his own experience. Pulled back through the psychic recesses of personal memory, the spoonbait gathers a heretofore unimaginable luminosity, and subtly reflects Heaney's conception of writing: "I see it as a process of continual going back in to what you have, changing it and coming out changed."[14]

In his elegy for Robert Fitzgerald, Heaney mythologizes the death of his friend, whose translations of the *Iliad* and *Odyssey* superceded those of Richmond Lattimore. "In Memoriam: Robert Fitzgerald" takes the form of a sonnet built around an obsessive lexicon:

> The socket of each axehead like the squared
> Doorway to a megalithic tomb
> With its slabbed passage that keeps opening forward
> To face another corbelled stone-faced door
> That opens on a third. There is no last door,
> Just threshold stone, stone jambs, stone crossbeam
> Repeating *enter, enter, enter, enter.*
> Lintel and upright fly past in the dark.
>
> After the bowstring sang a swallow's note,
> The arrow whose migration is its mark
> Leaves a whispered breath in every socket.
> The great test over, while the gut's still humming,
> This time it travels out of all knowing
> Perfectly aimed towards the vacant centre.
>
> (*HL* 22)

The repetition of words such as "stone," "door," "face," and "*enter*" emphasizes Heaney's intention to mine the narrowest possible linguistic vein. He transforms the "iron axe-helve sockets, twelve in a line,"[15] through which Penelope's suitors were obliged to shoot an arrow from Odysseus's great horn bow, into the Neolithic or Bronze Age passage-graves at Newgrange. Thus Heaney conjoins Bronze Age Irish and Mycenaean architecture with one facile trope. Of course, the dissolute suitors fail the ordeal of the bow: only the hero, Odysseus, is able to thread the twelve axe-helve sockets with a single shot. Heaney sees Fitzgerald's translation, both spiritual and literary, as a movement from one realm to the next, a faring forth that is interminable: "threshold stone, stone jambs, stone crossbeam / Repeating *enter, enter, enter, enter.*" The poet paradoxically asserts that the endless journey is the goal of life as well as art. Perhaps Henry Hart best limns the meaning of Heaney's metaphorical eulogy:

> As Heaney tells the story of Fitzgerald retracing original Greek texts in his *Iliad* and *Odyssey,* which in turn are retracings of Homer's "whispered breath" and the breaths of the storytellers before Homer, he deconstructs the old hierarchies by emphasizing that writing and speech, textual tradition and oral tradition, inscribing arrow and whispered breath, presence and absence, end and origin, known world and unknown underworld, issue from the same "vacant centre," which could be the mysterious source of all being.[16]

Heaney forgoes the self-aggrandizing tone of Yeats's "The Municipal Gallery Re-visited"; his friend achieves apotheosis through the dwelling in

absence that words betoken. Pursuit of literary excellence is the common
bond between Heaney and Fitzgerald, and he sees the individual artist,
whether translator or original poet, as one subsuming and subsumed by the
Western canon. Moreover, his elegy acknowledges the increasing impact
of translation on his own poetic identity. His "versions" from the *Buile
Suibhne, Beowulf*, the *Divine Comedy*, and the *Aeneid* have offered new
means of divining parallels between the Northern crisis and other aspects
of human history, thus providing a consolation of sorts. If the image of
endless doorways recognizes Fitzgerald's "linguistic love-right" or desire
for "carrying a thing across" into another language, it also celebrates the
sense of continuity afforded by such an act of love: "a cultural, political,
historical in-placeness, a 'we are all in there together' feeling."[17] In Fitzgerald's translations, then, Heaney sees the achievement of his own poetic
goal: to move beyond the boundaries of nationality and religion, eventually
arriving at a poetry of universal significance.

Heaney resumes his search for identity in a series of commemorative
sonnets titled "Clearances," a sequence that confronts death on a level
more intensely personal than ever before. Unlike the elegy "Mid-Term
Break," this eight-poem cycle eschews the aspects of mourning that make
for a ritual estrangement, concentrating instead on moments of quiet
bonding between mother and son. The narrative elements tend to be circu-
lar, and we do not arrive at Margaret Kathleen Heaney's deathbed until the
third sonnet. Even as the parish priest goes "hammer and tongs at the
prayers for the dying," Heaney recalls mornings spent with his mother
while the other family members were away at Mass: "I was all hers as we
peeled potatoes. / They broke the silence, let fall one by one / Like solder
weeping off the soldering iron" (*HL* 27). Sonnet six remembers the "high-
points of our *Sons and Lovers* phase. / The midnight fire. The paschal can-
dlestick" (*HL* 30). The fourth sonnet speaks to Heaney's ever-present
anxiety about his intellectual attainments, revealing a discomfort that belongs not entirely to him: "Fear of affectation made her affect / Inade-
quacy whenever it came to / Pronouncing words 'beyond her.' *Bertold
Brek*" (*HL* 28). But the most poignant sonnet appears second in the sequence. Here Heaney skillfully bridges the temporal and eternal, suggesting that cherished memories cannot be eclipsed by time. Every object
described in the octave emanates a pristine light, thus clarifying and af-
firming the idyllic bond between mother and son. The sestet implies that
Heaney has at last found the true "door into the light," an unspoken
covenant binding the generations of his house, father and daughter,
mother and son:

Polished linoleum shone there. Brass taps shone.
The china cups were very white and big—
An unchipped set with sugar bowl and jug.
The kettle whistled. Sandwich and tea scone
Were present and correct. In case it run,
The butter must be kept out of the sun.
And don't be dropping crumbs. Don't tilt your chair.
Don't reach. Don't point. Don't make noise when you stir.

It is Number 5, New Row, Land of the Dead,
Where grandfather is rising from his place
With spectacles pushed back on a clean bald head
To welcome a bewildered homing daughter
Before she even knocks. "What's this? What's this?"
And they sit down in the shining room together.

(*HL* 26)

The room of light seems to belong to "the still point of the turning world."[18] But this familial haven represents a center that cannot hold, and in the seventh sonnet Heaney confronts the moment of death head-on. The sudden absence of his mother so overwhelms him that she becomes a presence or representation: "The space we stood around had been emptied / Into us to keep, it penetrated / Clearances that suddenly stood open." Indeed, Hart asserts that Heaney's Aristotelian sensibility inevitably comes to the fore: "Imitating nature, Heaney's imagination abhors a vacuum. When presences turn ineluctably to absences, representations rush in to replace them."[19] In the eighth sonnet of "Clearances," Heaney likens the absence of his mother to the cutting down of a chestnut tree that had taken root in the year of his birth:

I heard the hatchet's differentiated
Accurate cut, the crack, the sigh
And collapse of what luxuriated
Through the shocked tips and wreckage of it all.
Deep planted and long gone, my coeval
Chestnut from a jam jar in a hole,
Its heft and hush become a bright nowhere,
A soul ramifying and forever
Silent, beyond silence listened for.

(*HL* 32)

In an essay entitled "The Placeless Heaven," Heaney recalls how one of his aunts planted a chestnut in a jam jar; when it began to sprout, she broke the jar and transplanted the seedling under a hedge in front of the Mossbawn home: "Over the years, the seedling shot up into a young tree that rose taller and taller above the boxwood hedge. And over the years I came to identify my own life with the life of the chestnut tree" (*GT* 3). The family moved from Mossbawn while the poet was still in his teens, and the tree was eventually cut down. The luxuriating chestnut acquires full significance as a symbol of his identity only in retrospect, with the event of his mother's death. In Sonnet VIII, the felling and displacement of the tree becomes a metaphor for the abrupt removal of the poet's mother from the center of his life. The loss of his mother utterly transforms Heaney's sense of poetic and familial identity, as Michael Parker notes:

> In contemplating "the space where the tree had been or would have been" some thirty years later, the poet was able to come to terms with his own unrootedness, his feelings of "luminous emptiness" in the wake of his mother's death. Out of the "cut, the crack, the sigh / and collapse," he begins a new phase of self-translation, working other intense moments of "childhood sensation" / adult experience into wonders.[20]

A number of critics accurately labelled *The Haw Lantern* a transitional volume, a working out of a new poetic style. According to Andrew Waterman, some considered the book overtly self-conscious, "weakened precisely by its author's awareness of himself as a public figure."[21] Yet Waterman also asserts that the collection marks a significant stage in Heaney's evolution, displaying no small measure of innovation, though the risks taken occasionally end in failure. His assessment of *The Haw Lantern* deems "its experimentation bracing, and often fruitful, the diverse nature of its successes more notable than in any of this poet's previous volumes."[22] By the final sonnet of "Clearances," Heaney's transition to a new poetic phase is complete. Redefining his identity by making his past "take the strain of adult experience,"[23] Heaney achieves a visionary stance that celebrates mutability and transcendence, and imbues his poetry with a renewed yet relaxed vitality. In his subsequent volumes of poetry, as in *The Haw Lantern*, Heaney increasingly draws strength from the Western literary tradition, and seeks a place for himself within its community. In *The Cure at Troy* (1991), his "version" of Sophocles' *Philoctetes*, he points to resemblances between the Trojan War and the Northern crisis. The poems in *Seeing Things*, framed by translations from the *Aeneid* and the *Inferno*, display the full fruition of Heaney's new vision, as he confronts his father's death, beginning "the journey back / Into the heartland of the ordinary" and finding himself finally able "to credit / Marvels." The journey continues in

The Spirit Level: images of release and renewal abound, as Heaney endows river gravel, cactus stalks, and well water with a resonance that is elemental, hence spiritual. But revisitings of his own epiphanic moments are balanced by delvings into a more historical past. "Mycenae Lookout," the volume's most ambitious entry, depicts the intrigue and bloodlust that pervaded Agamemnon's court at the close of the Trojan War, thus finding in Aeschylus's timeless tragedy a rich analogue to the Northern crisis. Heaney's gift for metaphor, his ability to draw stunning correspondences between images and experiences, enlivens poem after poem in this phase of his career.

The Cure at Troy, first performed by the Field Day Theatre Company in Derry in the fall of 1990, affirms the continuing effect of translation on Heaney's poetic development. Published in 1991 and dedicated to the memory of Robert Fitzgerald, Heaney's translation of Sophocles' *Philoctetes* reaffirms his identification with the alienated, the isolated, and the dispossessed. Moreover, the Greek drama enables Heaney to address the Northern crisis without didacticism. In drawing parallels between contemporary Ireland and the Trojan War, he envisions an end to conflict in the North. As he reveals in a 1989 interview with Barry White for the *Belfast Telegraph*, the boundaries symbolically broken down throughout the poetry of his middle career represent actual barriers that the poet and his contemporaries had always longed to transcend:

> I never think [in terms] of the Unionist community in Northern Ireland, nor the Nationalist community. . . . The writers of my generation, from the Protestant and Catholic side, all thought of ourselves as transcending those things. The desire was to get through the thicket, not to represent it.[24]

Imagining an end to the crisis, Heaney offers the possibility of freedom from the constraints it has imposed on the lives of its citizens; as he remarked in the interview above, "The human spirit is a much ampler and more resonant faculty and everyone feels within themselves a yearning and a possibility that it's much bigger than the terms that are offered."[25] Indeed, the onset of changes in Europe in 1989 partly inspired Heaney's rendering of *Philoctetes* and its spirit of hope.

Because of his wounded foot, Philoctetes is left on the isle of Lemnos by Odysseus and the Greeks. A decade later, Odysseus returns with Neoptolemus for the bow given to Philoctetes by Hercules; according to legend, Troy would not fall unless Neoptolemus and the bow were present. At Odysseus's behest, Neoptolemus deceives Philoctetes, but soon returns the afflicted warrior's bow and promises to take him home. Hercules, through the voice of the chorus, finally persuades both to go to Troy. Heaney's translation emphasizes the individual's responsibility; Philoctetes, though technically innocent of any wrongdoing, becomes bitter and vengeful during his exile. As Phyllis Carey observes, *The Cure at Troy* urges the Northern Irish to examine their own complicity in the Troubles, suggesting that all must relinquish the role of victim for the crisis to end: "The blurring of distinctions between hero and victim, between divine and human, underscores the pathetic nature of the social context when preoccupation with past wounds and perpetuation of more injustices render the entire society paralyzed, at an impasse."[26] Heaney's chorus symbolizes poetry and its potential, the power of art to assuage and to give the "hope for a great sea-change / On the far side of revenge" (*CT* 77). *The Cure at Troy* is an outgrowth of the poet's belief in the necessity of redefining one's own identity, initially expressed in the interview with Barry White in 1989:

> Everyone lives near the roots. It's not a matter of people not knowing who they are. Everyone knows exactly who they are. It's a matter of rethinking what you know and transforming yourself. . . . Firm roots are terrific. But they can also hamper you transforming yourself.[27]

As Craig Raine notes, *The Cure at Troy* fared better with London critics than Irish audiences.[28] Whatever its critical reception, however, *The Cure at Troy* had a significant effect on Heaney's poetic identity. Indeed, Neoptolemus's advice to Philoctetes to "Stop just licking your wounds. Start seeing things" (*CT* 74), provides a resonance between Heaney's translation and the volume of his original poetry published in 1991. Though translation is typically perceived as a sidelight of the poet's development, Alan Peacock sees the two 1991 volumes as intimately connected:

> Possibly, this successful assumption of a public, dramatic voice in endorsing hope and a belief in the "miracle" of reconciliation has freed Heaney, to an extent, to seek similar resolutions in the private and familial sphere in his non-dramatic poetry.[29]

The perspectives of European literary tradition, the prevailing tone of hope or "*uplift*," in Heaney's words, and the more public voice of *Seeing Things* stamp it as a close relation of *The Cure at Troy*.

Seeing Things, Heaney's eleventh volume of poetry, opens with a translation from the sixth book of the *Aeneid*. Declaring that he has already "foreseen and foresuffered all," Aeneas pleads with the Sibyl for "one look, one face-to-face meeting with my dear father." Thus Virgil's passage underscores Heaney's grief for his own father, whose death awakened in him "a whole new awareness of adulthood as life in a roofless universe, a prospect both liberating and terrifying."[30] The Sibyl's answer to the son of Anchises reveals that the descent is the least difficult part of the journey: "But to retrace your steps and get back to upper air, / This is the real task and the real undertaking." In this context, her subsequent instructions for plucking the Golden Bough affirm both Heaney's aesthetic stance and his identity as artist and poet: "If fate has called you, / The bough will come away easily, of its own accord." But the bough will move only for the chosen ones. If the possession of the golden bough here signifies entitlement, then Heaney becomes by implication one of those few called by fate to the role of the poet. His earlier persona of Incertus moves to the background as he begins to identify with the great artists of the Western tradition. Perhaps the branch replete with gold leaf supplants the pen Heaney used to "dig with" early on in his career; at this point, his adeptness surely equals his father's and grandfather's skilled spadework. While the role of poet may not earn Heaney a "face-to-face meeting" with his father, an encounter similar to the one so earnestly sought by Aeneas, it enables him to see his father again in a variety of ways, with imaginative powers that heighten and transform memory. Indeed, as Elmer Andrews notes in "The Spirit's Protest," Heaney's *Seeing Things* "celebrates the possibility of 'translation,' of change and metamorphosis, of transfiguration, of being carried out of oneself."[31] The poet apprehends anew the things of this world and the images that dominate memory.

In *Seeing Things*, Heaney likens the crimped satin lining of a priest's biretta to a delicately wrought miniature vessel found among Bronze Age artifacts in Broigher, County Derry:

> that small boat out of the Bronze Age
> Where the oars are needles and the worked gold frail
> As the intact half of a hatched-out shell,
> Refined beyond the dross into sheer image.
>
> ("The Biretta," *ST* 29)

Heaney contemplates the exquisite needlework, the burnished satin that shines but mirrors nothing. He feels the poet's inevitable compulsion towards metaphor, and adroitly pulls from the priest's hat the replica of a seafaring craft over three thousand years old. The transformation of biretta to boat is as startling as Homer's transfiguration of the oar in book 11 of the *Odyssey*, when the Bronze Age hero is told that he must placate the fuming sea deity Poseidon by wandering inland on foot until a stranger accosts him and asks, "What winnowing fan is that upon your shoulder?" If the journey back to Odysseus's time is something Heaney seems to perform in a twinkling, the knack for celebrating mutability through resemblances perceived in the imagination is invariably hard-won. Indeed, Heaney cannot so blithely slough the tendency to identify the biretta with the religious uncertainty of his own milieu: "The first time I saw one, I heard a shout / As an El Greco ascetic rose before me / Preaching hellfire, saurian and stormy" (*ST* 28). Even as Father Arnall terrorized Stephen Dedalus in Joyce's *A Portrait of the Artist as a Young Man*, the raging ascetic, if we can trust Heaney's account, "put the wind up me and my generation." Transcending his Roman Catholic identity, even through the magic of metaphor, proves virtually impossible for Heaney. However, the urge towards change or transcendence seems less difficult in other poems. In "Markings," for example, the emblems of agrarian life, once dominant throughout Heaney's work, have shifted their values so much that they seem to carry the poet out of his usual element:

> A mower parted the bronze sea of corn.
> A windlass hauled the centre out of water.
> Two men with a cross-cut kept it swimming
> Into a felled beech backwards and forwards
> So that they seemed to row the steady earth.
>
> (*ST* 11)

Here Heaney pulls free of his old moorings in the pastoral tradition with deceptive ease; nor is his sail bent this time for Denmark, the Orkneys, or the Faeroes, as it was in *North*. Although his sense of mutability still inclines to the elegiac, his ongoing engagement with what Eliot called the "mythic method" derives increasingly from the European epic of Homer, Virgil, and Dante.

Just as Heaney addresses his mother's mortality in a sonnet sequence central to *The Haw Lantern* (1987), a number of the poems in *Seeing Things* confront his father's recent death. Patrick Heaney figures as a powerful presence and source of identity even very early in Heaney's work. While the poet's affection is apparent, the father often seems a taciturn figure, a victim of the "famous / Northern reticence" that discourages open emotion. Though the poet had long since given over a childish awe of and pride in his father, the old man's death dramatically affects Heaney's sense of identity, occasioning a new understanding and reassessment of their relationship. "The Ash Plant," perhaps the best of the poems for his father, recalls how Patrick Heaney observed from his upstairs vantage point the familiar sights come to life each morning: "First milk-lorries, first smoke,

cattle, trees / In damp opulence above damp hedges— / He has it to himself." The dying man lies in bed, "Disencumbered as a breaking comber,"
but even as he perceives himself at the brink, he searches the center of his
being for some twinge of recognition, a deft anchoring in the sea of light:

> As his head goes light with light, his wasting hand
> Gropes desperately and finds the phantom limb
> Of an ash plant in his grasp, which steadies him.
> Now he has found his touch he can stand his ground
>
> Or wield the stick like a silver bough and come
> Walking again among us: the quoted judge.
> *I could have cut a better man out of the hedge!*
> God might have said the same, remembering Adam.
>
> (*ST* 21)

The ash plant becomes the patriarch's staff, the Greek psychopomp's
wand, the satiric bishop's crosier brandished by Stephen Dedalus in the
Night Town brothels of Joyce's *Ulysses*. For an Irish poet steeped in the
classics as well as the literature of his native land, the ash plant has more
varied associations than Aaron's rod after it turned into a serpent at
Pharaoh's feet. Moreover, here and throughout the volume, Heaney comes
to terms with his father's human qualities—and his own. In the subsequent
three-liner, "1.1.87," Heaney strips away metaphoric and symbolic implications, lending mutability and familial identity an expression no less eloquent for its pared-down quiescence: "Dangerous pavements. / But I face
the ice this year / With my father's stick" (*ST* 22). The dream fragment,
"An August Night," treats mutability as an ethereal phenomenon: "His
hands were warm and small and knowledgeable. / When I saw them again
last night, they were two ferrets, / Playing all by themselves in a moonlit
field" (*ST* 23). The poet envisions how the old laborer's hands, no longer
aching from spadework, take up svelte scurryings in another life; they
change into ferrets, irrepressible and mischievous, their pelts licking radiance from the moon.

   "Glanmore Revisited," a grouping of sonnets obviously intended as an
epilogue to the renowned cycle that originally appeared in *Field Work*, in-
corporates as a *donnée* the subtle mystique of transience and change. Once
again, Heaney defines his identity through his interactions with family and
friends at the cottage in County Wicklow, which he now calls his "place of
writing." An *in memoriam* for archaeologist Tom Delaney, whose shade
surfaced earlier in *Station Island*, "Scrabble" conjures winter evenings
spent at the Glanmore retreat in the company of his old friend:

Bare flags. Pump water. Winter-evening cold.
Our backs might never warm up but our faces
Burned from the hearth-blaze and the hot whiskeys.
It felt remembered even then, an old
Rightness half-imagined or foretold,
As green sticks hissed and spat into the ashes
And whatever rampaged out there couldn't reach us,
Firelit, shuttered, slated and stone-walled.

(*ST* 33)

Naked flagstones, subterranean water, the bolted-down cold of a freezing night: these images find antithesis in the rising whiskey-glow, the sputtering sap, the seething half-rhyme of "ashes / reach us." However, the idyllic refuge of comparative youth is also subject to mutability:

Year after year, our game of Scrabble: love
Taken for granted like any other word
That was chanced on and allowed within the rules.
So "scrabble" let it be. Intransitive.
Meaning to scratch or rake at something hard.
Which is what he hears. Our scraping, clinking tools.

(*ST* 33)

In his sestet, Heaney doubles the meaning of "scrabble": it could signify a parlor game played with wooden counters or a verb incapable of taking an object. In either case, he feels impotent to communicate beyond this life. He scrapes at the candescent firelog with a poker, the brittle embers splintering like glass on the grate. In "The Skylight," Heaney at first opposes fitting a canopy of stars above the bed: "I liked the snuff-dry feeling, / The perfect, trunk-lid fit of the old ceiling." As in the first Glanmore sequence, his wife Marie steps into the foreground to open the poet to new perspectives and possibilities. She thus takes an active hand in helping Heaney rethink and reshape his identity. Initially apprehensive about change, he prefers the battened-down, almost coffin-like interior, until she insists on having her way: "But when the slates came off, extravagant / Sky entered and held surprise wide open." Here mutability or change acquires a revelatory aspect, a lightening of circumstance nearly equal to transfiguration:

For days I felt like an inhabitant
Of that house where the man sick of the palsy
Was lowered through the roof, had his sins forgiven,
Was healed, took up his bed and walked away.

(*ST* 39)

With its biblical resonances and "cascade of light," "The Skylight" enacts a transcendence all its own.

Of the seven sonnets in the "Glanmore Revisited" sequence, "Scene Shifts" treats mutability and identity in a manner most direct, albeit highly allusive. The poet recalls raising hell with his brood years ago because they stripped from an ash tree the segment of bark whereon a friend had carved his name: "I was flailing round the house like a man berserk." Now Heaney gazes at the atrophied scar, at bark "thick-eared and welted," and he suddenly remembers how the incident laid bare his feelings. The shock of self-recognition is overwhelming, and he compares the sensation to Eurycleia's response when she saw again the old gash a boar's tusk once inflicted on Odysseus's thigh:

> a recognition scene
> In which old nurse sees old wound, then clasps brow
> (Astonished at what all this starts to mean)
> And tears surprise the veteran of the war.
>
> (*ST* 35)

Pain is its own signature, fresh and blinding, decades after the fact. Heaney compares the scar, both literal and figurative, left by the peeled inscription of his friend's name to the identifying mark on Odysseus's flesh, and thus raises the parochial to the level of the universal. Increasingly, he fuses his personal destiny with the masters of Western literature. As a reviewer for *The Library Journal* remarked when *Seeing Things* first appeared: "Among living poets, Heaney is one of the very few who dares blend his voice with the chorus of Immortals, and one of the fewer still who earns the honor."[32]

In "Wheels within Wheels," Heaney revives the old *agon* with Yeats, albeit with a tongue-in-cheek whimsy that betrays his continuing lack of reverence for the Sligo poet's mystical gyres. Heaney locates a defining moment in childhood, describing how he turned his bicycle upside down and turned the pedals by hand, letting a new momentum enter his consciousness "Like an access of free power, as if belief / Caught up and spun the objects of belief / In an orbit coterminous with longing." For Heaney, however, visionary splendor is always a combination of the sublime and the quotidian:

> I loved the disappearance of the spokes,
> The way the space between the hub and rim
> Hummed with transparency. If you threw

A potato into it, the hooped air
Spun mush and drizzle back into your face;
If you touched it with a straw, the straw frittered.

(*ST* 48)

Not content with turning the national tuber to mulch in a slur and stutter of spokes, young Heaney removes his bicycle to a shallow sump-bed: "The world-refreshing and immersed back wheel / Spun lace and dirt-suds there before my eyes / And showered me in my own regenerate clays." Earthy and life-affirming, to say the least, the image eventually accrues some element of the numinous: "For weeks I made a nimbus of old glit." "Glit" is a thin green spume of algae, a mercurial greenness that slips mysteriously between the fingers, and leaves only its emerald essence behind.[33] Delving into the Ulster word-hoard, as well as the clabber and glaur of the sump-bed, Heaney evokes his own equivalent of Yeats's "flame that cannot singe a sleeve."[34] He ably demonstrates that the sogged clay of the Northern bogs and fens with which critics so closely identify him can also emit an ethereal glow. Like Yeats at mid-career, we see Heaney engaged in remaking himself through a visionary poetics.

Despite employing a consciously geometric form (twelve poems consisting of twelve lines each), Heaney's long four-part sequence, "Squarings," refuses to impose a strict thematic or chronological ordering on the second half of *Seeing Things*. However, identity and mutability remain dominant motifs, as Heaney couples a poetics of loss with a Dantesque striving towards spiritual enlightenment. According to William Doreski,

> Mortality and form . . . remain firmly linked throughout his work; but this unity, these new poems suggest, seems more and more an allegory for the "squaring" or placement of the self in the landscape of spiritual, intellectual, and moral possibility. Most elegiacally, these poems of memory, epiphany, and insistently earthen imagery discover joy not only despite but in the fixed and affixing presence of death.[35]

The presence of death, recently embodied for Heaney by the loss of his parents, not only acquires a more personal meaning but also takes on a new perceptual and aesthetic dimension described by the poet as "the emboldening of language toward the ineffable areas." The final poem of the first sequence, subtitled "Lightenings," speaks of "A phenomenal instant when the spirit flares / With pure exhilaration before death— / The good thief in us harking to the promise!" For Heaney, the word "lightening" transcends mere disburdenment and aspires to the instant of transmutation. Here are the closing tercets:

So paint him on Christ's right hand, on a promontory
Scanning empty space, so body-racked he seems
Untranslatable into the bliss

Ached for at the moon-rim of his forehead,
By nail-craters on the dark side of his brain:
This day thou shalt be with Me in Paradise.

(*ST* 66)

We sense vividly the cruel torque of each sinew and muscle, the separate limbs wracked and battered by spasms. Moreover, the cool nimbus, the "moon-rim" of the thief's forehead, seems to arise from cadences, "Ached," "nail-craters," "dark side of his brain," somehow alien to the intelligence or will. A similar mystical aura surrounds certain pieces in "Settings," the second grouping within the overall sequence. Heaney converts Irish lore into a pastiche of Aristotelian zoology and Ovidian metamorphosis when he ponders the "virtues" of an eelskin: "What / Was the eel itself? A rib of water drawn / Out of the water, an ell yielded up // From glooms and whorls and slatings." The eel appears nothing less than muscle peeled from the dense rib-sheath of a slashing torrent, a source of vital replenishment yielded up by earth and water,

Rediscovered once it had been skinned.
When a wrist was bound with eelskin, energy

Redounded in that arm, a waterwheel
Turned in the shoulder, mill-races poured
And made your elbow giddy.

(*ST* 71)

In both poems, language involves the transfer of pure energy, what Heaney eventually defines as the "Body's deep obedience / To all its shifting tenses." Although his voice is primarily elegiac, he views the "shifting brilliancies" of this life with expectation and exhilaration. Moreover, his seemingly tireless anticipation of Charon, ferryman to Virgil and Dante, throughout the last two sections of "Squarings" implies a subtle awareness of his own place within the steadily evolving Western literary tradition. And yet Heaney ultimately opts for "a poem of utter evening," a seat nearer the medieval *skalds* of Iceland:

The thirteenth century, weird midnight sun
Setting at eye-level with Snorri Sturluson,

Who has come out to bathe in a hot spring
And sit through the stillness after milking time,
Laved and ensconced in the throne-room of his mind.

(*ST* 77)

Lest we imagine that Heaney aspires too humbly, the position seems already equal to the one Yeats claimed for himself beside Landor and Donne.

At 576 lines, "Squarings" is Heaney's longest effort to date. Within the poem, the remaking or "re-envisaging" of his personal and poetic identity emerges as an act of transcendence. Heaney creates an imaginative synthesis based on his early "fossil poetry of hob and slate"; he now instructs himself to alter subtly the scenes of his earlier life and writing: "Re-enter this as the adult of solitude, / The silence-forder and the definite / Presence you sensed withdrawing first time round" (*ST* 67). As Henry Hart asserts, "for Heaney the appeal of metaphysical visions and voyages is countered by a similar devotion to the quotidian."[36] Heaney therefore locates the sublime in whatever lies beyond known boundaries: "His poems continually draw attention to gates, thresholds, borders, limits, lines, ceilings, roofs, circles, squares. The situation he obsessively delineates is one where the mind comes up against a confining boundary, is checked by it, but then is stimulated to transcend it."[37] As an example of the poet's impulse toward transcendence, section xv is worth quoting entire:

And strike this scene in gold too, in relief,
So that a greedy eye cannot exhaust it:
Stable straw, Rembrandt-gleam and burnish

Where my father bends to a tea-chest packed with salt,
The hurricane lamp held up at eye-level
In his bunched left fist, his right hand foraging

For the unbleeding, vivid-fleshed bacon,
Home-cured hocks pulled up into the light
For pondering awhile and putting back.

That night I owned the piled grain of Egypt.
I watched the sentry's torchlight on the hoard.
I stood in the door, unseen and blazed upon.

(*ST* 69)

As in his earlier poems, Heaney's penchant for composition of place continues unabated, but the subtle patina, the "Rembrandt-gleam" teased out of common stable straw, is something new. The scene does indeed seem struck in gold relief, a vivid depiction of the humble bounty that lay at the heart of Heaney's youth. His father inspects his private trove—livestock fatted, slaughtered, apportioned, and cured on his own homestead—the choice cuts packed in the mineral glint of salt illuminated by a hurricane lamp. His expert eye ponders the rich hues of "unbleeding, vivid-fleshed bacon," but he puts aside the lean slabs for a more fortuitous time. If the doorway seems a less than confining boundary, the youngster's secret, late-night glimpse of his father checking the stores amounts to a moment of initiation. He suddenly apprehends the nature of adulthood and parenthood: while his father is the keeper of provender for his family, he seems less king than sentry—an image that appears earlier, in "The Ash Plant." Far from disappointed by the scene, Heaney enshrines the moment of seeing in memory: he converts the Midas-gleam of his father's hoard to "the piled grain of Egypt," an abundance he partakes of vicariously, "unseen and blazed upon." He remains invisible and eventually unpacks these striking images in the strongroom of language. Thus Heaney achieves full poetic identity through his ability to preserve and transmute half-forgotten experiences into vignettes that "Do not waver into language" and "Do not waver in it."

Heaney's father appears again in sections xxvii and xxxii of "Squarings." In the former, Heaney celebrates mutability and transcendence, blending the tutelary presence of the god Hermes with his own ancestry and locale:
'

> Everything flows. Even a solid man,
> A pillar to himself and to his trade,
> All yellow boots and stick and soft felt hat,
>
> Can sprout wings at the ankle and grow fleet.
>
> (ST 81)

The poet's image of the "solid man" become "god of fair-days, stone posts, roads and crossroads, / Guardian of travellers and psychopomp" undoubtedly derives from his father, now deceased. But the sense of mystery and other-worldliness with which Heaney invests his progenitor expands to embrace a *comitatus* of his kind, to whom he can entrust others: "'Look for a man with an ash plant on the boat,' / My father told his sister setting out / For London, 'and stay near him all night'" (*ST* 81). As Benedict Kiely notes, "The cattle dealer's stick was his lance, his sabre, his staff of office,"[38] apparently obsolete by the time of Heaney's first collection of poetry. In *Death of a Naturalist*, "Ancestral Photograph" recorded how his father learned the cattle trade from his uncle, and the inevitable sadness at the passing of cattle fairs. Moreover, in "The Strand at Lough Beg," Heaney traced the influence of this once tentative heritage: both he and his cousin "fought shy" of any part in the Troubles, precisely because they descended from "Big-voiced scullions" and were thus unsuited to "crack the whip or seize the day" (FW 17). In this section of "Squarings," the reticent father possesses a sacred wisdom. Heaney's rendering of "the mysteries of dealing men with sticks" extends the sense of continuity he feels between his father and himself, and posits a fitting analogue for his own imaginative power and poetic gifts. In section xxxii, Heaney turns to the idiom of his native Ulster, defining terms such as "kesh": "A kesh could mean the track some called a *causey* / Raised above the wetness of the bog, / Or the causey where it bridged old drains and streams." For the poet, the explanations have an assuaging effect: "It steadies me to tell these things." More potent than the landscape itself, however, are the familial associations bound up with it:

> I cannot mention keshes or the ford
> Without my father's shade appearing to me
>
> On a path towards sunset, eyeing spades and clothes
> That turfcutters stowed perhaps or souls cast off
> Before they crossed the log that spans the burn.
>
> (ST 86)

The poem echoes another aspect of Heaney's identity explored earlier, in "Digging": his father's ability to "handle a spade" in the potato drills harks back to the poet's grandfather, who "cut more turf in a day / Than any other man on Toner's bog." Though Heaney no longer seems uncertain or apologetic about his means to "follow men like them," his sense of ancestry remains a potent force in shaping his own identity. What Michael Parker terms the "energies of generation" continue to surface in the poetry. Moreover, if Patrick Heaney takes on the role of soul guide, he yet remains a turf-cutter, close to the life-affirming earth. Once again, the poet trusts the mystery to arise from the commonplace, achieving transcendence through a combination of the sublime and the quotidian.

Heaney conjures the numinous recollections of childhood in section xli, evoking the damp marl, sandy loam, and shifting gravel-beds so abundant in his County Derry demesne: "Sand-bed, they said. And gravel-bed. Before / I knew river shallows or river pleasures / I knew the ore of longing in those words" (ST 95). The poet celebrates the alluvial deposits common to the Ulster landscape, as ripple-ribbed sandbars and bright mosaics of gravel deposits become dynamic manifestations of "Sweet transience."As always, Heaney refuses to trace the lineaments of the ineffable from any realm other than the substantive. In section xlii, he consolidates the ongoing tendency to identify with the inhabitants of his native turf when he describes the rural laborers of his youth as apparitions still haunting a familiar landscape:

> Heather and kesh and turf stacks reappear
> Summer by summer still, grasshoppers and all,
> The same yet rarer: fields of the nearly blessed
>
> Where gaunt ones in their shirtsleeves stooped and dug
> Or stood alone at dusk surveying bog-banks—
> Apparitions now, yet active still
>
> And territorial, still sure of their ground.
>
> (*ST* 96)

The rhythms of life never abate, not even in the face of mutability and death. Thus the rude vigor and constant vigilance so characteristic of Heaney's forebears render them "Still interested, not knowing how far / The country of the shades has been pushed back." The old inhabitants of the land remain vital presences with whom the poet can identify long after they cease to be mortal. Like all shades, they exist out of time: "Caught like a far hill in a freak of sunshine," they cling to the land as a shadow cleaves to the light. Indeed, light is the phenomenon that makes vision and the visionary possible throughout *Seeing Things*. In the final section of "Squarings," Heaney plays on the polytropic potential of the word:

> Strange how things in the offing, once they're sensed,
> Convert to things foreknown;
> And how what's come upon is manifest
>
> Only in light of what has been gone through.
> Seventh heaven may be
> The whole truth of a sixth sense come to pass.
>
> At any rate, when light breaks over me
> The way it did on the road beyond Coleraine
> Where wind got saltier, the sky more hurried
>
> And silver lamé shivered on the Bann
> Out in mid-channel between the painted poles,
> That day I'll be in step with what escaped me.
>
> (*ST* 102)

In the first line of the second tercet, Heaney underscores the metaphorical implications of "light," implying a particular aspect or appearance presented to view. In the third tercet, "light" becomes literal, but also connotes the awakening of a sixth sense, a moment of sudden illumination when the sunstruck Bann glimmers like brocade shot through with silver thread. Moreover, the moment of transcendence is held in delicate equipoise by the briny aftertaste of a stiff breeze. Heaney thus conjoins the sublime and the quotidian to startling effect. As Douglas Dunn observes in his essay "Quotidian Miracles," "Vision becomes the intellectual, sentient, imaginative substance of the visionary."[39]

Heaney concludes *Seeing Things* with "The Crossing," a translation from the third canto of Dante's *Inferno*. Like the section from the *Aeneid* that opens the volume, the passage from Dante reinforces the sense of being chosen. Virgil emerges again, this time as Dante's guide. Indeed, Virgil's gentle admonition ("No good spirits ever pass this way / And therefore, if Charon objects to you, / You should understand well what his words imply") echoes the ferryman's earlier pronouncement ("A lighter boat must be your carrier"). The presiding spirits of Virgil and Dante provide *Seeing Things* with a powerful sense of continuity, suggesting that Heaney has enacted his own crossing by the end of the book—perhaps even an eventual crossing over to poetic immortality. With this volume, he has at least solved the problem of identity he described in "Place and Displacement" as common to Northern Irish poets: "The poet is stretched between politics and transcendence, and is often displaced from a confidence in a single position by his disposition to be affected by all positions, negatively rather than positively capable."[40] If Heaney has arrived at "the virtue of an art that knows its mind," it is because he now trusts and protects his poetic art completely. As Lachlan MacKinnon notes, the poet achieves a significant measure of independence in *Seeing Things*, freeing himself from "[t]he burden of being Seamus Heaney, of which Heaney has always been uniquely conscious." Once he excuses himself from "the extra-poetic authority of civic and largely externally imposed responsibility . . . he is the more liberatingly able to answer it."[41] As a result, the Troubles rarely surface in the poetry of *Seeing Things*; while the threat of violence may occasion discomfort, it seldom provokes the emotional turmoil or paralysis Heaney experienced earlier in his poetic career. In much the same way, Heaney's increasing distance from Roman Catholicism, expressed in forthright comments about the afterlife in "Squarings" ("There is no next-time-round," *"All gone into the world of light?"*), intensifies his capacity for evoking the spiritual. To the poet, at least, such imaginative autonomy seems long overdue: "Me waiting until I was nearly fifty / to credit marvels." Moreover, it is inevitably hard-earned; according to Henry Hart, Heaney himself implies that "the lightening—one of his favorite words in *Seeing Things*—would never have come if he hadn't felt weighed down by the political, religious, and poetic 'doldrums of what happens.'"[42] With *Seeing Things*, the poet has brought the various strands of his identity— personal, familial, literary, religious and political—closer together than in any volume since *Field Work*.

Having disembarked for a brief sojourn in Homer's Aegean during the late autumn of 1995, Heaney received word while at Sparta that he had been awarded the Nobel Prize for Literature. His subsequent address to the Swedish Academy and the Nobel Foundation focused on the shaping of a poetic identity, describing his upbringing in a three-room thatched farmstead in County Derry as a "creaturely existence" more or less insulated from the outside world. In the published lecture entitled *Crediting Poetry* (1996), the poet remembers his earliest childhood with a combination of nostalgia and misgiving, characterizing it as "[a]historical, pre-sexual, in suspension between the archaic and the modern" (4). But through his father's ingenuity and the grafting of technology to nature ("an aerial wire attached to the topmost branch" of a chestnut tree and running into the "innards" of the kitchen wireless), Heaney's encounter with language and the larger cosmos waxed daily: "a little pandemonium of burbles and squeaks would give way to the voice of a BBC newsreader speaking out of the unexpected like a *deus ex machina*" (5). Years later, as his mind began to discern the subtle nexus between words and the phenomenal world, each subsequent attempt to write poetry became an enactment of desire that consumed Heaney's childhood timidity. Indeed, Robert Langbaum insists that "desire is the single impulse or energy . . . that binds together an identity."[43] Of course, to ascribe the poetry of desire to libidinal yearnings would be a mistake in emphasis. For Heaney, the making of a singular poetic identity increasingly entails the longing to achieve an imaginative synthesis between subjective and objective truth: "there are times when a deeper need enters, when we want the poem to be not only pleasurably right but compellingly wise, not only a surprising variation played upon the world but a retuning of the world itself" (*CP* 20).

In *The Spirit Level*, Heaney's twelfth book-length volume and his first to appear since he was awarded the 1995 Nobel Prize for Literature, identity remains a vital theme. In a childhood reminiscence about snipping sprigs of mint, the poet avers: "My last things will be first things slipping from me." If the pronouncement echoes Eliot's brooding mixture of memory and desire in *The Waste Land,* Heaney proves somewhat more buoyant and open in his outlook ("Yet let all things go free that have survived"). In "The

Rain Stick," he exchanges his traditional ashplant for a cactus stalk, and takes some unusual soundings: "Upend the rain stick and what happens next / Is a music that you never would have known / To listen for." Heaney listens generously:

> Downpour, sluice-rush, spillage and backwash
> Come flowing through. You stand there like a pipe
> Being played by water, you shake it again lightly
>
> And diminuendo runs through all its scales
> Like a gutter stopping trickling. And now here comes
> A sprinkle of drops out of the freshened leaves,
>
> Then subtle little wets off grass and daisies;
> Then glitter-drizzle, almost-breaths of air.
>
> (*SL* 3)

The onomatopoeic quality of "drops" and "wets" darkens the foliage until it is struck off the prismatic hardness of "glitter-drizzle"; the poet pushes these images to the brink of extravagance before diffusing them into "almost-breaths of air." Only toward the end does he comment: "Who cares if all the music that transpires // Is the fall of grit or dry seeds through a cactus?" For Eliot, such aridity signified spiritual dryness and decadence. But Heaney seizes on the instrument at hand, transforming the brittle marrow of the cactus stalk into a rain-replenished landscape. The power of redemption stems from the imagination and the music of what happens: "You are like a rich man entering heaven / Through the ear of a raindrop. Listen now again" (*SL* 3).

In "To a Dutch Potter in Ireland," a two-part poem dedicated to Sonja Landweer, Heaney's desire to grasp the mystique of an art form other than his own is set against the backdrop of World War II. As in the poems for artists written earlier in his career, Heaney draws strength from a bond of kinship with other craftsmen, especially those who endure and overcome the ordeals of their day. The piece opens with a six-line prologue that insists on a more dynamic relationship between language and the plastic arts than Keats urges in the "Ode on a Grecian Urn": *"Then I entered a strongroom of vocabulary / Where words like urns that had come through the fire / Stood in their bone-dry alcoves next a kiln"* (*SL* 4). Heaney recalls entering a sanctum sanctorum, "a strongroom of vocabulary," where words standing in "bone-dry alcoves" momentarily suggest the brittle aridity of funeral amphorae endlessly sifting bone flakes and ash. But he emerges enlightened and converted, like the Roman sentry who witnessed the fusion

of clay and spirit "in a diamond-blaze of air." In section 1, he recalls his
childhood fascination with Bann clay:

> Like wet daylight
> Or viscous satin under the felt and frieze
> Of humus layers. The true diatomite
>
> Discovered in a little sucky hole,
> Grey-blue, dull-shining, scentless, touchable—
> Like the earth's old ointment box, sticky and cool.
>
> (*SL* 4)

The siliceous residue running beneath the Bann Valley river bottoms becomes "viscous satin," a slick layer that gluts and holds. Heaney extends
the motif of resurrection when he refers to the grey-blue stratum as "the
earth's old ointment box," an allusion to the ointment and cool spices
brought to the Holy Sepulcher for the anointing of Jesus' body.

Heaney changes both setting and tone when he addresses Landweer directly: "At that stage you were swimming in the sea / . . . A nymph of phosphor by the Norder Zee, // A vestal of the goddess Silica" (*SL* 4–5). Pagan
epithets—playful, to be sure—introduce an element of yearning: "We
might have known each other then, in that / Cold gleam-life under
ground." Heaney's reverie about his fellow artist is tinged with desire: the
two "might have done the small forbidden things— / Worked at mud-pies
or gone too high on swings, / Played 'secrets' in the hedge or 'touching
tongues'" (*SL* 5). But his lifelong affinity for the soil, especially Bann clay
with its clutch of Mesolithic flints, provides the real impetus behind these
lines. His aesthetic, like the potter's, has always focused on the four elements—earth, water, fire, and air—and although his medium is language,
his art equally involves shaping:

> Night after night instead, in the Netherlands,
> You watched the bombers kill; then, heaven-sent,
>
> Came backlit from the fire through war and wartime
> And ever after, every blessed time,
> Through glazes of fired quartz and iron and lime.
>
> (*SL* 5)

Heaney's analogy between the incendiary bombings and the finishing
process of fire-glazing implies that those who mold earthenware or "words
like urns" must pass through the flames of violence and suffering. He goes
on to capture in language the phenomenon of clay thrown on a potter's

wheel: "And if glazes, as you say, bring down the sun, / Your potter's wheel is bringing up the earth. / *Hosannah ex infernis*. Burning wells." We sense the power of both centripetal and centrifugal force as the plastic substance erupts and responds to the potter's knowing touch. Heaney's evocation of the Harrowing of Hell—"*Hosannah ex infernis*"—is more controlled than enraptured, especially since his metric remains as steady as a foot on a treadle. He renews the resurrection motif with the image of grain rising from crystalline soil near the bombed-out rubble: "Hosannah in clean sand and kaolin / and, 'now that the rye crop waves beside the ruins', / In ash-pits, oxides, shards and chlorophylls" (*SL* 5). As Paul Breslin remarks in "Heaney's Redress," the image of native clay that initially emerged in the penultimate poem of *Door into the Dark* illustrates how the poet's sense of identity has shifted:

> What has changed, since "Bann Clay," is the exclusive focus on archaic origins as the lost source of art and identity, to be recovered and celebrated. . . . Not solely in some ahistorical primal past, hidden beneath the changing surface, but through the collision of what is primal and timeless with the turbulent weather of the surface, its transforming air, light, and fire, can the clay become an urn, rough-hewn or well-wrought as one's aesthetics may demand. The result is and should be impure—the primal contaminated and reshaped by the temporal, irreconcilables mixed.[44]

In section 2, Heaney offers his version of "After Liberation," a poem from the Dutch of J. C. Bloem: "In a pearly clarity that bathes the fields / Things as they were come back; slow horses / Plough the fallow, war rumbles away" (*SL* 5). Not even prolonged strife and suffering can delay the resurrection that comes with peace, and Heaney returns his previous image of renewal to its original context: "And complaint is wrong, the slightest complaint at all, / Now that the rye crop waves beside the ruins" (*SL* 6). The Irish poet's translation from the Dutch attempts to leap linguistic and cultural barriers, and to strengthen the bond between himself and Landweer. When he praises her ability to harness the immutable laws of rotation and gravity, to make the clay rise between her hands into "a diamond-blaze of air," he also celebrates the shaping spirit inherent in all forms of art. Moreover, he intimates that the fires of war—like the fires of a kiln—are actually generative, and can call forth works that transcend skill and even mastery. Heaney's gift for metaphor, for divining resemblances between seemingly disparate modes of creation, is the driving force behind "To a Dutch Potter in Ireland."

In *The Spirit Level*, Heaney continues his search for parallels between the Troubles and the crises of the past. "Mycenae Lookout," which probably owes its inception to his earlier version of Sophocles' *Philoctetes*, draws again on the fall of Troy. The most ambitious poem of the volume, "Mycenae Lookout" enacts desire in a language of bloodlust and turmoil. Heaney's speaker is the tower sentry of Aeschylus's *Agamemnon*, a common soldier sent aloft by Clytemnestra to watch for the victory beacon from Troy. Like a number of Heaney's speakers in his earlier work, the lookout expresses both reluctance and complicity; his position in the watchtower affords alienation, but little detachment. His knowledge of the queen's protracted affair with Aegisthus, Agamemnon's cousin, pricks his conscience as much as the war's eventual outcome:

> And [I] saw it coming, clouds bloodshot with the red
> Of victory fires, the raw wound of that dawn
> Igniting and erupting, bearing down
> Like lava on a fleeing population . . .
> Up on my elbows, head back, shutting out
> The agony of Clytemnestra's love-shout
> That rose through the palace like the yell of troops
> Hurled by King Agamemnon from the ships.
>
> (*SL* 35)

Through metaphor, Heaney compares the final conflict to a seething magma bearing down on the Trojan citadel; by juxtaposition, Clytemnestra's lust seems no less apocalyptic. For the speaker, both the war and the royal liaison are a carnal nightmare: "I'd dream of blood in bright webs in a ford, / Of bodies raining down like tattered meat."

In part 2, we never see Agamemnon struggle in the web and tackling of Aegisthus's net or the fatal blow struck home by Clytemnestra. Instead, the speaker focuses on Cassandra, "a lamb / at lambing time, // bleat of clair- / voyant dread," eventually dubbing her the "Little rent / cunt of their guilt" (*SL* 38). The cruel metonym refers not only to the brutal rape of the Trojan priestess, but also evokes the fatal wounds inflicted on her while attending Agamemnon's bath. With a savage mingling of eros and thanatos, Heaney thus enacts the perverse fate that overtakes both the warrior and his coveted spoil:

> in she went
> to the knife,
> to the killer wife,
>
> to the net over
> her and her slaver,
> the Troy reaver,

saying, "A wipe
of the sponge,
that's it.

The shadow-hinge
swings unpredict-
ably and the light's

blanked out."

(*SL* 38–39)

The terse enjambment and trickling metric suggest blood seeping across glazed tiles. In part 3, Heaney's narrative harks back to the war, and his speaker's visual acuity sharpens to a foreknowledge similar to Cassandra's. The sentry conjures the Trojan plain during brief periods of armistice with startling clarity: "The little violets' heads bowed on their stems, / The pre-dawn gossamers, all dew and scrim / And star-lace." These lulls are all the more painful for what they presage. He describes the blood-letting on the battlefield as a series of isolated vignettes, each confrontation a choreographed horror:

I saw cities of grass,
Valleys of longing, tombs, a wind-swept brightness,
And far-off, in a hilly, ominous place,

Small crowds of people watching as a man
Jumped a fresh earth-wall and another ran
Amorously, it seemed, to strike him down.

(*SL* 40-41)

The individual combats between warriors, recast in a language of desire, become brutal trysts with death.

In part 4, the speaker remembers his inability to dispel the image of the doomed Mycenaean king: "My own mind was a bull-pen / where horned King Agamemnon / had stamped his weight in gold" (*SL* 44). As lord marshal of the Greek coalition, Agamemnon dons the aspect of a bull, but his helmet ridge also bears the cuckold's horns. Indeed, nothing will assuage the speaker's conscience for his silent complicity in the regicide plotted by Aegisthus and Clytemnestra: "I moved beyond bad faith: / for his bullion bars, his bonus / was a rope-net and a blood-bath" (*SL* 44). Throughout "Mycenae Lookout," memory perverts desire: the queen yearns for Agamemnon's death because he sacrificed their daughter Iphigenia to gain a fair wind for Troy; the Greeks crave vengeance for the abduction of

Helen. Some Irish critics have suggested that Heaney's rewriting of Aeschylus is an analogue for the endless cycle of sectarian reprisals in Northern Ireland. To be sure, the theme of blood feud or vendetta applies to both cultures; moreover, when factions hanker for rapine and murder in the name of retribution, it is often the innocent who suffer, as the sentry recognizes:

> When the captains in the horse
> felt Helen's hand caress
> its wooden boards and belly
> they nearly rode each other.
> But in the end Troy's mothers
> bore their brunt in alley,
> bloodied cot and bed.
>
> (*SL* 43)

Heaney closes the poem with a reverie about his recent visits to the Aegean: "At Troy, at Athens, what I most clearly / see and nearly smell / is the fresh water" (*SL* 45). As in "The Rain Stick," the aquatic motif becomes a source of redemption and imaginative plenitude. He remembers his boyhood in County Derry, and the laborers who sank a well-shaft near the Mossbawn homestead: "finders, keepers, seers of fresh water / in the bountiful round mouths of iron pumps / and gushing taps" (*SL* 46).

But Heaney seldom addresses the Troubles by way of analogue elsewhere in *The Spirit Level*. Indeed, he seems to treat them more directly than ever: in the sestina "Two Lorries," the old lorry of Agnew the coalman, who sweet-talks Heaney's young mother while making his delivery at Mossbawn, blurs into a more recent one, "with a payload / That will blow the bus station to dust and ashes." "Keeping Going," a poem for his brother Hugh, who still works the family farm at Derry, describes the gruesome death of a police reservist whose brains are literally blown out in a drive-by shooting. Moreover, in section 4 of "The Flight Path," Heaney recalls his own encounter with an acquaintance who belonged to the I.R.A. on a train bound for Belfast in May 1979. The man demands to know when the poet will "write / Something for us," and Heaney retorts, "If I do write something, / Whatever it is, I'll be writing for myself" (*SL* 29). In relating the incident, the poet marks a shifting of his ground, an open defiance of the claims of solidarity that others would impose upon the artist. In a 1987 interview with Thomas Foster, Heaney emphasized that the poet writing in the midst of cultural crisis bore the additional responsibilities of dealing "with truth and justice" and of not exacerbating the conflict: "you [must] beware of the fallout of your words, and perhaps I've been unduly aware of that, of the relationship between lyric and life, of the responsibility for what you say."[45] Although Heaney doubtless still stands by his belief that the writer must assume responsibility for the effect of his work, he increasingly insists on his poetic independence. He closes the passage with a segment from his earlier translation of Dante's Ugolino canto, surely intended as an ironic answer to his I.R.A. acquaintance: "*When he had said all this, his eyes rolled / And his teeth, like a dog's teeth clamping round a bone, / Bit into the skull and again took hold*" (*SL* 30).

Fraught with assertions of artistic independence, translations from Dutch and Romanian, and poems dedicated to authors, scholars, and artists of other nationalities, *The Spirit Level* signals Heaney's arrival at an international identity. Doubtless his recent travel and teaching at Harvard and Oxford have opened him to the possibility of a more inclusive cultural identity, a direction he was already moving toward in *Seeing Things*. Heaney's ongoing interest in the potential resolution of the Northern crisis and the notion of cultural identity find their fullest expression in his most recent book of criticism, *The Redress of Poetry* (1995). His essay "Frontiers of Writing" encourages a more flexible and positive sense of identity for Protestant and Catholic alike: "There is nothing extraordinary about the challenge to be in two minds" (*RP* 202). In a poem written a decade earlier for the editors of *The Penguin Book of Contemporary British Poetry*, Heaney had declared "my passport's green." Though his passport is now "a Euro-, but not an imperial, purple," the initial discussion of its color was meant "to maintain the right to diversity *within* the border":

> Those who want to share that name [Irish] and identity in Britain's Ireland should not be penalized or resented or suspected of a sinister motive because they draw cultural and psychic sustenance from an elsewhere supplementary to the one across the water. (*RP* 201)

Both sides must cultivate a mutual respect. Moreover, Protestants must adopt the "two-mindedness" that Catholics have always felt because of their position within the dominant British culture; they should "conceive of themselves within—rather than beyond—the Irish element" and "make their imagination press back against the pressure of reality and re-enter the whole country of Ireland imaginatively" (*RP* 202). Heaney's essay thus echoes Erik Erikson's call in 1969 for a wider sense of identity, "a development by which two groups who previously had come to depend on each other's negative identities . . . join their identities in such a way that new potentials are activated in both."[46] Whether Heaney's neighbors will reconfigure their cultural identities, casting off the negative roles of oppressor and oppressed, is another matter. As *The Spirit Level* and *The Redress of*

Poetry demonstrate, even at this point in Heaney's career, sectarian conflict remains a part of his cultural, religious, and familial heritage, to which he inevitably returns; however, to define him strictly in terms of the Northern crisis, as "a poet of one problem,"[47] is to underrate the accomplishment of *The Haw Lantern*, *Seeing Things*, and *The Spirit Level*.

Heaney's shorter poems in *The Spirit Level* demonstrate his love of language and return us to those "first things" that moved like an unbidden joy through his earlier work. In "The Gravel Walks," he recounts childhood forays among pebbles at the river's margin: "The flints and sandstone-bits / Worked themselves smooth and smaller in a sparkle // Of shallow, hurrying barley-sugar water" (*SL* 48). Indeed, the alluvial runoff becomes his private treasure-trove: "Pebbles of caramel, hailstone, mackerel-blue." But what appears to be an exercise in pure linguistic revel, a sensual delight in words and the things of this world, comes to an abrupt halt. Amid a sprinkling of minnows, a tractor drops "its link-box in the gravel bed," and workmen plunder the gleaming hoard: "men in dungarees, like captive shades, / Mixed concrete, loaded, wheeled, turned, wheeled, as if / The Pharaoh's brickyards burned inside their heads." Numb obeisance fuels this activity, and it is no wonder that the men move about like "captive shades" forever sundered from the desires of the flesh. However, the world's mutability fails to daunt the poet. In "The Walk," which begins with a photograph of the young Heaney and his parents, but gives way to an early portrait of the poet and his wife, he proclaims the resilience of a relationship occasionally sapped by the passage of time:

> So here is another longshot. Black and white.
> A negative this time, in dazzle-dark,
> Smudge and pallor where we make out you and me,
> The selves we struggled with and struggled out of,
> Two shades who have consumed each other's fire,
> Two flames in sunlight that can sear and singe,
> But seem like wisps of enervated air,
> After-wavers, feathery ether-shifts . . .
> Yet apt still to rekindle suddenly
> If we find along the way charred grass and sticks
> And an old fire-fragrance lingering on,
> Erotic woodsmoke, witchery, intrigue,
> Leaving us none the wiser, just better primed
> To speed the plough again and feed the flame.

> (*SL* 74–75)

Heaney can scarcely identify the apparitions in the negative's "Smudge and pallor," but through the sparks and flares of spoken fricatives, sibilants, and aspirates, he nurtures the flame back to life. Here, as in his earlier work, the poet's relationship with his wife remains a crucial part of his identity, a source of inspiration and regeneration.

In many ways, Heaney's quest for identity has come full circle in *The Spirit Level*. "Damson" marks another phase of his abiding obsession with various artisans ranging from thatchers and blacksmiths to plasterers and potters. That Heaney still equates the mastery of tools with lyric acumen so many decades after "Digging" should not surprise. Indeed, Albert Camus insists in the preface to *Lyrical and Critical Essays* (1968) that "a man's work is nothing but this slow trek to rediscover, through the detours of art, those two or three great and simple images in whose presence his heart first opened."[48] For once, however, Heaney's skilled artisan has erred, cutting himself through sheer insouciance: "Gules and cement dust. A matte tacky blood / On the bricklayer's knuckles, like the damson stain / That seeped through his packed lunch." Blood, the sticky infusion of life, betrays the momentary fallibility of this agile "scaffold-stepper," so that Heaney still marvels at the "Wound that I saw / In glutinous colour fifty years ago." By comparing the consistency of spilt blood to jam rendered from blue damsons and staining the bricklayer's lunch bag, the poet provides us with an image at once malign and gorgeous, a wound bright with portent: "Damson as omen, weird, a dream to read— / Is weeping with the held-at-arm's-length dead / From everywhere and nowhere, here and now." Heaney then shifts to a vignette detailing the bricklayer's wonted expertise: "the bricks / Jiggled and settled, tocked and tapped in line." The exquisite tympany of "tocked" and "tapped" plays off the more mundane elements of the line like echoes in a stone chantry. The poet simply cannot forego reverence for any task well performed:

> I loved especially the trowel's shine,
> Its edge and apex always coming clean
> And brightening itself by mucking in.
> It looked light but felt heavy as a weapon.
> Yet when he lifted it there was no strain.
> It was all point and skim and float and glisten
> Until he washed and lapped it tight in sacking
> Like a cult blade that had to be kept hidden.
>
> (*SL* 19–20)

Heaney's identification with the injured masonry worker deepens in the poem's third section, as he likens the trowel to the ritual blade Odysseus used to cut the throats of ram and ewe on the threshold of Hades: "Ghosts with their tongues out for a lick of blood / Are crowding up the ladder, all unhealed, / And some of them still rigged in bloody gear." In book 10 of Homer's *Odyssey*, the grizzled veteran of the Trojan war is forewarned by Circe to force the ravenous spirits of the dead back from the sacrificial blood: "Meanwhile draw sword from hip, crouch down, ward off / the surging phantoms from the bloody pit / Until you know the presence of Tiresias."[49] Not until the blind prophet speaks can Odysseus learn the way back to Ithaca, thus freeing himself from the travails of war and endless wandering. Heaney therefore admonishes the bricklayer to fend off the outnumbering dead, the victims of sectarian strife in Northern Ireland:

> Trowel-wielder, woundie, drive them off
> Like Odysseus in Hades lashing out
> With his sword that dug the trench and cut the throat
> Of the sacrificial lamb.
>
>   But not like him—
> Builder, not sacker, your shield the mortar board.
>
>   (*SL* 20)

Heaney desires the injured artisan to remember his role as builder or maker, to ply his trowel with loving severity so that a new Belfast might rise from the bombed-out rubble of the old. He implores the bricklayer to herd the dead back to the turf-fires of home, to return them to the ameliorating warmth of the hearth and the rich odor of damsons stewing in a cauldron: "Drive them back to the wine-dark taste of home, / The smell of damsons simmering in a pot, / Jam ladled thick and steaming down the sunlight." As in "Mycenae Lookout," Heaney draws on the matter of Troy as an analogue for the Troubles in Northern Ireland. Moreover, he reaffirms not only his tendency to identify with the simple artisans of his homeland, but also his place in the lineage extending from Homer to Joyce to the present.

As in *Seeing Things*, a number of poems in *The Spirit Level* confront the death of Patrick Heaney, the poet's father. In "The Sharping Stone," "The Strand," and "A Call," an elegiac yet celebratory tone is pervasive. But a different picture of the poet's father emerges. Heretofore, the father had appeared as a somewhat stern, reticent figure in Heaney's poetry, with the recollection in "Mossbawn" offering a rare glimpse of the elder Heaney's affectionate sense of humor. In "The Errand," which provides the title for *The Spirit Level*, the father's attempt to dispatch his young son on a fool's errand exposes a convivial trickster:

> "On you go now! Run, son, like the devil
> And tell your mother to try
> To find me a bubble for the spirit level
> And a new knot for this tie."
>
> But still he was glad, I know, when I stood my ground,
> Putting it up to him
> With a smile that trumped his smile and his fool's errand,
> Waiting for the next move in the game.
>
> (SL 65)

Already young Heaney realizes the subtle nature of the things that surround him: sartorially, the intricate four-in-hand slipknot (perhaps of the Windsor variety) completes the man for a specific occasion, but he remains a plainspoken rural patriarch. The spirit level, too, maintains a sure equilibrium. Its center—the bubble of ether or alcohol that never freezes—will not need replacing, unless the glass tube containing it cracks or shatters. The encounter implies that the young boy has absorbed not only "the merriment / in the spirit level's eye," as Heaney phrases it in *Station Island* ("The Sandpit," 54), but also its mysteries of balance and proportion: beginning with the rough-hewn contours of wood and stone, carpenters and masons have raised vast cathedrals beneath the spirit level's auspicious gaze. The ongoing "game" of testing and answering between father and son here mimics the shifting and balancing of the instrument's bubble. Fecund with possibilities, its true analogue is the "magnified and bouyant ovum" of "Alphabets" rather than the frozen "bleb" of "North." Indeed, the volume's title connotes both the plane of existence on which Heaney now communes with the shades of his past and his continuing "drama of self-measuring and revelation" begun in *Seeing Things*.[50]

In *The Spirit Level*, Heaney faces more squarely than ever the new possibilities provided by growth and change. Such possibilities often focus on the problematic question of national identity. "The Flight Path" charts the negotiations the poet makes between Mossbawn, Wicklow, New York, California, Belfast, and Rocadamour, but also between the concepts of a national and an international identity. While a certain continuity persists ("Sweeney astray in home truths out of Horace: / *Skies change, not cares, for those who cross the seas*"), the poet himself realizes the impact of change at a roadblock, when he answers "far away" to a policeman who asks where he comes from: "And now it is—both where I have been living / And where I left" (*SL* 30). The experience proves oddly exhilarating rather than dislocating: the poet compares himself to "starlight that is light years on the go / From far away and takes light years arriving." As Michael

Molino remarks, "Rather than immersing himself exclusively in the local, regional, or traditional, Heaney has discovered that liberation and peregrination go hand in hand,"[51] a formulation initially arrived at with *Sweeney Astray.* Yet Heaney's current ability to achieve such continuity is painstakingly earned, arising out of the crisis of identity that dates back to his earliest poetry. In "Tollund," the penultimate poem of *The Spirit Level,* the poet revisits the setting and tone of "The Tollund Man" after the recently begun ceasefire in Northern Ireland:

> we stood footloose, at home beyond the tribe,
>
> More scouts than strangers, ghosts who'd walked abroad
> Unfazed by light, to make a new beginning
> And make a go of it, alive and sinning,
> Ourselves again, free-willed again, not bad.
>
> (*SL* 80–81)

If Heaney finds himself "at home beyond the tribe," the ceasefire has created a mood of hope, in which he embraces his cultural identity: "Ourselves again, free-willed again, not bad." Thus the poet affirms the potential of his nation to escape the seemingly endless ravages of sectarian strife—in Seamus Deane's words, "to overcome history by overcoming what history has made of us."[52]

In his 1995 Nobel lecture, Heaney characterizes some of the conflicting origins that naturally contributed to the initial onset of his crisis of identity:

> Without needing to be theoretically instructed, consciousness quickly realizes that it is the site of variously contending discourses. The child in the bedroom listening simultaneously to the domestic idiom of his Irish home and the official idioms of the British broadcaster while picking up from behind both the signals of some other distress—that child was already being schooled for the complexities of his adult predicament, a future where he would have to adjudicate between promptings variously ethical, aesthetical, moral, political, metrical, sceptical, cultural, topical, typical, post-colonial. (*CP* 15–16)

While such competing influences might have proven overwhelming at times, they have also allowed for tremendous personal and poetic growth. Heaney's quest for continuity has transcended the confines of time and space, taking him from Mossbawn to County Wicklow and St. Patrick's Purgatory but also to Iron Age Jutland and Bronze Age Greece and Troy. The poet's struggle to come to grips with various oppositions, his awareness of the complexities of his own identity, has allowed him finally to collapse some of the polarities—or at least, to make them more permeable.[53] Indeed, as Heaney's frequent travel and his poetics of transcendence have affirmed, our notions of identity are not necessarily as fixed as they may seem. Thus the poet is able to assert that "There is nothing extraordinary about the challenge to be in two minds" *(RP* 202), suggesting a more flexible cultural identity, one that might allow citizens of Northern Ireland to transcend the Troubles.

Yet Heaney's origins remain a vital part of his identity, as he notes in his Nobel lecture:

> This temperamental disposition towards an art that was earnest and devoted to things as they are was corroborated by the experience of having been born and brought up in Northern Ireland and of having lived with that place even though I have lived out of it for the past quarter of a century. No place in the world prides itself more on its vigilance and realism, no place considers itself more qualified to censure any flourish of rhetoric or extravagance of aspiration. (*CP* 13)

If such an upbringing initially led to an avoidance or undervaluing of Stevens, Rilke, Dickinson, and Eliot, it occasioned an outright renunciation of Yeats. The young poet intuitively rejected both Yeats's imaginative excesses and his disdain of the Catholic minority, preferring the example of Wordsworth, whose influence pervades his early work as well as the "Glanmore Sonnets." Indeed, Yeats functioned as an important negative identity for Heaney early on, providing him with a clear portrait of what he felt poetry should not do. Though he moved out of Yeats's shadow with *North*, he also began to accord Yeats more respect, having come to appreciate his predecessor's struggle for identity in the midst of civil war. Heaney has since found much to admire in Yeats, especially "the humility of his artistic mastery before the mystery of life and death" (*Pr* 111), and the self-fashioning required for continued poetic growth. Yet Heaney inevitably derives his poetic sensibility from Joyce, whose ability to infuse the particular with the resonance of the universal continues unparalleled among Irish writers in this century. Heaney's increasing tendency to turn to Homer, Virgil, and Dante reflects a desire to place himself squarely within the Western literary tradition, to achieve a continuity that transcends nationality and religion.

Heaney's personal and political crises have in many respects aided in resolving his aesthetic dilemmas. Indeed, in the latest phase of his career, Heaney is engaged in a remaking of his poetic identity. In "The Settle Bed," he remarks that "whatever is given // Can always be reimagined" (*ST* 31). While the various strands of his identity—familial, religious, cultural, and literary—remain intertwined, the poet achieves continuity through the power of the poetic imagination to animate and transform memory. He still draws parallels between his parents' rural labors and his poetic craft, but more than ever he tests the possibilities of metaphor, re-envisioning his relationship with his parents anew nearly a decade after their respective deaths. He revisits the settings of Derry and Wicklow, which remain fertile imaginative ground, though he recognizes the inevitable nature of change in *Seeing Things*: "The places I go back to have not failed / But will not last" (*ST* 95). The rural environs of his youth continue to be crucial to his poetry, far more so than the Northern conflict, as Kieran Quinlan notes: "Indeed, while the Ulster crisis has been at the heart of Heaney's progress and has deepened his sense of his own purpose, it has also stood as a distraction from the original impulse of his work."[54] Heaney's desire to recover "the small pieties and petty restrictions and simple elations" of rural Ireland in the 1940s and 1950s, "an Ireland of almost preindustrial consciousness and of a now-nostalgically remembered unworldliness," still manifests itself in his poetry.[55] However, Heaney defines the current remaking of his poetic identity as "walking on air" (*CP* 9), a phrase that carries a variety of meanings beyond the obvious: "For Heaney, it also conveys an effort of determination and defiance, as much remaking as relaxing. . . . it is about defying the ingrained, the expected, the natural."[56] Thus the poet seeks to throw off his "temperamental disposition towards an art that was earnest and devoted to things as they are," so as to transcend the rooted, Antean character of his earliest poetry and to achieve the power of the imagination first glimpsed in *Seeing Things*: "To walk on air is to be both mobile and suspended, free to soar or sink, to be able to move between the concrete and the immaterial, to be on both sides or in between."[57] From an achieved equipoise between realms subjective and objective, corporeal and spiritual, mundane and sublime, arises the imaginative power to shape the ineffable into words.

Epilogue:
Beowulf and *Electric Light*

THE SEPTEMBER 1994 TRUCE BETWEEN THE I.R.A. PROVISIONALS AND the Ulster paramilitaries precipitated "Tollund," the penultimate poem in *The Spirit Level,* in which Seamus Heaney imagines himself and his wife "footloose, at home beyond the tribe" (*SL* 80). But the tenuous peace accords in the North were abruptly shattered by the resumption of violence, forcing Heaney to forego unalloyed optimism in lieu of a vision annealed not only by time and maturity but also by bitter experience. Not even the official accolades garnered during the December 1995 festivities in Stockholm could assuage the conflicts, both internal and external, that would continue to shape Heaney's identity as an artist and an individual. In "The Famous Seamus," a deeply insightful biographical sketch published in the 20 March 2000 *New Yorker*, fellow countryman and lifelong friend Seamus Deane remembers that virtually no one attending the Nobel presentation could have predicted how Heaney's translation of *Beowulf* "would intensify the earlier conflict in his work between a serene freedom and a haunting violence."[1] Indeed, Heaney's most recent undertakings compel scholars—including the author of the present study—to reconsider the impact of the Northern crisis on the poet's overall development. Perhaps Deane offers the most succinct appraisal of the Old English poem as Heaney renders it:

> *Beowulf* (1999) . . . reminded readers of the battle that lies at the heart of his work. The deadly combat between the dragon and Beowulf is not only a story of a fight with a monstrous evil force. It is also an emblem of the struggle between civilization and its opposite. If freedom has the air as its natural habitat, violence clings to the ground. Yet, like the dragon, it can rise from its buried lair and infect the air: the "ground-burner" is also the "sky-roamer."[2]

Deane also cites Heaney's abiding enthusiasm for *Beowulf*, an obsession that he traces back to their undergraduate days. We cannot gainsay his assertion that Heaney's translation serves as "one further act of retrieval, taking an Old English poem into the ambit of Northern Ireland, where the ancient combat between monstrous violence and the search for peace is even now being refought at a political level."[3] But if the Irish laureate's concerns are both personal and cultural, some measure of aesthetic aspiration likewise prompted his recent confrontation with the Anglo-Saxon epic. In the process of "retrieving" *Beowulf*, Heaney subtly recasts and renews the passion for tribal culture, etymologies, Aristotelian philosophy, history, archaeology, and artisanal mastery that forged the Iron Age bog poems and the Viking sequence of *North*. He breathes new vitality into the most mordant of Western masterpieces, and thus simultaneously imbues his original work with a certain canonical validity. As Eliot observes in "Tradition and the Individual Talent": "the past should be altered by the present as much as the present is directed by the past."[4] Because of intertextual resonances struck between *North* and Heaney's version of *Beowulf*, we will never again read the Old English saga in quite the same way.

As Heaney comments in the introduction to his translation, "It is impossible to attain a full understanding and estimate of *Beowulf* without recourse to [an] immense body of commentary and elucidation" (*B* xi). He assents to the current theory that the poem is the work of a single Christian poet who imposed order and synthesis on a body of pre-existing pagan Germanic poetry. English in language and origin, the textual *Beowulf* nevertheless focuses on the heroic culture of Scandinavian forebears whose fifth and sixth century migrations from the northwest European continent eventually led to the formation of the Anglo-Saxon Heptarchy that included the insular petty kingdoms of Northumbria, Kent, Mercia, East Anglia, Essex, Sussex, and Wessex. Set down in a monastery scriptorium on unadorned parchment, the poem's flinty dictions were illuminated by sparks in 1731 when a fire gutted the building that housed Sir Robert Bruce Cotton's collection of medieval English manuscripts. The charred text survived mainly intact, a fortunate circumstance, in Heaney's estimation: "Its narrative elements may belong to a previous age but as a work of art it lives in its own continuous present, equal to our knowledge of reality in the present time" (*B* ix). Therefore it is not surprising that Heaney's sense of connectedness to this extraordinary linguistic artifact adheres, at least in part, to the critical paradigm established by J. R. R. Tolkien's "*Beowulf*: The Monsters and the Critics" (1936):

He [Tolkien] assumed that the poet had felt his way through the inherited material—the fabulous elements and the traditional accounts of an heroic past—and by a combination of creative intuition and conscious structuring had arrived at a unity of effect and a balanced order. He assumed, in other words, that the *Beowulf* poet was an *imaginative* writer rather than some kind of back-formation derived from nineteenth-century folklore and philology. Tolkien's brilliant literary treatment changed the way the poem was valued and initiated a new era—and new terms—of appreciation. (xi)

Like Tolkien, Heaney conceives of the *Beowulf* poet as a highly imaginative craftsman rather than a glorified chronicler of genealogies and narrative episodes both historical and apocryphal. He believes that the Geatish prince's successive *agons* with preternaturally formidable manifestations of evil—the homicidal, man-eating Grendel, his mere-dwelling troll-dam, and the incendiary dragon—acquire personal and universal significance largely because the separate combats transpire in "three archetypal sites of fear: the barricaded night-house, the infested underwater current, and the reptile-haunted rocks of a wilderness" (*B* xii). Moreover, if Heaney's Tollund Man and Bog Queen of Moira are victims of cult violence and ghoulish rapine, their archaeological veracity and mythical status in Heaney's Northern reliquary make the specter of Grendel and his mother prowling the fens and mist-shrouded moors doubly chilling. Those who have read Heaney's *North* require little suspension of disbelief to see the grim marauders of Heorot sweeping "forward into the global village of the third millennium" (*B* xiii).

Throughout *Beowulf,* the protean and transitory nature of identity proves a sustaining leitmotif, a theme so dominant that Heaney alters the name of the Danish ring-lord who founds the Scylding dynasty to Shield Sheafson, a designation nominally evoking his own agrarian ancestry. The opening burial ship passage, revised since its publication as "A Ship of Death" in *The Haw Lantern*, echoes the burdensome ritual of initiation enacted on a personal level in "Funeral Rites": "they shouldered him out to the sea's flood, / the chief they revered who had long ruled them" (ll. 30–31; 5). Heaney is seldom loath to ring variations on the four-stress alliterative line of Old English, cleaving to the traditional medial caesura only when it seems rhythmically expedient:

> A ring-whorled prow rode in the harbour,
> ice-clad, outbound, a craft for a prince.
> They stretched their beloved lord in his boat,
> laid out by the mast, amidships,
> the great ring-giver. Far-fetched treasures

were piled upon him, and precious gear.
I never heard before of a ship so well furbished
with battle tackle, bladed weapons
and coats of mail. The massed treasure
was loaded on top of him: it would travel far
on out into the ocean's sway.

(ll. 32–42; 5)

In cadences appropriate to a solemn processional, Heaney vividly depicts the well-tempered blades and splendidly wrought armor that identify Shield Sheafson as the much revered warrior-lord of a thriving *comitatus*. Heaney's translation avoids lexicographic lockstep, thus capturing the sublime tone and visual immediacy of the original. His enthusiasm for the fabulous or "imaginative" elements of *Beowulf* notwithstanding, the Irish poet once again reveals his affinity for artistic expression arising from "the locus of the given world." In 1939, just three years after Tolkien's watershed essay, archaeologists excavating burial mounds on an escarpment overlooking the Devon river estuary in Suffolk discovered the twenty-seven meter outline of a clinker-built rowing ship. Although hundreds of iron rivets *in situ* were the only remnants of the craft's hull, the burial chamber located amidships yielded "the richest treasure ever dug from British soil, and the most important archaeological document yet found in Europe for the era of the migrations of the Germanic peoples (5th to 7th centuries A.D.) in which the settlement of England . . . was an episode."[5] Mound One on the Sutton Hoo estate, long suspected to be the ancestral burial ground of the East Anglian Wuffingas, relinquished a veritable trove of pre-Viking artifacts: sword, baldric, shield, helmet, mailcoat, axe hammer, lyre, intricate fittings for drinking horns—all exhibiting exquisite workmanship. Students of the Old English epic who once considered the funeral tableau exceedingly fanciful now conceded that it could embody a genuine bardic memory. In "Royal Power and Royal Symbols in *Beowulf*," Barbara Raw notes: "For literary scholars, Sutton Hoo provided confirmation that the allusions to wealth and splendour in *Beowulf* were not the result of poetic exaggeration; for archaeologists, the description of Scyld's funeral at the beginning of *Beowulf* offered a context for the objects excavated at Sutton Hoo."[6] Many grave goods of gold, silver, garnet, bronze, and iron—especially weapons and armor—were of Scandinavian origin or influence. Like the hallowed occupant of the Sutton Hoo mound, Shield Sheafson receives a pagan Germanic funeral complete with pattern-welded sword and richly inlaid battle regalia. Indeed, the *Beowulf* poet's continual reference to a Judeo-Christian god cannot quell his ardor for a Northern heritage at once lurid and beautiful. According to Martin Carver,

> [T]he message of the cemetery, like that of *Beowulf*, is heroic and interna-
> tional; in praise of enterprise, achievement and fame, of a life that is mem-
> orable even if short. . . . The allegiance is to Scandinavia and a Germanic
> pagan brotherhood of the North Sea. . . . Rome and Christianity themselves
> are not to be served but resisted; and in this perhaps Sutton Hoo differs
> from *Beowulf*, at least in the form that the latter has come down to us.[7]

Heaney never alludes to Sutton Hoo in his introduction to *Beowulf*, although it is probably no less familiar to him than the Danish bog corpses
disgorged at Tollund Fen or the Viking funeral ships exhumed at Gokstad
and Oseberg in Norway. Throughout *North*, the bog victims and the relics
of Viking colonialism unearthed at Wood Quay in Dublin served to vali-
date his vision of a centuries-old archetypal pattern of violence embracing
all of northwest Europe, a brilliant and painstakingly evolved analogue for
sectarian war in the Ulster province. Because Heaney ultimately deplores
this internecine strife, he must see the anonymous *Beowulf* poet (whether
East Anglian, Mercian, or Northumbrian), as one whose "doctrinal certitude" endows him with sufficient distance and moral rectitude to admonish
the foibles of his heroic, albeit heathen forebears: "the poet can view the
story-time of his poem with a certain historical detachment and even censure the ways of those who lived *in illo tempore*" (*B* xvi):

> Sometimes at pagan shrines they vowed
> offerings to idols, swore oaths
> that the killer of souls might come to their aid
> and save the people. That was their way,
> their heathenish hope; deep in their hearts
> they remembered hell.
>
>   (ll. 175–80; xvi)

But did the original *Beowulf* poet and the segment of society that comprised his audience own the same doctrinal certitude and historical detachment? In the seventh century, Archbishop Theodore's *Penitential* cites a
number of heathen practices relevant to Anglo-Saxon England: "he who
sacrifices to demons in trivial matters shall do penance for one year; but he
who [does so] in serious matters shall do penance for ten years."[8] Conversion to Christianity was notoriously slow among the Anglo-Saxons. Even
the Alfred Jewel, commissioned by Alfred the Great and symbolic of the
culture of Christian Saxon England, terminates in a gold boar's-head
socket evocative of a pagan past. Perhaps it is Heaney himself, his crisis of
identity approaching aesthetic resolution, who possesses the "imaginative
sympathy" to lend full rhetorical force to Beowulf's intonation of the
Northern warrior's implacable ethos:

> It is always better
> to avenge dear ones than to indulge in mourning.
> For every one of us, living in this world
> means waiting for our end. Let whoever can
> win glory before death. When a warrior is gone,
> that will be his best and only bulwark.
>
> (ll. 1384–89; xvi–xvii)

Heaney enters into a subtle collaboration with the *Beowulf* poet, groping this side of the millennium for a voice that approximates the austere tone and sovereignty of spirit characteristic of the Old English epic. Not surprisingly, he remembers the Ulster accents of his father's relatives, men he has previously dubbed the "big voiced Scullions":

> the words they uttered came across with a weighty distinctness, phonetic units as separate and defined as delph platters displayed on a dresser shelf. A simple sentence such as "We cut the corn to-day" took on immense dignity when one of the Scullions spoke it. (*B* xxvii)

Moreover, he discreetly subverts the aristocratic hauteur of the original, introducing a note vestigially colloquial but unerringly appropriate to certain portions of the narrative: "So, after nightfall, Grendel set out / for the lofty house, to see how the Ring-Danes / were settling into it after their drink" (ll. 115–17; 9, 11). The bloodthirsty and covetous Grendel is the vessel of consciousness for these lines. He cares nothing for the sanctity of Hrothgar's mead-hall, where the *scop* sings of the Creation and the old Danish king shows his largesse, bestowing rings and torques of twisted gold on his young retainers and hearth-companions. Heorot, the gabled "bawn" above the moors, seems the only place in *Beowulf* where the communal values of Mediterranean Christianity and the Germanic warrior fraternity converge. As Heaney remarks in his prologue: "Here is heat and light, rank and ceremony, human solidarity and culture" (*B* xv). His yearning for the turf-fire snugness of the Gaeltacht, a source of tribal and etymological identity for Heaney, emerges in an earlier passage describing the arrival of Beowulf and his Geats at the Danish stronghold:

> So they duly arrived
> in their grim war-graith and gear at the hall,
> and, weary from the sea, stacked wide shields
> of the toughest hardwood against the wall,
> then collapsed on the benches; battle-dress
> and weapons clashed. They collected their spears
> in a seafarers' stook, a stand of greyish

> tapering ash. And the troops themselves
> were as good as their weapons.
>
> (ll. 321–31; 23)

Although Beowulf and his followers belong to a warrior elite, Heaney infuses his version with a more intimate sensibility, yoking Irish locutions to words of Old High German origin, thus forming new kennings such as "war-graith" and "seafarers' stook." Some critics accuse Heaney of introducing "what one might call political dialect into the Modern English version that is not in the Old English version. The original does not use words from one specific dialect to make a larger political and poetic claim."[9] This is a telling observation, but it ignores Heaney's attempt to recover some semblance of the folk idioms initially available to the Old English *scop*. Despite the highly formulaic structure of the kenning in later Old Icelandic verse, the minstrel who plucks his *hearpestreng* in Hrothgar's hall awakens a chord buried deep in the *Völkerwanderungun* or "migration of the peoples."

Doubtless Heaney's attraction to *Beowulf* stems in part from the issue of identity within the world of the poem itself. Unlike Hrothgar, Grendel bears an onerous genealogy; he is a descendant of Cain, the first fratricide, an exile from the Lord's favor and the fellowship of men. He cannot abide "the din of the loud banquet" or the *scop*'s variation on "Caedmon's Hymn": "how the Almighty had made the earth / a gleaming plain girdled with waters" (ll. 92–93; 9). Even in prose, Heaney describes him as a malignant aberration, "a kind of dog-breath in the dark, a fear of collision with some hard-boned and immensely strong android frame, a mixture of Caliban and hoplite" (*B* xviii). Grendel revels perversely in his negative identity, gorging himself on the sleeping members of the Danish *comitatus* during his nightly raids on Heorot. Moreover, he scorns the rule of law, and refuses to pay the *wergild* or "man-price" for those he mauls and devours piecemeal. To requite a debt his father owes Hrothgar and for the sake of fame that will live on in the choicest gleanings of the word-hoard, Beowulf sets sail for the land of the Spear-Danes. In his *beot* before Hrothgar's mead-bench, the young Geat pledges to vanquish Grendel without weapons. Heaney makes the most of the monster's approach to the bolted-down, horn-rigged manor where the youthful hero and his men settle in at moonrise:

> In off the moors, down through the mist bands
> God-cursed Grendel came greedily loping.
> The bane of the race of men roamed forth,
> hunting for a prey in the high hall.

> Under the cloud-murk he moved towards it
> until it shone above him, a sheer keep
> of fortified gold. Nor was that the first time
> he had scouted the grounds of Hrothgar's dwelling—
> although never in his life, before or since,
> did he find harder fortune or hall-defenders.
>
> (ll. 710–19; 49)

A variable alliteration sustains the headlong momentum of these lines, but kennings such as "God-cursed" and "cloud-murk"—each liquid-vowelled and bracketed by hard consonants—conjure aurally the oozing footprints of Grendel on the move. Heaney is at his best when Beowulf and the "hell-serf" actually come to grips in the dark hall: "the alert hero's / comeback and armlock forestalled him utterly." Indeed, he taps the essence of the Old English kenning for the body, *ban-hus* or "bone-house," as Grendel's joints quake in preamble to the desperate brawl that shakes Heorot to its foundations: "Every bone in his body / quailed and recoiled, but he could not escape" (ll. 752–53; 51). In a despairing attempt to flee, the monster sunders himself from himself: "a tremendous wound / appeared on his shoulder. Sinews split / and the bone-lappings burst" (ll. 815–17; 55). Plosives, specifically *p* and *b*, convey the socket-ripping, soul-destroying gravity of Grendel's hurt. Blundering back to his lair in the fen, he learns that death's grip is stronger than the Geatish warrior's: "With his death upon him, he had dived deep / into his marsh-den, drowned out his life / and his heathen soul: hell claimed him there" (ll. 849–51; 57). Heaney's sedulous attention to every nuance of language captures the terrible intimacy of the *agon* between Beowulf and Grendel more memorably than any other translation.

The exorcism of so fierce a visitant as Grendel occasions pure joy in the aftermath. Beowulf nails the moorwalker's shoulder, arm, and taloned hand to a high beam in Heorot. He regales Hrothgar with a detailed account of his victory over the monster: "He is hasped and hooped and hirpling with pain" (l. 975; 65). Heaney comes down unusually hard on the metrical register, and his choice of Gaelic idioms, especially "hirpling," proves at once harrowing and estranging, eliciting fear but no pity. This is altogether apt, as the *Beowulf* poet conflates pagan Germanic and Judeo-Christian elements, foregrounding not only the "scoretaking" Northern ethos but also the Old Testament tribal values of "an eye for an eye, a tooth for a tooth." Oddly enough, Hrothgar—not the court poet—speaks Beowulf's apotheosis, declaring his birth little short of a world-transforming event:

> Whoever she was
> who brought forth this flower of manhood,
> if she is still alive, that woman can say
> that in her labour the Lord of Ages
> bestowed a grace on her.
>
> (ll. 941–45; 63)

No less an authority than Samuel Johnson observes: "We must try its effect as an English poem; that is the way to judge the merit of a translation."[10] In his modern version, Heaney plays aurally on the phrase "Lord of Ages," thus generating a subtle homophone for "Lord of Aegis." In *Beowulf*, as in other Old English poetry, God is often likened to a celestial ring-lord, one under whose auspices or aegis the good warrior fights. Rather than resort to blatant epithets like "Warden of men," Heaney prefers to express such conceits *sotto voce*, adding layers of depth and meaning to his own rendition. Beowulf receives a new identity, as Hrothgar announces a formal bond of kinship: "I adopt you in my heart as a dear son. / Nourish and maintain this new connection" (ll. 946–47; 63). He then delves into the coffers of his strongroom, lavishing gifts of cunning metalwork on the Geatish prince, each one "both precious object and token of honor." Heaney cannot forego his old love of artisanal mastery, detailing adornments both intricate and utilitarian on headgear reminiscent of the Sutton Hoo helmet:

> An embossed ridge, a band lapped with wire
> arched over the helmet: head-protection
> to keep the keen-ground cutting edge
> from damaging it when danger threatened
> and the man was battling behind his shield.
>
> (ll. 1029–33; 69)

In a narrative digression that ominously portends the appearance of Grendel's mother hankering for revenge, the *scop* sings of the "Finnsburg episode," in which the Danish "peace-bride," Hildeburh, sees her brother Hnaef and her unnamed son killed in the stronghold of her husband, the Frisian king, Finn. An unforeseen brawl erupts between Frisians and visiting Danes in Finn's mead-hall; many retainers die on both sides, and an uneasy truce is negotiated between Finn and Hengest, *secundus* to the slain Danish ring-lord, Hnaef. Critics often mistake Hildeburh for a hapless victim, but her strategic side-by-side placement of brother and son on a funeral pyre heaped with corpses and weapons provides an incitement to the coming blood-feud:

> *Then Hildeburh*
> > *ordered her own*
> *son's body*
> > *be burnt with Hnaef's,*
> *the flesh on his bones*
> > *to sputter and blaze*
> *beside his uncle's.*
> > *The woman wailed*
> *and sang keens,*
> > *the warrior went up.*
> *Carcass flame*
> > *swirled and fumed,*
> *they stood round the burial*
> > *mound and howled*
> *as heads melted,*
> > *crusted gashes*
> *spattered and ran*
> > *bloody matter.*
> > > (ll. 1115–23; 77)

Hildeburh apparently considers blood kinship stronger than any connubial ties; indeed, her son doubtless belonged to her brother's *comitatus*, a peculiar tribal relationship noted by Tacitus in his *Germania*: "Sister's sons are held in as much esteem by their uncles as by their fathers; indeed, some regard the relation as even more sacred and binding."[11] Hildeburh's ritual plaint for succor and vengeance consumes Hengest until the spring thaw frees him to seek reinforcements and hew down the Frisian king:

> > *Finn was cut down,*
> *the queen brought away,*
> > *and everything*
> *the Shieldings could find*
> > *inside Finn's walls—*
> *the Frisian king's*
> > *gold collars and gemstones—*
> *swept off to the ship.*
> > *Over sea-lanes then*
> *back to Daneland*
> > *the warrior troop*
> *bore that lady home.*
> > > (ll. 1152–58; 81)

If the "Finnsburg episode" implies the unusual mobility of women within medieval Scandinavian kin groups, it also emphasizes the complexities of identity in times of strife. Heaney stresses the importance of this interior drama in his introduction:

> The "Finnsburg episode" envelops us in a society that is at once honour-bound and blood-stained, presided over by the laws of the blood-feud, where the kin of a person slain are bound to exact a price for the death. . . . [B]loodshed begets further bloodshed, the wheel turns, the generations tread and tread and tread. . . . [T]he Finnsburg passage is central to the historical and imaginative world of the poem as a whole. (*B* xiii–xiv)

The inexorable shedding of blood in the name of a culturally sanctioned code of reciprocity in *Beowulf* underscores a recurrent theme in Heaney's Viking and bog poems, hence expanding his vast analogue for the recent cycle of violence involving Protestant and Catholic paramilitary groups in Northern Ireland. But the nexus between Heaney's translation of the first English epic and his mythopoeic volume *North* resides as much in the Irish poet's remarkable facility with words and their etymological origins as in the dramatic incidents that comprise *Beowulf*. To subtly align his own corpus with a monolithic precursor bespeaks lofty aspirations, but the cognitive power, mastery of figurative language, exuberance of diction, and superlative craftsmanship that characterize Heaney's original poetry have long since validated his presence in the ever-evolving canon of Western literature. Moreover, his poetic vision cannot be arbitrarily separated from the cultural and political milieu that fostered it.

Appropriately, the spectral visage of Grendel's mother set on revenge for her son's recent death appears soon after the recitation of the Finnsburg passage. Although Heaney adopts epithets such as "hell-dam" and "tarn-hag" to denote her true nature, he lends her the aspect of a warrior upon her abrupt entry to the slumbering mead-hall:

> Her onslaught was less
> only by as much as an amazon warrior's
> strength is less than an armed man's
> when the hefted sword, its hammered edge
> and gleaming blade slathered in blood,
> razes the sturdy boar-ridge off a helmet.
>
> (ll. 1282–87; 91)

An extended metaphor of Homeric complexity replete with highly evocative locutions typical of Heaney—"slathered" and "razes," for example—the simile invests the troll-dam's nocturnal raid with a tacit legitimacy underscored by the compelling demands of the blood-feud. Even Hrothgar

attributes the ensuing abduction and brutal murder of his beloved coun-
selor, Aeschere, to unwitting provocation as he recounts the mayhem to
Beowulf the next morning: "she has taken up the feud / because of last
night, when you killed Grendel, / wrestled and racked him in ruinous
combat" (ll. 1333–35; 93). The aging Danish ring-lord must search his
memory for her place of abode, an ominous tract of fens and bogs never
before broached by men:

> A few miles from here
> a frost-stiffened wood waits and keeps watch
> above a mere; the overhanging bank
> is a maze of tree-roots mirrored in its surface.
> At night there, something uncanny happens:
> the water burns. And the mere bottom
> has never been sounded by the sons of men.
>
> (ll. 1361–67; 95)

The wood is a sentinel suspended in frost, its tangle of roots repeated on the
mere's glazed surface. Phosphor burns in the murky depths each night. By
proxy of the *Beowulf* poet, Heaney reprises the closure of his otherwise innocuous "Bogland": "The bogholes might be Atlantic seepage. / The wet
centre is bottomless" (*Poems* 86). For most of a day, Beowulf descends
these eerie waters in forge-linked battle harness, a luminescence that spares
his flesh the buffetings of tusked "sea-beasts." Indeed, the chain-mail coat
turns the edge of a hideous dagger wielded by Grendel's mother. The
Geatish prince almost perishes in terra incognita, and only a wondrous
sword fashioned by antediluvian giants enables him to fell the ogress in her
rock-vaulted chamber. When he turns and lops Grendel's head from its life-
less trunk, the damascened blade begins to "wilt into gory icicles, / to
slather and thaw" (ll. 1606–7; 111). Beowulf later presents the massive
hilt—its gem-encrusted pommel and scrollworked guard—to his Danish
patron: "In pure gold inlay on the sword-guards / there were rune-markings
correctly incised" (ll. 1694–95; 117). The ancient heirloom confirms Beowulf's identity as a hero; just as no one in Homer's *Iliad* save the transcendent warrior Achilles could heft the bronze-tipped Pelian ash, only
Beowulf could effectively strike with the fabulous blade, which ironically
will strike no more. According to George Clark, the weapon becomes an
extension of Beowulf's will: "[I]n the depths of Grendel's mere, the gigan-
tic sword almost becomes Beowulf's other self, its power, spirit, and mood
matching his. The instrument of victory and the victor fuse as the hero's
mind acquires the character of the weapon and the weapon seems to exult
like its wielder."[12] Moreover, Heaney redeems vicariously bog victims such

as the Tollund Man from the pre-Christian Germanic earth goddess, Nerthus. In an article entitled "The Germanic Earth Goddess in *Beowulf*," Frank Battaglia cites cultural and etymological studies associating Grendel's mother with a Danish variant of the *genius loci* guarding all bogs, fens, meres, and tarns in North Europe: "H. M. Chadwick identified early Anglian Nerthus, Scandinavian Freyia, and Danish Gefion as 'local forms of the chthonic [female] deity . . . whose cult was known to all Teutonic peoples.'"[13] Heaney's well-known bog sequence identifies him in contemporary consciousness as both reluctant celebrant and implacable foe of the goddess.

Beowulf exchanges pledges of enduring friendship with Hrothgar, and returns over the sea to southern Sweden and the fortified hall of his uncle and king, Hygelac. The young warrior presents his own ring-lord with the splendid tokens he won in Denmark, including a priceless torque that rivals "the Brosings' neck-chain." Hygelac lavishes on Beowulf a gold-chased patrilineal blade, "and then reward[s] him with land as well, / seven thousand hides, and a hall and a throne" (ll. 2195–96; 149). The young hero eventually succeeds his kinsman's son as king of the Weather-Geats. Beowulf winters into wisdom, and in his fiftieth regnal year, a dragon begins to scorch the thatched roofs of the countryside. Neither Grendel nor his troll-dam intrigue Heaney as much as the winged firedrake. In his prologue, he describes it as a "Fourth of July effulgence fire-working its path across the night sky" (*B* xix). Although somewhat anthropomorphized by the *Beowulf* poet—a fugitive who pilfers a precious cup from its subterranean treasure-hoard touches off the dragon's twilight pyrotechnics—the beast's capacity to embody both the marvellous and the mundane enthralls Heaney. If the dragon can breast the cold blasts and updrafts of a north wind off the fjord, it prefers to slumber amid the radiance of its trove in "a dry-stone vault" uncannily similar to the megalithic passage tombs toward which the glacial black motorcade advances in part three of "Funeral Rites." Earthen barrows with interiors braced by hand-hewn masonry, the ancient burial mounds add up to mutual psychic terrain for Heaney and the *Beowulf* poet.

These tumuli mark the landscape of northwest Europe from the British Isles to Scandinavia, and for more than a thousand years have sheltered refugees and surreptitious wealth. In "A Fear of the Past: The Place of the Prehistoric Burial Mound in the Ideology of Middle and Later Anglo-Saxon England," Sarah Semple remarks:

> [E]ven in the thirteenth century, the barrow was a place where outcasts could hide. Perhaps this was because there was still a widespread fear of the supernatural occupants of such places. One could regard the discovery

of some hoards of Anglo-Saxon and Viking metalwork from the vicinity of barrows as reflecting a clever decision to hide treasure where no one would dare to look.[14]

Shrouded in occult lore and myth, the dragon's lair remains bedded in archaeological and historical fact. Determined to confront and slay the saurian marauder, Beowulf orders his weapon smith to purge all dross from the most obdurate of ores:

> The warriors' protector, prince of the hall-troop,
> ordered a marvellous all-iron shield
> from his smithy works. He well knew
> that linden boards would let him down
> and timber burn. After many trials,
> he was destined to face the end of his days
> in this mortal world; as was the dragon,
> for all his long leasehold on the treasure.
>
> (ll. 2337–44; 159)

Eloquent in the plainness of its design, the unblazoned iron shield betokens the old ring-lord's wry knowledge of his adversary; moreover, it betrays his sense of a heretofore unaccustomed vulnerability. Beowulf's fate is upon him. The dragon is a force of nature, a metamorphic "stratum of the earth," to borrow Heaney's turn of phrase. At once dormant and volatile, it flows to the attack like molten lava—"a gushing stream / that burst from the barrow, blazing and wafting / a deadly heat" (ll. 2545–47; 173)—yet turns a cool "enamelled scale" to Beowulf's sword point. A shape-shifting creature of "spasm and spout," the dragon overwhelms Beowulf, even as he and young Wiglaf quell its heat with thrusting blades. Thus the values of the *comitatus* are reaffirmed: "[T]hat pair of kinsmen, partners in nobility, / had destroyed the foe" (ll. 2707–8; 183). Among translators of *Beowulf*, none captures so well as Heaney the steadfast gnomic utterance at the heart of the hero's farewell:

> For fifty years
> I ruled this nation. No king
> of any neighbouring clan would dare
> face me with troops, none had the power
> to intimidate me. I took what came,
> cared for and stood by things in my keeping,
> never fomented quarrels, never
> swore to a lie. All this consoles me,
> doomed as I am and sickening for death;

because of my right ways, the Ruler of mankind
need never blame me when the breath leaves my body.
(ll. 2732–42; 185)

Beowulf's death bodes ill for the Geats, now bereft of their king's extraordinary martial prowess, his matchless leadership in the *wael-raes* or
"rush of battle-slaughter." Merovingian and Swedish factions long to gain
revenge for Hygelac's former incursions, to renew the blood-feud held in
abeyance for a generation. Wiglaf knows intuitively that the great funeral
barrow soon to be raised on the headland at Hronesness will double as Beowulf's memorial and a guide to enemy raiding ships. Like Shield Sheafson, the Geatish hero receives a pagan Germanic funeral, his "four-square"
pyre decked with boar-crested helmets, richly embossed shields, and
gleaming war-graith:

> On a height they kindled the hugest of all
> funeral fires; fumes of woodsmoke
> billowed darkly up, the blaze roared
> and drowned out their weeping, wind died down
> and flames wrought havoc in the hot bone-house,
> burning it to the core. They were disconsolate
> and wailed aloud for their lord's decease.
> A Geat woman too sang out in grief;
> with hair bound up, she unburdened herself
> of her worst fears, a wild litany
> of nightmare and lament: her nation invaded,
> enemies on the rampage, bodies in piles,
> slavery and abasement. Heaven swallowed the smoke.
> (ll. 3143–55; 211)

Heaney adheres more scrupulously to the traditional alliterative and quali-
tative line of Old English in this passage. In the first line above, the repetition of aspirate *h* quickens a run of fricatives, specifically initial *f* sounds,
in the ensuing line. Coaxed to life phonetically, sparks flare and seethe to a
crescendo in "flames wrought havoc": cored from within, the metaphorical
"bone-house" collapses. Even as the ashes disperse, the anonymous Geat
woman's threnody soars, a "wild litany" in which she envisions boundaries
violated, bondage imposed, and the utter abjection of defeat. Doubtless
such a cry went up in the camps below Nineveh when Alexander passed
from delirium to immortality. But Heaney emphasizes the odd contemporaneity of the scenario:

The Geat woman who cries out in dread as the flames consume the body of
her dead lord could come straight from a late-twentieth-century news

report, from Rwanda or Kosovo; her keen is a nightmare glimpse into the minds of people who have survived traumatic, even monstrous events and who are now being exposed to a comfortless future. (*B* xxi)

The *topos* of the keening woman is as ancient as epic poetry; in *Beowulf,* the ideal incarnation would be a nubile blonde in a dyed cloak pinned with disk brooches, her chatelain gaudy with the latchkeys of rank and privilege. But Heaney's commentary promises a starker picture. Renewal of the ubiquitious blood-feud threatens most immediately the creatural existence of the common folk. Moreover, the eulogy for Beowulf implies both a compassionate vigilance and a largesse of spirit rare in any age: "They said of all the kings upon the earth / he was the man most gracious and fair-minded, / kindest to his people and keenest to win fame" (ll. 3180–82; 213).

Nicholas Howe insists that Heaney's translation of *Beowulf* "tends to flatten or elongate the Old English line, to make it seem heavy with words rather than direct and flowing."[15] On the contrary, Heaney avoids the jog-trot rhythms of those translators who invariably conform to the alliterative template of early medieval prosody. He enriches his version of *Beowulf* with a subtle interplay of assonance and consonance, but avoids a surfeit of polysyllabic locutions that would cause his rhythms to founder. As a result, his narrative line comes across as both straightforward and mellifluous. Although Heaney's spare interpolation of words from his native Ulster dialect—"wean," "bawn," "bothies," "brehon," "hoke," and "graith"—is not without polemical undertones, it also replicates the idiomatic permutations of a poem originally appropriated from a centuries-old oral tradition. Nor does the Irish laureate necessarily claim the final say in these matters, as the epigraph to his introduction makes clear:

> And now this is "an inheritance"—
> Upright, rudimentary, unshiftably planked
> In the long ago, yet willable forward
>
> Again and again and again.
>
> (*B* ix)

In *Electric Light* (2001), Heaney's most recent volume of original verse, the poet foregrounds the issue of identity in a wide array of dramatic settings that range from the Mossbawn scullery to the sandstone grottoes and mineral tricklings of the Castalian Spring in "Sonnets from Hellas." The collection's valedictory tone notwithstanding, Heaney's personal origins continue to inform his essential poetic vision, a circumstance he addresses in a recent interview with Karl Miller: "A writer's sense of the

world is admittedly going to derive from the intimacies and attitudes given
to him by his hearth culture. That colouring of the sensibility is fundamental and precious, maybe the ultimate *sine qua non* in the gift."[16] In "Out of
the Bag," Heaney revisits the psychic crucible of childhood, embellishing
a myth common to the Irish Catholic household in a more innocent age:
"All of us came in Doctor Kerlin's bag" (*EL* 6). He describes the physician's bag as "a plump ark," an image recalling the beautifully carved
wooden reliquaries of the medieval Celts and Saxons. However, the brooding receptacle—its brusque "trap-sprung mouth / Unsnibbed and gaping
wide"—hoards no precious relics: it opens to the hypnotic glint of surgical
tools, thus leading young Heaney to conjure the prosthetic chill of "teat-
hued infant parts." Doctor Kerlin is a prestidigitator, his "nosy, rosy, big,
soft hands" slick and plausive as he laves up before and after:

> Getting the water ready, that was next—
> Not plumping hot, and not lukewarm, but soft,
> Sud-luscious, saved for him from the rain-butt
>
> And savoured by him afterwards, all thanks
> Denied as he towelled hard and fast,
> Then held his arms out suddenly behind him
>
> To be squired and silk-lined into the camel coat.
> At which point he once turned his eyes upon me,
> Hyperborean, beyond-the-north-wind blue.
>
> (*EL* 7)

The boy waits like a footman for the doctor to finish his ablutions, and we
glimpse a vestige of the old deference that prompted Heaney to sign his
first poems Incertus. The doctor's "Hyperborean" gaze lingers, a look searing as the blandishments of his silk-lined coat. The youthful speaker imagines, in the physician's inner sanctum, infant parts "Strung neatly from a
line up near the ceiling— / A toe, a foot and shin, an arm, a cock // A bit like
the rosebud in his buttonhole" (*EL* 8). Nipped in the metaphorical bud, the
diminutive phallus is both a generative organ and a boutonniere, the
emblem of a sublime and esoteric order. Heaney's whimsical trope subverts Doctor Kerlin's punctilious manner, his self-assured claim on the art
of creation.

     In the poem's second section, Heaney crosscuts to a sanitorium in Epi-
daurus. He describes the Greek baths as a "site of incubation, where 'incubation' / Was technical and ritual, meaning sleep / When epiphany
occurred and you met the god" (*EL* 8). Although he alludes to Asclepius

early on, the heat and humidity induce a hallucination wherein he sees "Doctor Kerlin at the steamed-up glass / Of our scullery window, starting in to draw" (*EL* 9). The physician inscribes the dense condensation on the panes with the figures of men and women, "giving them all / A set of droopy sausage-arms and legs // That soon began to run." When Heaney likens arms and legs to "sausage," the carnal lapses into the carnivalesque, but the ensuing stanzas converge in a genuine epiphany:

> And then as he dipped and laved
> In the generous suds again, *miraculum*:
> The baby bits all came together swimming
>
> Into his soapy big hygienic hands
> And I myself came to, blinded with sweat,
> Blinking and shaky in the windless light.
>
> (*EL* 9–10)

Within Heaney's numinous reverie, the rude natal hieroglyphs melting down the scullery glass symbolize the sacred encoding that all poetry embodies. Thus Heaney's crisis of identity is resolved in the self-fashioning potential of the creative imagination. He can now contemplate with gentle amusement his youthful misprision regarding the doctor's role in childbirth. But the poet's innate humility leads him back to the true source, as he watches his mother sleeping "In sheets put on for the doctor, wedding presents / That showed up again and again, bridal / And usual and useful at births and deaths." The eldest of nine siblings, Heaney commingles birth and death to poignant effect. The speaker approaches his exhausted mother, a willing participant in the game:

> I would enter every time, to assist and be asked
> In that hoarsened whisper of triumph,
>
> "And what do you think
> Of the new wee baby the doctor brought for us all
> When I was asleep?"
>
> (*EL* 11)

In "The Border Campaign," Heaney confirms his lifelong obsession with *Beowulf*, imparting a tendency to identify with the beleaguered inhabitants of Hrothgar's mead-hall in the wake of Grendel's depredations. His title relates specifically to a series of I.R.A. strikes in ten different locales along the borders of the North Six counties on the night of 12 December

1956.[17] Most targets were demolished with gelignite stolen from quarries in the Republic by I.R.A. operatives, but Heaney's opening lines apparently refer to the Magherafelt Quarter Sessions Courthouse in County Derry, a structure that perished in flames: "Soot-streaks down the courthouse wall, a hole / Smashed in the roof, the rafters in the rain / Still smouldering." Heaney is a seventeen-year-old boarder at St. Columb's College when the violence erupts:

> when I heard the word "attack"
> In St. Columb's College in nineteen fifty-six
> It left me winded, left nothing between me
> And the sky that moved beyond my boarder's dormer
> The way it would have moved the morning after
> Savagery in Heorot, its reflection placid
> In those waterlogged huge pawmarks Grendel left
> On the boreen to the marsh.
>
> (*EL* 21)

In the first five lines above, Heaney subordinates auditory imagery to physical and visual perceptions. Hearing the hard-bitten articulation of the word "attack" rips the breath from his lungs; the gray winter sky moves with a stunned grandeur beyond his window. However, the long *e* sound in the Anglo-Irish locution "boreen" mimics aurally the slow seepage of cloud-murk into the "huge pawmarks" on the narrow pathway to the marsh. Once again, Heaney seeks an analogue for Ireland's civil strife in the Norse code of "scoretaking" reciprocity. Significantly, the youthful poet identifies with men who adhere to the rule of law and oppose unprovoked violence:

> All that was written
> And to come I was a part of then,
> At one with clan chiefs galloping down paths
> To gaze at the talon Beowulf had nailed
> High on the gable, the sky still moving grandly.
>
> (*EL* 21)

The poem's coda is a potent variation on Heaney's translation of *Beowulf*: "*Every nail and claw-spike, every spur / And hackle and hand-barb on that heathen brute / Was like a steel prong in the morning dew*" (*EL* 21). Words such as "spike", "spur," "hackle," and "barb" crackle with a malign vigor that almost reanimates the hate-dismembered limb. Not even "prong" can sound the knell for a sundered appendage that is more spiked truncheon than battle trophy.

Heaney explores the exigencies of identity in "The Real Names," a retrospective about the amateur yet ardent theatrical productions of his days at St. Columb's. The poem is not so much an elliptical narrative as a series of vignettes wherein Heaney remembers his schoolfellows casting off the daily round and putting on the extravagant guises and manifold passions of Shakespeare's creations. Interestingly, he opens with a scene from *The Tempest*, thus appropriating for himself the role of Prospero, the figure of the *magus* who by dint of deep learning, cloistered discipline, and assured skill could command the mysterious forces of both natural and supernatural worlds. In control of the play from beginning to end, Prospero is the Shakespearian character that scholars most closely identify with author and director:

> Enter Owen Kelly, loping and gowling,
> His underlip and lower jaw ill-set,
> A mad turn in his eye, his shot-putter's
> Neck and shoulders still a schoolboy's.
>
> (*EL* 52)

Kelly enacts the part of Caliban, progeny of the foul witch Sycorax, a truculent half-man, half-beast that Heaney compared to Grendel in his introduction to *Beowulf*: "The hard sticks / He dumped down at the opening of the scene / Raised a stour off the boards." When Heaney uses the term "stour," akin to the Old High German *sturm* or "storm," he deepens etymologically the connection between Caliban and Grendel. But the poet delights in Owen Kelly's assumed identity, his "turnip fists" and "ripped tarpaulin smock." Kelly's heathen brute is an avid delver in the potato drills, one who probes the soil for tubers like nuggets: "I won't forget his Sperrins Caliban, / His bag-aproned, potato-gatherer's Shakespeare: / *And I with my long nails will dig thee pig-nuts*" (*EL* 52). Heaney's verse memoir momentarily banishes the specter of Grendel's terrible prehensile claw. The person who plays the naive and pubescent Miranda—"Flaxen, credible, incredible"—reprises the role amidst an all-male enrollment, exactly as he would have in Shakespeare's day: "He was a she angelic in the light / We couldn't take our eyes off" (*EL* 52). Other times Heaney's reminiscence conflates disparate characters such as the foolish steward Malvolio of *Twelfth Night* and the Scots warrior so fierce he could unseam a foe "from the knave to th' chops" with a single sword stroke: "The previous year / Gerry had been Macbeth, green football socks / Cross-gartered to his Thane of Cawdor knees" (*EL* 53). But the most cherished moment that Heaney culls from memory involves a textual encounter with Shakespeare's capacious wit:

> The smell of the new book. The peep ahead
> At words not quite beyond you. At which time
> *A CARRIER, with a lantern in his hand*
> Entered the small hours, speaking low-life prose,
>   And a light that sparked when I read that Charles's Wain
> Was *over the new chimney* has never stopped
> Arriving ever since.
>
>   (*EL* 53)

The palpable heft and scent of the new volume, the clandestine "peep ahead," imply that young Heaney's aesthetic sensibility was primed and ready for the coarse albeit scintillant raillery of a horse-packer outside an ostlery in the opening lines of Act 2, scene 1, *1 Henry IV.* "Charles's Wain" is the constellation now known as the Plough, a configuration fit to strike sparks in the poet's mind. More importantly, the effulgent image offers Heaney an aperture to his remote past:

> Sometimes it was as if a chink had opened
> Upon a scene foreseen and enterable—
> Like the perpetual that shone in the sparks going up
> From MacNicholl's chimney:
>   I was crossing the yard
> When I saw them that one time,
> Babe in the world, up to my eyes in it,
> Up and about in the winter milker's darkness,
> Hand held by one with a lantern in her hand.
>
>   (*EL* 53–54)

Shakespeare's *tableau vivant* allowed the youthful Heaney to divine correspondences between art and the phenomenal world, an illumination that shaped his poetic identity as surely as watching his grandfather cut peat on Toner's bog. The muse he walks with hand in hand is his own mother.

In "Castalian Spring," the fifth of Heaney's "Sonnets from Hellas," the poet achieves self-actualization as an artist by transgressing the strictures of cultural custodianship and recent tourism. Located at Delphi in the sanctuary of Apollo excavated by French archaeologists in the mid-twentieth century, the Castalian Spring is a sacred font pouring from a fissure in the lower slopes of Mount Parnassus. Heaney has made his arduous pilgrimage; he mounts the slow, exalted grade familiar to inhabitants of the Graeco-Roman world since the seventh century B.C., only to be stonewalled by a modern caricature of the ancient Sibyl: "Thunderface. Not Zeus's ire, but hers / Refusing entry, and mine mounting from it" (*EL* 49). The often dubious sanctions of oracular utterance hold little consequence for Heaney; indeed, he intends to undergo a ritual of self-affirmation:

> This one thing I had vowed: to drink the waters
> Of the Castalian Spring, to arrogate
> That much to myself and be the poet
> Under the god Apollo's giddy cliff.

(EL 49)

Always plagued by excessive humility, Heaney means to drink of Apollo's spring, thus confirming once and for all his identity as a poet: "But the inner water sanctum was roped off / When we arrived. Well then, to hell with that." He refuses to be balked by official barriers or the keeper's outraged sense of propriety:

> So up the steps then, into the sandstone grottoes,
> The seeps and dreeps, the shallow pools, the mosses,
> Come from beyond, and come far, with this useless
> Anger draining away, on terraces
> Where I bowed and mouthed in sweetness and defiance.

(EL 49)

Heaney's apotheosis involves an ascent to alcoves of porous sandstone brimming with the sweetness of plenitude, all echoes muted by luxuriant mosses underfoot. Does bowing to partake of the source preclude obeisance? The poet tastes, and becomes whole beyond anger or confusion.

In "Electric Light," the volume's title poem, Heaney strives to manifest "that order of poetry where we can at last grow up to that which we stored up as we grew" (*CP* 32–33). Indeed, a photograph of Thomas Alva Edison's first electric light bulb ornaments the book's dust jacket, the latest metaphor in a progression that leads from "bleb" to "ovum" to "bubble" to filament-lit glass-blown globe. Heaney traces the orbit of a single creative lifetime in three dramatic sections describing his earliest encounter with artificial light, a phenomenon somewhat rare in the North Six counties during World War II: "[R]ural electrification is further advanced in the Republic, and you can tell by the large number of poles and overhead wires where you are."[18] When the poem opens, the speaker is no more than three or four years old, an overnight visitor in his grandmother's Ulster homestead:

> Candle-grease congealed, dark-streaked with wick-soot . . .
> The smashed thumb-nail
> Of that ancient mangled thumb was puckered pearl,
>
> Rucked quartz, a littered Cumae.
> In the first house where I saw electric light
> She sat with her fur-lined felt slippers unzipped.

(EL 96)

The soft gutturals of internal rhyme in line one—"grease" and "con-gealed"—coagulate around *k* sounds in "dark-streaked" and "wick-soot." Long ago the thumb snuffed the pash of tallow, printed indelibly the ac-cumlation of molten nacre. Thus, in the speaker's impressionable mind, the "smashed thumb-nail" takes on the semblance "puckered pearl," hard-ens to a glint of "rucked quartz." The metaphor "a littered Cumae" seems problematic until we liken the cracked and glimmering "thumb-nail" to the shrivelled husks of leaves blown about the cave of the Sibyl of Cumae whenever a questor enters, a tableau evoked by the Trojan seer Helenus in book 3, lines 450–72 of Virgil's *Aeneid.* According to Vir-gil by proxy of Aeneas's cousin, the priestess refuses to rearrange the prophetic signs and symbols that she scripted on the leaves, and men depart "hat[ing] / The Sibyl's dwelling."[19] Heaney remembers how his grandmother sat in the same chair year after year, and "whispered / In a voice that at its loudest did nothing else / But whisper" (*EL* 96). Both grandparent and child are equally distraught at his uncomprehending de-spair:

> The night I was left to stay, when I wept and wept
> Under the clothes, under the waste of light
> Left turned on in the bedroom. "What ails you, child,
>
> What ails you, for God's sake?" Urgent, sibilant
> *Ails,* far off and old. Scaresome cavern waters
> Lapping a boatslip. Her helplessness no help.

(EL 96)

The speaker's embryonic sensibility recoils at the sheer urgency of aspi-rates and sibilants in the refrain, "What ails you?" He hearkens instead to the ominous muttering of subterranean waters.

In the poem's second section, Heaney begins to parlay his grand-mother's "Lisp and relapse" into the harsh accents and liquid sonorities of spoken English: "I would come alive in time // As ferries churned and turned down Belfast Lough / Towards the brow-to-glass transport of a morning train" (*EL* 97). His faring forth is both literal and metaphorical, an enactment of the Greek *metapherein*, "to transfer." He seeks—not without a certain wry cynicism—the "very 'there-you-are-and-where-are-you?' // of poetry itself" in the language and landscape of Empire:

> Backs of houses
> Like the back of hers, meat-safes and mangles
> In the railway-facing yards of fleeting England,

Then fields of grain like the Field of the Cloth of Gold.
To Southwark too I came, from tube-mouth into sunlight,
Moyola-breath by Thames's "straunge stronde."

(EL 97)

From the window of a train chuffing cross-country through post-industrial England, Heaney watches a succession of familiar images glide past. The adjective-noun combination "meat-safes" is superficially foreboding in proximity to "mangles"—rollers for pressing damp linen, which may explain his grandmother's maimed thumb-nail—and the discreetly framed backyard vignettes give way to the panoramic "fields of grain like the Field of the Cloth of Gold." Here the poem becomes densely allusive: Heaney's ebullient simile refers to the rendezvous of Henry VIII and Francis I of France near the Pas-de-Calais in June 1520 at the Field of the Cloth of Gold, named for the sumptuously embroidered garments and pavilions of the two kings and their respective retinues. Indeed, Shakespeare conjures the two weeks of negotiating, feasting, jousting, and dancing in Act 1, scene 1, of *Henry VIII*:

> Today the French,
> All clinquant all in gold, like heathen gods
> Shone down the English; and tomorrow they
> Made Britain India. Every man that stood
> Showed like a mine.[20]

Shakespeare's metaphorical turn of phrase—"tomorrow they / Made Britain India"— meant in 1613 that the English contingent outfaced the French by making Britain appear as fabulously wealthy as India or the West Indies, an ironically prescient figure of speech when one remembers that a large portion of the West Indies and the subcontinent of India would eventually become colonial possessions of Great Britain. Of course, Shakespeare's purpose was to present to the court of James Stuart a tragicomic romance detailing the ostentation and excess of the Tudor monarchs. But does Heaney's passing reference to the Field of the Cloth of Gold merely offer a glimpse into the extravagant consciousness of a young Irish poet upon his first arrival in storied Albion? Not likely; indeed, who could forget that Henry Tudor's dynastic and imperial ambitions were the virtual flashpoint of sectarian strife in the British Isles? In his biography *Henry VIII* (1964), John Bowle states that

> in June 1541 [Henry] had himself proclaimed by the Irish Parliament as
> king, not merely lord, of Ireland—a title originally conferred by the Pope

—and confirmed as head of the Irish Church. The great chieftains were flattered and conciliated, encouraged to surrender their lands, regranted on terms better for them than for their people.[21]

Heaney crosscuts smoothly from the countryside, emerging from a South-wark "tube-mouth" in time to catch a breath of his own Moyola River rising off the Thames. The Middle English expression "straunge stronde" means "foreign shores," and derives from line 13 of the prologue to Geof-frey Chaucer's *Canterbury Tales*: "And palmeres for to seeken straunge strondes." Heaney's journey is indeed a pilgrimage, an attempt to locate his poetic identity in the English tradition by citing those cultural and his-torical circumstances wherein his life and those of his major precursors in-tersect. The young Chaucer was a page in the household of Elizabeth, Countess of Ulster and Connaught. In an era when many of his contempo-raries were writing in French and Latin, Chaucer's recourse to English in *Troilus and Criseyde* and *The Canterbury Tales* established the vernacular as a viable medium for serious poetry. On the other hand, a great number of words and phrases, many of French origin, appear for the first time in his writings. Almost six hundred years later, Heaney would follow Chaucer's example, introducing the argot of his native Ulster and the Gaeltacht into contemporary poetry. Clearly, Heaney's awakening in section 2 of "Elec-tric Light" celebrates more than the masque and pageant of the turning sea-sons.

In the third and final section of the title poem, Heaney returns to his youth and his grandmother's rural home in County Derry, where electricity runs in easy harness with older technologies:

> If I stood on the bow-backed chair, I could reach
> The light switch. They let me and they watched me.
> A touch of the little pip would work the magic.
>
> A turn of their wireless knob and light came on
> In the dial. They let me and they watched me
> As I roamed at will the stations of the world.
>
> (*EL* 98)

If a touch of the "little pip" produces the magic of incandescent light, a turn of the "wireless knob" summons a luminescence and amplitude that frees young Heaney to roam—like Prospero's Ariel—the secular "stations of the world." Once more he discerns the universal in the parochial, as he listens to the BBC weatherman intone the old litany: Dogger, Rockall, Malin, Shetland, Faroes, and Finisterre. He savors in the subtle orchestration and cadences of language both noble accents and lucid, inescapable rhythms. Abruptly, his parents depart:

> Then they were gone and Big Ben and the news
> Were over. The set had been switched off,
> All quiet behind the blackout except for
>
> Knitting needles ticking, wind in the flue.
> She sat with her fur-lined felt slippers unzipped,
> Electric light shone over us, I feared
>
> The dirt-tracked flint and fissure of her nail,
> So plectrum-hard, glit-glittery, it must still keep
> Among beads and vertebrae in the Derry ground.
>
> (*EL* 98)

Heaney plays initial fricatives off glyptic *t* in "flint" and sibilant *s* in "fissure," the merest spark insinuating the mythic eloquence of his grandmother's sibylline whisper. The horn-sheath of her thumb persists, "plectrum-hard," a musical inheritance striking the full spectrum of color from the poet's imagination. The nail endures, "glit-glittery," a palpitating translucence among scattered beads and displaced vertebrae beneath the cold clay of County Derry. Fusing aural and visual tropes, Heaney's penultimate line proves deftly synaesthetic, thus transmuting an object of childhood fear into an emblem of lyric transcendence. Cumulative layers of meaning are nothing new to his structural methodology, but Heaney's use of synchronic imagery, including such cinematic techniques as the crosscut and slow dissolve—not to mention comparatively oblique historical and textual allusions—endow "Electric Light" with a quasi-modernist aura. No longer reluctant to embrace the peculiarly English aspects of his poetic identity, he nevertheless includes Virgil along with Chaucer and Shakespeare in an elliptical poem that defies strict chronology. Between the smoldering wick in a nub of tallow and the incubating warmth of a bulb shaped by intellect and high artifice, the poet's unique sensibility continues to grow.

Heaney's translation of *Beowulf* evinces his ongoing quest for fidelity to "the nature of the English language" as well as his own "non-English origin." According to the poet, overcoming the tendency "to conceive of English and Irish as adversarial tongues" was a gradual process, beginning in earnest with his study of the history of the English language as a student at Queens University, Belfast. Nevertheless, the poems in *Electric Light* demonstrate that translating *Beowulf* has enabled Heaney to fully accept the English language as part of his cultural heritage and "voice-right." He describes the process of translating *Beowulf* not as a retrieval or reclamation but as "a coming to terms," a struggle with "that complex history of conquest and colony, absorption and resistance, integrity and antagonism, a history which has to be clearly acknowledged by all concerned" (*B* xxx). The old exhilaration of being placed between "'the demesne' and 'the bog'" remains a vital component of Heaney's poetic identity, enhancing his ability to convert personal experience into a singular and sustaining vision.

Notes

CHAPTER I

1. Homer, *The Odyssey*, trans. Robert Fitzgerald (New York: Doubleday, 1961), 416.
2. Ibid., 418.
3. Harold Bloom, *The Western Canon: Books and Schools for the Ages* (New York: Harcourt Brace, 1994), 6.
4. Ibid., 7.
5. Robert Penn Warren, *Who Speaks for the Negro?* (New York: Random House, 1965), 17.
6. Heaney, "Land-Locked," *Irish Press* (1 June 1974), 6.
7. Erik Erikson, *Identity, Youth and Crisis* (New York: Norton, 1968), 208.
8. Ibid., 16.
9. Elmer Andrews, *The Poetry of Seamus Heaney: All the Realms of Whisper* (New York: St. Martin's Press, 1988), 35.
10. Polly Devlin, *All of Us There* (Belfast: Blackstaff Press, 1994), 38–40.
11. Richard Kearney, *Transitions: Narratives in Modern Irish Culture* (Manchester: Manchester University Press, 1988), 9.
12. Andrews, *The Poetry*, 157.
13. Erikson, *Identity*, 298.
14. Kearney, *Transitions*, 14.
15. Penn Warren, *Who Speaks*, 17.
16. Andrews, *The Poetry*, 16.
17. Blake Morrison, *Seamus Heaney* (London: Methuen, 1982), 29.
18. W. B. Yeats, *The Autobiography of William Butler Yeats* (New York: Macmillan, 1938), 16.
19. W. B. Yeats, "The Lake Isle of Innisfree," *The Poems of W. B. Yeats* (New York: Macmillan, 1983), 39.
20. A. Norman Jeffares, *W. B. Yeats* (New York: Farrar, Straus, and Giroux, 1988), 33.
21. W. B. Yeats, *The Variorum Edition of the Plays of W. B. Yeats* (London: Macmillan, 1966), 290: 528–35.
22. Yeats, *The Poems*, 127.
23. Ibid., 134.
24. W. B. Yeats, *A Vision* (New York: Collier, 1966), 8.
25. Richard Ellmann, *The Identity of Yeats* (New York: Oxford University Press, 1954), 150.

26. W. B. Yeats, *Autobiographies* (London: Macmillan, 1979), 70–71.

27. Terence Brown, "A Northern Voice," in *Seamus Heaney*, ed. Harold Bloom (New York: Chelsea House, 1986), 34.

28. Yeats, *The Poems*, 201.

29. Terence Brown, "The Counter-Revival, 1930–65: Poetry," in *The Field Day Anthology of Irish Writing,* ed. Seamus Deane (Derry: Field Day Publications, 1991), 3:129.

30. E. H. Mikhail, ed., *W. B. Yeats: Interviews and Recollections* (London: Macmillan, 1977), 2:243.

31. Yeats, *The Poems*, 321.

32. Patrick Kavanagh, *Collected Poems* (New York: Norton, 1964), 34.

33. Ibid., 35.

34. Ibid., 53.

35. Ibid., 53.

36. Yeats, *The Poems*, 327.

37. Fitzgerald, "Seamus Heaney: An Appreciation," in *Seamus Heaney*, ed. Harold Bloom (New York: Chelsea House, 1986), 39–40.

38. Terence Brown, "The Counter-Revival, 1930–65: Poetry," in *The Field Day Anthology,* ed. Seamus Deane (Derry: Field Day Publications, 1991), 3:131.

39. Yeats, *The Poems*, 237.

40. Kavanagh, *Collected Poems*, 53.

41. Harold Bloom, *The Anxiety of Influence: A Theory of Poetry* (New York: Oxford University Press, 1973), 15.

42. Yeats, "Towards Break of Day," *The Poems*, 185.

43. Andrews, *The Poetry*, 36.

44. Hugh Kenner, *The Pound Era* (Berkeley: University of California Press, 1971), 42.

45. Ibid., 47.

46. Ibid., 44.

47. Richard Ellmann, *James Joyce* (Oxford: Oxford University Press, 1983), 505.

48. Dillon Johnston, *Irish Poetry After Joyce* (Notre Dame, IN: University of Notre Dame Press, 1985), 53.

49. Fitzgerald, "Seamus Heaney: An Appreciation," in *Seamus Heaney,* ed. Harold Bloom, 40–41.

50. James Joyce, *A Portrait of the Artist as a Young Man* (New York: Penguin, 1988), 35.

51. Helen Vendler, *The Music of What Happens* (Cambridge: Harvard University Press, 1988), 163.

52. Devlin, *All of Us There,* 158.

53. Andrews, *Seamus Heaney,* 43.

54. Joyce, *Portrait,* 241.

55. Michael Parker, *Seamus Heaney: The Making of a Poet* (Iowa City: University of Iowa Press, 1993), 9.

56. Seamus Heaney, "Unhappy and at Home," interview by Seamus Deane, *Crane Bag* 1, no. 1 (1977), 66.

57. Parker, *Seamus Heaney: The Making*, 18.

58. William Wordsworth, *The Prelude*, in *English Romantic Writers,* ed. David Perkins (New York: Harcourt Brace, 1967), 1: 484–90; 218–19.

59. Graham Storey, *A Preface to Hopkins* (New York: Longman, 1981), 34.

60. Gerard Manley Hopkins, "As Kingfishers Catch Fire, Dragonflies Draw Flame," in *The Norton Anthology of Poetry,* ed. Alexander W. Allison et. al. (New York: W. W. Norton, 1983), 1064.

61. Seamus Heaney, interview by James Randall, *Ploughshares* 5, no. 3 (1979), 14.

62. Wordsworth, *The Prelude,* 280.

63. E. Estyn Evans, *Irish Folk Ways* (New York: Devin-Adair, 1957), 159.

64. Ibid., 188.

65. Kavanagh, *Collected Poems,* xiv.

66. Evans, *Irish Folk Ways,* 11.

67. Kavanagh, *The Green Fool* (New York: Harper and Brothers, 1939), 81.

68. Neil Corcoran, *Seamus Heaney* (London: Faber and Faber, 1986), 47.

69. Evans, *Irish Folk Ways,* 142.

70. Ibid., 263.

71. Henry Hart, *Seamus Heaney: Poet of Contrary Progressions* (New York: Syracuse University Press, 1992), 27.

72. Cecil Woodham-Smith, *The Great Hunger* (New York: Old Town Books, 1989), 30.

73. Ibid., 44.

74. Ibid., 85.

75. Andrews, *The Poetry,* 18.

76. Parker, *Seamus Heaney: The Making,* 72.

77. Robert Buttel, *Seamus Heaney* (Lewisburg, PA: Bucknell University Press, 1975), 47.

78. Barry Raftery, *Pagan Celtic Ireland* (London: Thames and Hudson, 1994), 183.

79. Thomas Foster, *Seamus Heaney* (Boston: Twayne, 1989), 23.

80. Evans, *Irish Folk Ways,* 71.

81. Burris, *The Poetry of Resistance: Seamus Heaney and the Pastoral Tradition* (Athens: Ohio University Press, 1990), 82.

82. Seamus Heaney, interview by John Haffenden, in *Viewpoints* (London: Faber and Faber, 1981), 63.

83. Andrews, *The Poetry,* 20.

CHAPTER 2

1. Yeats, *The Poems,* 195.

2. See Robert Fitzgerald, "Seamus Heaney: An Appreciation," in *Seamus Heaney,* ed. Harold Bloom (New York: Chelsea House, 1986), 44.

3. Andrews, *The Poetry,* 35.

4. R. F. Foster, ed., *The Oxford Illustrated History of Ireland* (New York: Oxford University Press, 1989), 273.

5. Seamus Heaney, interview by James Randall, *Ploughshares* 5, no. 3 (1979): 18.

6. P. V. Glob, *The Bog People: Iron Age Man Preserved* (New York: Cornell University Press, 1969), 101.

7. Field Day Theatre Company, *Ireland's Field Day* (Notre Dame, IN: Notre Dame University Press, 1986), 71.

8. Deane, *Field Day Anthology,* 2:525.

9. E. Estyn Evans, *The Personality of Ireland: Habitat, Heritage, and History* (Cambridge: Cambridge University Press), 14.

10. Yeats, *Variorum Edition of the Plays,* 1063; 214–19.

11. Evans, *Personality of Ireland,* 47.

12. Tim Pat Coogan, *The I.R.A.: A History* (Niwot: Roberts Rinehart, 1994), 455.

13. W. B. Yeats, *Autobiographies,* (London: Macmillan, 1955), 101.

14. Thomas Heffernan, *Wood Quay: The Clash over Dublin's Viking Past* (Austin: University of Texas Press, 1988), 20.

15. Ibid., 21.

16. J. R. Green, *The Making of England* (London: Macmillan, 1910), vii.

17. Yeats, *Variorum Edition of the Plays*, 232.

18. Ibid., 226.

19. Ibid., 231.

20. Kearney, *Transitions*, 106.

21. See R. F. Foster, *Oxford Illustrated History of Ireland,* 289.

22. James Joyce, *Ulysses: The Corrected Text* (New York: Vintage Books of Random House, 1986), 14.

23. Ibid., 17.

24. See Hart, *Seamus Heaney*, 61.

25. Thomas Kinsella, trans., *The Táin* (New York: Irish University Press, 1969), 252.

26. Burris, *Seamus Heaney: The Poetry of Resistance*, 12.

27. See Sean O' Ríordáin, *Antiquities of the Irish Countryside* (London: Methuen, 1953), 33.

28. Anne Ross, *Pagan Celtic Britain* (London: Routledge and Kegan Paul, 1967), 126.

29. Seamus Heaney, "Unhappy and At Home," interview by Seamus Deane, 70.

30. Evans, *Irish Folk Ways*, 268.

31. *Henry V*, revised Pelican edition, ed. Alfred Harbage (Baltimore: Penguin Books, 1969), 3.2.113–114.

32. Joyce, *Ulysses*, 272.

33. Hart, *Seamus Heaney*, 69.

34. Cecil Woodham-Smith, *The Great Hunger*, 27.

35. Parker, *Seamus Heaney: The Making*, 89–90.

36. Jeanne Cooper Foster, *Ulster Folklore* (Belfast: H. R. Carter Publications, 1951), 35.

37. Thomas Hardy, *The Return of the Native* (New York: Norton, 1969), 106.

38. R. F. Foster, *Oxford Illustrated History*, 161.

39. Seamus Heaney, "Place, Pastness, Poems: A Triptych," *Salmagundi* (Fall–Winter 1985–86), 37.

40. Glob, *The Bog People*, 18.

41. See Parker, *Seamus Heaney: The Making*, 107.

42. Tony Curtis, ed., *The Art of Seamus Heaney* (Bridgend, Mid Glamorgan: Poetry Wales, 1994), 47.

43. Ibid., 47.

44. Geoffrey Hill, *New and Collected Poems, 1952–1992* (New York: Houghton Mifflin, 1994), 93.

45. Ibid., 99.

46. Ibid., 102.

47. Ibid., 105.

48. Ibid., 111, 121.

49. Morrison, *Seamus Heaney*, 51.

50. Catharine Malloy and Phyllis Carey, eds., *Seamus Heaney: The Shaping Spirit* (Newark: University of Delaware Press, 1996), 82.

51. James Graham-Campbell and Dafydd Kidd, *The Vikings* (London: British Museum Publications, 1980), 25.

52. R. F. Foster, *Oxford Illustrated History*, 31.

53. Ibid., 33.

54. Andrews, *The Poetry*, 53.

55. Hart, *Seamus Heaney*, 79.

56. Graham-Campbell and Kydd, *The Vikings*, 179.

57. Hart, *Seamus Heaney*, 81.

58. Graham-Campbell and Kydd, *The Vikings*, 173.

59. Heffernan, *Wood Quay*, 12.

60. R. F. Foster, *Oxford Illustrated History*, 35.

61. Birgit Sawyer and Peter Sawyer, *Medieval Scandinavia: From Conversion to Reformation, circa 800–1500* (Minneapolis: University of Minnesota Press, 1993), 26.

62. Joyce, *Portrait*, 253.

63. Heffernan, *Wood Quay*, 21.

64. Peter Sacks, *The English Elegy: Studies in the Genre from Spenser to Yeats* (Baltimore: Johns Hopkins University Press, 1985), 299.

65. O' Ríordáin, *Antiquities*, 101.

66. Andrews, *The Poetry*, 16.

67. Corcoran, *Seamus Heaney*, 111.

68. Heaney, "The Interesting Case of John Alphonsus Mulrennan," *Planet* (January 1978), 40.

69. Thomas Foster, *Seamus Heaney*, 57.

70. Ibid., 58–59.

71. Shakespeare, *Hamlet*, Harbage, 1.257–58.

72. David Jones, *The Dying Gaul and Other Writings* (London: Faber and Faber, 1978), 50.

73. Coogan, *The I.R.A.*, 341.

74. T. S. Eliot, *Selected Prose of T. S. Eliot* (New York: Harcourt Brace, 1975), 177.

75. Heffernan, *Wood Quay*, 10.

76. Hart, *Seamus Heaney*, 92.

77. Andrews, *The Poetry*, 96.

78. Hart, *Seamus Heaney*, 95.

79. Glob, *The Bog People*, 180.

80. Hart, *Seamus Heaney*, 95.

81. Andrews, *Seamus Heaney*, 96.

82. Yeats, *The Poems*, 181.

83. Parker, *Seamus Heaney: The Making*, 255 n. 203.

84. Devlin, *All of Us There*, 39.

85. Andrews, *Seamus Heaney*, 109.

86. Devlin, *All of Us There*, 158.

87. Padraig O'Malley, *The Uncivil Wars: Ireland Today* (Boston: Houghton Mifflin, 1983), 208.

88. Charles Rzepka, *The Self as Mind: Vision and Identity in Wordsworth, Coleridge, and Keats* (Cambridge: Harvard University Press, 1986), 22.

89. Devlin, *All of Us There*, 131.

90. See Ian Gibson, *Federico Garcia Lorca: A Life* (New York: Pantheon, 1989), 466.

91. Joyce, *Portrait*, 203.

92. Erikson, *Identity*, 297. (Erikson, who appropriates the term "surrendered identity" from C. Vann Woodward, notes that its recovery is especially important for writers.)

93. Jahan Ramazani, *Poetry of Mourning: The Modern Elegy from Hardy to Heaney* (Chicago: University of Chicago Press, 1994), 343.

94. Devlin, *All of Us There*, 123–24.

95. Erikson, *Identity*, 25.

CHAPTER 3

1. Morrison, *Seamus Heaney*, 42, 68.

2. Thomas Foster, *Seamus Heaney*, 55.

3. Parker, *Seamus Heaney: The Making*, 7.

4. Seamus Heaney, interview by James Randall, 20.

5. Evans, *Irish Folk Ways*, 48.

6. See Anthony Bailey, "A Gift for Being in Touch," *Quest* (January–February 1978), 44.

7. Seamus Heaney, interview by James Randall, 20.

8. Lawrence Lipking, *The Life of the Poet* (Chicago: University of Chicago Press, 1981), vii–viii.

9. Richard Tillinghast, *Robert Lowell's Life and Work: Damaged Grandeur* (Ann Arbor: University of Michigan Press, 1995), 88.

10. Lowell, "Reading Myself," *Selected Poems* (New York: Noonday, 1992), 183.

11. Hart, *Seamus Heaney*, 137.

12. Thomas Foster, *Seamus Heaney*, 81.

13. Seamus Heaney, interview by James Randall, 21.

14. Ibid., 21.

15. Jahan Ramazani, *Poetry of Mourning*, 345.

16. Andrews, *The Poetry*, 137.

17. Devlin, *All of Us There*, 94.

18. Coogan, *The I.R.A.*, 439.

19. Corcoran, *Seamus Heaney*, 138.

20. Andrews, *The Poetry*, 128.

21. Paul Mariani, *Lost Puritan: A Life of Robert Lowell* (New York: Norton, 1994), 436.

22. Alice Curtayne, *Francis Ledwidge: A Life of the Poet* (London: Martin Brian and O'Keeffe, 1972), 190.

23. Wilfred Owen, *The Collected Poems of Wilfred Owen*, ed. C. Day Lewis (New York: New Directions, 1965), 35.

24. Curtayne, *Francis Ledwidge*, 180.

25. Ibid., 164.

26. Heaney, "An Open Letter," *Ireland's Field Day*, 25.

27. Lowell, "For the Union Dead," *Selected Poems*, 135.

28. Robert Langbaum, *The Mysteries of Identity: A Theme in Modern Literature* (New York: Oxford University Press, 1977), 7.

29. Ibid., 44.

30. Andrews, *The Poetry*, 138.

31. Seamus Heaney, interview with Bel Mooney, *Turning Points*, BBC Radio 4, 15 November 1988.

32. Dante, *Paradiso*, trans. John Ciardi (New York: Mentor, 1970), canto 31, ll. 16–18.

33. Richard Ellmann and Charles Fiedelson, ed., *The Modern Tradition: Backgrounds of Modern Literature* (New York: Oxford University Press), 4.

34. Morrison, *Seamus Heaney*, 74.

35. Langbaum, *Mysteries of Identity*, 53.

36. Ibid., 47.

37. *Oxford English Dictionary* (Oxford: Clarendon Press, 1989), 2: 401.

38. *The Tempest*, Harbage, 1.2.296.

39. *Macbeth*, Harbage, 4.1.122–24.

40. Parker, *Seamus Heaney: The Making*, 171.

41. Burris, *The Poetry of Resistance*, 131–32.

42. Seamus Heaney, interview by Bel Mooney, 15 November 1988.

43. Langbaum, *Mysteries of Identity*, 61.

44. Seamus Heaney, "Unhappy and at Home," interview by Seamus Deane, 70.

45. Robert Graves, *The White Goddess* (New York: Farrar, Straus and Giroux, 1948), 455.

46. Hart, *Seamus Heaney*, 141.

47. Corcoran, *Seamus Heaney*, 153.

48. Andrews, *The Poetry,* 147.

49. Sammye Crawford Greer, "'Station Island' and the Poet's Progress," in *Seamus Heaney: The Shaping Spirit*, ed. Catharine Malloy and Phyllis Carey (Newark: University of Delaware Press, 1996), 106.

50. J. E., "St. Patrick's Purgatory," *Canadian Journal of Irish Studies* 10, no. 10 (1984), 17.

51. Parker, *Seamus Heaney: The Making*, 204.

52. Joyce, *Ulysses*, 175.

53. Stephen Hawlin, "Seamus Heaney's 'Station Island': The Shaping of a Modern Purgatory," *English Studies* 73 (1992), 40.

54. William Carleton, *Lough Dearg Pilgrim* (New York: Garland, 1979), 85.

55. Andrews, *The Poetry*, 160.

56. Ibid., 157.

57. Ibid., 159.

58. Heaney, "Place, Pastness, Poems: A Triptych," 34.

59. Ibid., 34.

60. Parker, *Seamus Heaney: The Making*, 196.

61. Andrews, *The Poetry*, 163.

62. Parker, *Seamus Heaney: The Making*, 29.

63. Andrews, *The Poetry*, 164.

64. Parker, *Seamus Heaney: The Making*, 55.

65. Patrick Kavanagh, *Lough Derg* (London: Martin Brian and O'Keeffe, 1978), 1.

66. Devlin, *All of Us There*, 119.

67. Hart, *Seamus Heaney*, 174.

68. Heaney, "Envies and Identifications: Dante and the Modern Poet," *Irish University Review* 15, no. 1 (1985), 19.

69. See Andrews, *The Poetry*, 167.

70. Coogan, *The I.R.A.*, 409–10.

71. O'Malley, *The Uncivil Wars*, 266, 267.

72. Coogan, *The I.R.A.*, 379.

73. Erikson, *Identity*, 25.

74. Heaney, *Stations*, 9.

75. Thomas Foster, *Seamus Heaney*, 128.

76. Joyce, *Portrait*, 251.

77. Greer, "'Station Island' and the Poet's Progress," in *Seamus Heaney: The Shaping Spirit*, ed. Catharine Malloy and Phyllis Carey, 115.

78. R. D., "Double Time," *The Boston Phoenix* (18 September 1981), sec. 3.3.

79. Declan Kiberd, *Inventing Ireland* (Cambridge: Harvard University Press, 1996), 594–95.

80. Corcoran, *Seamus Heaney*, 170.

81. Thomas Foster, *Seamus Heaney*, 127.

82. See Kiberd, *Inventing Ireland*, 591, 594.

83. Corcoran, *Seamus Heaney*, 155–56.

84. Heaney, "Envies and Identifications," 18.

85. Seamus Heaney, "Seamus Heaney: The Words Worth Saying," interview by Stephen Ratiner, *Christian Science Monitor* (7 October 1992), 17.

CHAPTER 4

1. Andrews, *Seamus Heaney*, 228.

2. Thomas Foster, *Seamus Heaney*, 133.

3. Seamus Heaney, "Seamus Heaney: The Words Worth Saying," interview by Steven Ratiner, 17.

4. Erikson, *Identity*, 105.

5. Ibid.

6. Parker, *Seamus Heaney: The Making*, 211–12.

7. Erikson, *Identity*, 141.

8. Hart, *Seamus Heaney*, 175.

9. Helen Vendler, *Soul Says* (Cambridge: Harvard University Press, 1995), 188.

10. Hart, "What is Heaney Seeing in *Seeing Things*?" *Colby Quarterly* 30 (1994), 33.

11. Vendler, *Soul Says*, 186.

12. Seamus Heaney, "Seamus Heaney: An Interview," interview by Rand Brandes, *Salmagundi* 80 (Fall 1988), 8.

13. Malloy and Carey, *Seamus Heaney: The Shaping Spirit*, 14.

14. Heaney, "Seamus Heaney: An Interview," interview by Rand Brandes, 19.

15. Robert Fitzgerald, trans., *Odyssey* 21:39; 405.

16. Hart, *Seamus Heaney*, 189.

17. Heaney, "Seamus Heaney: An Interview," interview by Rand Brandes, 12.

18. Eliot, "Burnt Norton," *Complete Poems and Plays, 1909–1950* (New York: Harcourt Brace, 1980), 119.

19. Hart, *Seamus Heaney*, 199.

20. Parker, *Seamus Heaney: The Making,* 217.

21. Waterman, "Keep it in the Six Counties, Heaney!," *PN Review* 15, no. 6 (1989), 37.

22. Ibid., 38.

23. Heaney, "Seamus Heaney: An Interview," interview by Rand Brandes, 19.

24. Seamus Heaney, interview by Barry White, *Belfast Telegraph* (29 June 1989), 9.

25. Ibid., 9.

26. Phyllis Carey, "Heaney and Havel: Parables of Politics," in *Seamus Heaney: The Shaping Spirit*, ed. Catharine Malloy and Phyllis Carey (Newark: University of Delaware Press, 1996), 140.

27. Heaney, interview by Barry White, 9.

28. See Craig Raine, "Famous Seamus," *Vanity Fair* 54, no. 12 (1991), 246.

29. Andrews, *Seamus Heaney*, 245.

30. John Breslin, "Vision and Revision: Seamus Heaney's New Poems," *America* 165 (7 December 1991): 438.

31. Andrews, *Seamus Heaney*, 220.

32. Fred Muratori, "Seeing Things," *Library Journal* 116, no. 9 (15 November 1991), 86.

33. See Devlin, *All of Us There*, 98.

34. Yeats, "Byzantium," *The Poems*, 248.

35. William Doreski, "Seeing Things," *Colorado Review* 19 (Spring–Summer 1992), 166.

36. Hart, "What is Heaney Seeing," 34.

37. Ibid., 36.

38. Benedict Kiely, "A Raid into Dark Corners: The Poems of Seamus Heaney," *The Hollins Critic* 4 (October 1970), 8.

39. Curtis, ed., *The Art of Seamus Heaney*, 213.

40. Heaney, "'Place and Displacement': Recent Poetry from Northern Ireland," *Wordsworth Circle* 16 (Spring 1985), 50–51.

41. Lachlan MacKinnon, "A Responsibility to Self," *Times Literary Supplement* 4601 (7 June 1991), 28.

42. Hart, "What is Heaney Seeing," 38.

43. Langbaum, *The Mysteries of Identity*, 65.

44. Paul Breslin, "Heaney's Redress," *Poetry* 168, no. 6 (1996), 343.

45. Thomas Foster, *Seamus Heaney,* 6.

46. Erikson, *Identity,* 315–16.

47. Paul Breslin, "Heaney's Redress," 337.

48. Albert Camus, *Lyrical and Critical Essays* (New York: Knopf, 1969), 17.

49. Fitzgerald, *Odyssey,* 193.

50. Maurice Harmon, "Seamus Heaney: Divisions and Allegiances," *Colby Quarterly* 30, no. 1 (1994), 16.

51. Michael Molino, "Charting an Uncertain Flight Path: Irish Writers and the Question of Nation, Identity, and Literature," *The Comparatist* 20 (May 1996), 47.

52. Deane, "Oranges and Lemons," *New Statesman and Society* 4 (5 April 1991), 19.

53. Nicholas Jenkins, "Walking on Air," *Times Literary Supplement,* (5 July 1996), 10.

54. Kieran Quinlan. "'Tracing Seamus Heaney," *World Literature Today* 69, no. 1 (1995), 65.

55. Ibid., 65.

56. Jenkins, 12.

57. Ibid.

Epilogue

1. Seamus Deane, "The Famous Seamus," *New Yorker* 76, no. 4 (2000), 69.

2. Ibid., 66.

3. Ibid.

4. T. S. Eliot, *Selected Prose of T. S. Eliot* (New York: Harcourt Brace, 1965), 39.

5. Rupert Bruce-Mitford, *The Sutton Hoo Ship Burial: A Handbook* (London, British Museum, 1972), 18.

6. Barbara Raw, "Royal Power and Royal Symbols in *Beowulf,*" in *The Age of Sutton Hoo: The Seventh Century in Northwestern Europe,* ed. Martin Carver (Suffolk: Boydell Press, 1992), 173.

7. Martin Carver, *Sutton Hoo: Burial Ground of Kings* (Philadelphia: University of Pennsylvania Press, 1998), 173–74.

8. Martin Carver, ed., *The Age of Sutton Hoo*, 122.

9. Nicholas Howe, "Scullionspeak," *The New Republic* 222, no. 9 (2000), 35.

10. James Boswell, *Life of Johnson* (Oxford: Oxford University Press, 1991), 921.

11. Tacitus, *The Complete Works of Tacitus* (New York: Random House / Modern Library, 1942), 719.

12. George Clark, *Beowulf* (Boston: Twayne Publishers, 1990), 103.

13. Frank Battaglia, "The Germanic Earth Goddess in Beowulf," *Mankind Quarterly* 35, no. 1–2 (1994), 39.

14. Sarah Semple, "A Fear of the Past: The Place of the Prehistoric Burial Mound in the Ideology of Middle and Later Anglo-Saxon England," *World Archaeology* 30, no. 1 (1998), 114.

15. Howe, "Scullionspeak," 35.

16. Seamus Heaney, interview by Karl Miller, in *Stand* 2, no. 2 (2000), 155.

17. See Coogan, *The I. R. A.,* 230.

18. Ibid., 225.

19. Virgil, *Aeneid,* ed. Brian Wilkie, trans. Rolfe Humphries (New York: Macmillan, 1987), ll. 462–63.

20. *Henry VIII,* Harbage, 1.1.18–22.

21. John Bowle, *Henry VIII* (Boston: Little, Brown, 1964), 244.

Bibliography

Alighieri, Dante. *The Paradiso*. Translated by John Ciardi. New York: Mentor, 1970.

Allison, Alexander W., et al., ed. *The Norton Anthology of Poetry*. 3d ed. New York: Norton, 1983.

Andrews, Elmer. *The Poetry of Seamus Heaney: All the Realms of Whisper*. New York: St. Martin's Press, 1988.

————, ed. *Seamus Heaney: A Collection of Critical Essays*. New York: St. Martin's Press, 1992.

Annwn, David. *Inhabited Voices: Myth and History in the Poetry of Geoffrey Hill, Seamus Heaney and George Mackay Brown*. Somerset: Bran's Head, 1984.

Bailey, Anthony. "A Gift for Being in Touch." *Quest* (January–February 1978): 33–46, 92–93.

Battaglia, Frank. "The Germanic Earth Goddess in *Beowulf*?" *Mankind Quarterly* 35, no. 1–2 (Fall/Winter 1994): 39–69.

Bengtsson, Frans G. *The Long Ships: A Saga of the Viking Age*. Translated by Michael Meyer. New York: Knopf, 1961.

Blamires, Harry. *The New Bloomsday Book: A Guide through Ulysses*. New York: Routledge, 1989.

Bloom, Harold. *The Anxiety of Influence: A Theory of Poetry*. New York: Oxford University Press, 1973.

————, ed. *Seamus Heaney*. New Haven: Chelsea House Publishers, 1986.

————. *The Western Canon: The Books and School of the Ages*. New York: Harcourt Brace, 1994.

Boswell, James. *Life of Johnson*. Edited by R. W. Chapman. Oxford: Oxford University Press, 1991.

Bowle, John. *Henry VIII: A Biography*. Boston: Little, Brown, 1964.

Breslin, John B. "Vision and Revision: Seamus Heaney's New Poems." *America* 165 (7 December 1991): 438–39.

Breslin, Paul. "Heaney's Redress." *Poetry* 168, no. 6 (1996): 337–51.

Brodsky, Joseph, Seamus Heaney, and Derek Walcott. "Poets' Round Table: A Common Language," by Michael Schmidt. Edited by Julian May. *PN Review* 15, no. 4 (1989): 39–47.

Brody, Alan. *The English Mummers and Their Plays: Traces of Ancient Mystery*. Philadelphia: University of Pennsylvania Press, 1970.

Brookes, Chris. *A Public Nuisance: A History of the Mummers Troupe*. St. John's: Memorial University of Newfoundland, 1988.

Brophy, James D., and Raymond J. Porter. *Contemporary Irish Writing*. Boston: Iona College Press, 1983.

Brown, Terence. "The Counter-Revival, 1930–65: Poetry." In *The Field Day Anthology of Irish Writing,* ed. Seamus Deane, 3:129–34. Derry: Field Day Publications, 1991.

——. "A Northern Voice." In *Seamus Heaney,* edited by Harold Bloom. New Haven: Chelsea House Publishers, 1986.

Bruce-Mitford, Rupert. *The Sutton Hoo Ship Burial: A Handbook*. 2d ed. London: British Museum, 1972.

Burris, Sidney. "An Empire of Poetry." *Southern Review* 27 (1991): 558–74.

——. "Heaney's Argufying: Subjects that Matter." *Shenandoah* 45 (1995): 27–46.

——. "The Pastoral Art of Seamus Heaney." Ph.D. diss., University of Virginia, 1986.

——. *The Poetry of Resistance: Seamus Heaney and the Pastoral Tradition*. Athens: Ohio University Press, 1990.

Buttel, Robert. *Seamus Heaney*. Lewisburg, PA: Bucknell University Press, 1975.

Camus, Albert. *Lyrical and Critical Essays*. New York: Knopf, 1969.

Carleton, William. *Father Butler: The Lough Dearg Pilgrim*. New York: Garland, 1979.

Carver, Martin, ed. *The Age of Sutton Hoo: The Seventh Century in North-Western Europe*. Suffolk: Boydell Press, 1992.

——. *Sutton Hoo: Burial Ground of Kings*. Philadelphia: University of Pennsylvania Press, 1998.

Castleden, Rodney. *Neolithic Britain: New Stone Age Sites of England, Scotland, and Wales*. London: Routledge, 1992.

Chambers, E. K. *The English Folk-Play*. Oxford: Clarendon Press, 1933.

Clark, George. *Beowulf*. Boston: Twayne Publishers, 1990.

Coogan, Tim Pat. *The I.R.A.: A History*. Niwot: Roberts Rinehart, 1994.

Corcoran, Neil. *Seamus Heaney*. London: Faber and Faber, 1986.

Curtayne, Alice. *Francis Ledwidge: A Life of the Poet (1887–1917)*. London: Martin Brian and O'Keeffe, 1972.

Curtis, Tony, ed. *The Art of Seamus Heaney*. Bridgend, Mid Glamorgan: Poetry Wales, 1994.

Deane, Seamus. "The Famous Seamus." *New Yorker* 76, no. 4 (2000): 54–69.

——, ed. *The Field Day Anthology of Irish Writing*. 3 vols. Derry: Field Day Publications, 1991.

——. "Oranges and Lemons." *New Statesman and Society* 4 (5 April 1991): 18–19.

Devlin, Polly. *All of Us There*. London: Weidenfeld and Nicolson, 1983.

Doreski, William. "Seeing Things." *Colorado Review* 19 (Spring–Summer 1992): 161–66.

Edwards, Nancy. *The Archaeology of Early Medieval Ireland*. Philadelphia: University of Pennsylvania Press, 1990.

Eliot, T. S. *Complete Poems and Plays, 1909–1950*. New York: Harcourt Brace, 1980.

——. *Selected Prose of T. S. Eliot*. New York: Harcourt Brace, 1975.

Ellmann, Richard. *The Identity of Yeats*. New York: Oxford University Press, 1954.

———. *James Joyce*. New and revised edition. Oxford: Oxford University Press, 1983.

Ellmann, Richard, and Charles Fiedelson, eds. *The Modern Tradition: Backgrounds of Modern Literature*. New York: Oxford University Press, 1980.

Erikson, Erik H. *Identity, Youth and Crisis*. New York: Norton, 1968.

Evans, E. Estyn. *Irish Folk Ways*. New York: Devin-Adair, 1957.

———. *The Personality of Ireland: Habitat, Heritage and History*. Cambridge: Cambridge University Press, 1973.

Eyler, Audrey S., and Robert F. Garratt, eds. *The Uses of the Past: Essays on Irish Culture*. Newark: University of Delaware Press, 1988.

Field Day Theatre Company. *Ireland's Field Day*. Notre Dame, IN: University of Notre Dame Press, 1986.

Fitzgerald, Robert, trans. *Odyssey*, by Homer. New York: Doubleday, 1961.

———. "Seamus Heaney: An Appreciation." In *Seamus Heaney*, edited by Harold Bloom, 39–44. New Haven: Chelsea House Publishers, 1986.

Foster, Jeanne Cooper. *Ulster Folklore*. Belfast: H. R. Carter Publications, 1951.

Foster, R. F., ed. *The Oxford Illustrated History of Ireland*. New York: Oxford University Press, 1989.

Foster, Thomas C. *Seamus Heaney*. Boston: Twayne, 1989.

Garratt, Robert F. *Modern Irish Poetry: Tradition and Continuity from Yeats to Heaney*. Berkeley: University of California Press, 1986.

Gassier, Pierre, and Juliet Wilson. *The Life and Complete Work of Francisco Goya*. Edited by Francois Lachenal. New York: Reynal & Company/William Morrow, 1971.

Gibson, Ian. *Federico Garcia Lorca: A Life*. New York: Pantheon, 1989.

Givens, Seon, ed. *James Joyce: Two Decades of Criticism*. New York: Vanguard Press, 1948.

Glob, P. V. *The Bog People: Iron-Age Man Preserved*. New York: Cornell University Press, 1969.

———. *The Mound People: Danish Bronze-Age Man Preserved*. New York: Cornell University Press, 1970.

Graham-Campbell, James, and Dafydd Kidd. *The Vikings*. London: British Museum Publications, 1980.

Graves, Robert. *The White Goddess*. New York: Farrar, Straus, & Giroux, 1948.

Hardy, Thomas. *The Return of the Native*. New York: Norton, 1969.

Harmon, Maurice. "Seamus Heaney: Divisions and Allegiances." *Colby Quarterly* 30, no. 1 (1994): 7–16.

Hart, Henry. *The Poetry of Geoffrey Hill*. Carbondale: Southern Illinois University Press, 1986.

———. *Seamus Heaney: Poet of Contrary Progressions*. New York: Syracuse University Press, 1992.

———. "What is Heaney Seeing in *Seeing Things?*" *Colby Quarterly* 30, no. 1 (1994): 33–42.

Hawlin, Stephan. "Seamus Heaney's 'Station Island': The Shaping of a Modern Purgatory." *English Studies* 73 (1992): 35–50.

Heaney, Seamus, trans. *Beowulf*. New York: W. W. Norton, 2000.

———. *Crediting Poetry: The Nobel Lecture*. New York: Farrar, Straus, & Giroux, 1995.

———. *The Cure at Troy: A Version of Sophocles'* Philoctetes. New York: Farrar, Straus and Giroux, 1991.

———. *Electric Light*. New York: Farrar, Straus, & Giroux, 2001.

———. "Envies and Identifications: Dante and the Modern Poet." *Irish University Review* 15, no. 1 (1985): 5–19.

———. *Field Work*. New York: Farrar, Straus, & Giroux, 1979.

———. *The Government of the Tongue: Selected Prose. 1978–1987*. New York: Farrar, Straus, & Giroux, 1988.

———. *The Haw Lantern*. New York: Farrar, Straus, & Giroux, 1987.

———. "The Interesting Case of John Alphonsus Mulrennan." *Planet* (January 1978): 34–40.

———. Interview by Barry White. *Belfast Telegraph* (29 June 1989): 9.

———. Interview by Bel Mooney. *Turning Points*. BBC Radio 4 (15 November 1988).

———. "An Interview with Seamus Heaney," by James Randall. *Ploughshares* 5, no. 3 (1979): 7–22.

———. "Land-Locked." Review of *The Mound People*, by P. V. Glob. *Irish Press* (1 June 1974): 6.

———. *North*. London: Faber and Faber, 1975.

———. "An Open Letter." *Ireland's Field Day*. Notre Dame, IN: University of Notre Dame Press, 1986.

———. "'Place and Displacement': Recent Poetry from Northern Ireland." *Wordsworth Circle* 16 (Spring 1985): 50–51.

———. "Place, Pastness, Poems: A Triptych." *Salmagundi* (Fall–Winter 1985–86): 30–47.

———. *The Place of Writing*. Atlanta, GA: Scholars Press, 1989.

———. *Poems 1965–1975*. New York: Farrar, Straus, & Giroux, 1980.

———. *Preoccupations: Selected Prose, 1968–1978*. New York: Farrar, Straus, & Giroux, 1980.

———. *The Redress of Poetry*. New York: Farrar, Straus, & Giroux, 1995.

———. "Seamus Heaney: An Interview," by Rand Brandes. *Salmagundi* 80 (Fall 1988): 4–21.

———. "Seamus Heaney: in Interview." By Karl Miller. *Stand* 2, no. 2 (2000): 151–56.

———. "Seamus Heaney: The Words Worth Saying." Interview by Steven Ratiner. *Christian Science Monitor* (7 October 1992): 16–17.

———. *Seeing Things*. New York: Farrar, Straus, & Giroux, 1991.

———. *Selected Poems 1966–1987*. New York: Farrar, Straus, & Giroux, 1990.

———. *The Spirit Level*. New York: Farrar, Straus, & Giroux, 1996.

———. *Station Island*. New York: Farrar, Straus, & Giroux, 1985.

———. *Stations*. Belfast: Ulsterman Publications, 1975.

———. *Sweeney's Flight*. London: Faber and Faber, 1992.

———. "Unhappy and at Home." Interview by Seamus Deane. *Crane Bag* 1, no. 1 (1977): 66–72.

Heffernan, Thomas Farel. *Wood Quay: The Clash over Dublin's Viking Past*. Austin: University of Texas Press, 1988.

Hildebidle, John. "A Decade of Seamus Heaney's Poetry." *Massachusetts Review* (1987): 393–409.

Hill, Geoffrey. *Mercian Hymns*. London: Deutsch, 1971.

Howe, Nicholas. "Scullionspeak." *The New Republic* 222, no. 9 (2000): 32–37.

J. E. "St. Patrick's Purgatory." *Canadian Journal of Irish Studies* 10, no. 1 (1984): 7–40.

Jeffares, A. Norman. *W. B. Yeats*. New York: Farrar, Straus, & Giroux, 1988.

Jenkins, Nicholas. "Walking on Air." *Times Literary Supplement* (5 July 1996): 10–12.

Johnston, Dillon. *Irish Poetry After Joyce*. Notre Dame, IN: University of Notre Dame Press, 1985.

Jones, David. *The Dying Gaul and Other Writings*. London: Faber and Faber, 1978.

Joyce, James. *A Portrait of the Artist as a Young Man*. New York: Penguin, 1988.

———. *Ulysses. The Corrected Text*. Edited by Hans Walter Gabler. New York: Vintage Books of Random House, 1986.

Joyce, P. W. *The Origin and History of Irish Names of Places*. 2 vols. Dublin: McGlashan & Gill, 1869.

Kavanagh, Patrick. *Collected Poems*. New York: Norton, 1964.

———. *The Green Fool*. New York: Harper and Brothers, 1939.

———. *Lough Derg*. London: Martin Brian and O'Keeffe, 1978.

Kearney, Richard. *Transitions: Narratives in Modern Irish Culture*. Manchester: Manchester University Press, 1988.

Keeley, Lawrence H. *War Before Civilization: The Myth of The Peaceful Savage*. New York: Oxford University Press, 1996.

Kenner, Hugh. *The Pound Era*. Berkeley: University of California Press, 1971.

Kiberd, Declan. *Inventing Ireland*. Cambridge: Harvard University Press, 1996.

Kiely, Benedict. "A Raid into Dark Corners: The Poems of Seamus Heaney." *The Hollins Critic* 4 (4 October 1970): 1–12.

Kinsella, Thomas, trans. *The Táin*. New York: Irish University Press, 1969.

Langbaum, Robert. *The Mysteries of Identity: A Theme in Modern Literature*. New York: Oxford University Press, 1977.

Lipking, Lawrence. *The Life of the Poet: Beginning and Ending Poetic Careers*. Chicago: University of Chicago Press, 1981.

Lloyd, David. "'Pap for the dispossessed': Seamus Heaney and the Poetics of Identity." In *Seamus Heaney: A Collection of Critical Essays*, edited by Elmer Andrews, 87–116. New York: St. Martin's Press, 1992.

Lowell, Robert. *Selected Poems*. New York: Noonday, 1992.

MacKinnon, Lachlan. "A Responsibility to Self." *Times Literary Supplement* 4601 (7 June 1991): 28.

Magnusson, Magnus, and Hermann Pálsson, trans. *Njal's Saga*. Harmondsworth: Penguin, 1960.

Mallory, J. P., and T. E. McNeill. *The Archaeology of Ulster from Colonization to Plantation*. Queen's University of Belfast: Institute of Irish Studies, 1991.

Malloy, Catharine, and Phyllis Carey, eds. *Seamus Heaney: The Shaping Spirit*. Newark: University of Delaware Press, 1996.

Mapp, Alf J. *The Golden Dragon: Alfred the Great and His Times*. La Salle, IL: Open Court, 1974.

Mariani, Paul. *Lost Puritan: A Life of Robert Lowell.* New York: Norton, 1994.

Mikhail, E. H., ed. *W. B. Yeats: Interviews and Recollections.* 2 vols. London: Macmillan, 1977.

Molino, Michael. "Charting an Uncertain Flight Path: Irish Writers and the Question of Nation, Identity, and Literature." *The Comparatist* 20 (May 1996): 41–49.

Morrison, Blake. *Seamus Heaney.* Contemporary Writers Series. Edited by Malcolm Bradbury and Christopher Bigsby. London: Methuen, 1982.

Muratori, Fred. "Seeing Things." *Library Journal* 16, no. 19 (1991): 86.

O'Malley, Padraig. *The Uncivil Wars: Ireland Today.* Boston: Houghton Mifflin, 1983.

O'Riórdáin, Sean. *Antiquities of the Irish Countryside.* London: Methuen, 1953.

Owen, Wilfred. *The Collected Poems of Wilfred Owen.* Edited by C. Day Lewis. New York: New Directions, 1965.

Oxford English Dictionary. 2nd ed. Oxford: Clarendon Press, 1989. 20 vols.

Parker, Michael. *Seamus Heaney: The Making of a Poet.* Iowa City: University of Iowa Press, 1993.

Peacock, Alan. "Mediations: Poet as Translator, Poet as Seer." In *Seamus Heaney: A Collection of Critical Essays*, edited by Elmer Andrews, 233–55. New York: St. Martin's Press, 1992.

Piepenburg, Robert. *The Spirit of the Clay.* Farmington Hills, MI: Pebble Press, 1996.

Preminger, Alex, and T. V. F. Brogan. *The New Princeton Encyclopedia of Poetry and Poetics.* Princeton: Princeton University Press, 1993.

Quinlan, Kieran. "Tracing Seamus Heaney." *World Literature Today* 69, no. 1 (1995): 63–68.

Raftery, Barry. *Pagan Celtic Ireland.* London: Thames and Hudson, 1994.

Raine, Craig. "Famous Seamus." *Vanity Fair* 54, no. 12 (1991): 244–47, 266–67.

Ramazani, Jahan. *Poetry of Mourning: The Modern Elegy from Hardy to Heaney.* Chicago: University of Chicago Press, 1994.

Raw, Barbara. "Royal Power and Royal Symbols in *Beowulf.*" In *The Age of Sutton Hoo*, edited by Martin Carver, 167–74. Suffolk: Boydell Press, 1992.

R. D. "Double Time." *The Boston Phoenix* (18 September 1987): sec. 3.3.

Reeves-Smyth, Terence, and Fred Hamond, eds. *Landscape Archaeology in Ireland.* Oxford: BAR British Series 116, 1983.

Rzepka, Charles J. *The Self as Mind: Vision and Identity in Wordsworth, Coleridge and Keats.* Cambridge: Harvard University Press, 1986.

Sacks, Peter. *The English Elegy: Studies in the Genre from Spenser to Yeats.* Baltimore: Johns Hopkins University Press, 1985.

Sawyer, Birgit, and Peter Sawyer. *Medieval Scandinavia: From Conversion to Reformation, circa 800–1500.* Minneapolis: University of Minnesota Press, 1993.

Semple, Sarah. "A Fear of the Past: The Place of the Prehistoric Burial Mound in the Ideology of Middle and Later Anglo-Saxon England." *World Archaeology* 30, no. 1 (1998): 109–26.

Shakespeare, William. *The Complete Works.* Edited by Alfred Harbage. The Pelican text revised. Baltimore: Penguin Books, 1969.

Spenser, Edmund. *A View of the Present State of Ireland.* Edited by W. L. Renwick. London: Scholartis Press, 1934.

Stockman, Gerard, ed. *Place-Names of Northern Ireland*. 3 vols. Belfast: Institute of Irish Studies, Queen's University, 1992.

Storey, Graham. *A Preface to Hopkins*. New York: Longman, 1981.

Stradling, Diana, and J. Garrison Stradling. *The Art of the Potter*. New York: Main Street/Universe Books, 1977.

Sturluson, Snorri. *The Poetic Edda*. Translated by Henry Adams Bellows. New York: American-Scandinavian Foundation, 1923.

———. *The Prose Edda*. Translated by Jean I. Young. Cambridge: Bowes and Bowes, 1954.

Tacitus. *The Complete Works of Tacitus*. Translated by Alfred John Church and William Jackson Brodribb. Edited by Moses Hadas. New York: Random House, Modern Library, 1942.

Tillinghast, Richard. *Robert Lowell's Life and Work: Damaged Grandeur*. Ann Arbor: University of Michigan Press, 1995.

Ulster Folk Museum. *Ulster Dialects: An Introductory Symposium*. Belfast: Ulster Folk Museum, 1964.

Vendler, Helen. *The Music of What Happens*. Cambridge: Harvard University Press, 1988.

———. *Soul Says*. Cambridge: Harvard University Press, 1995.

Virgil. *The Aeneid*. Translated by Rolfe Humphries. Edited by Brian Wilkie. New York: Macmillan, 1987.

Wallace, Patrick F. *The Viking Age Buildings of Dublin*. Parts 1 and 2. Dublin: Royal Irish Academy, 1992.

Warren, Robert Penn. *Who Speaks for the Negro?* New York: Random House, 1965.

Waterman, Andrew. "Keep it in the Six Counties, Heaney!" *PN Review* 15, no. 6 (1989): 37–41.

Wildenhain, Marguerite. *Pottery: Form and Expression*. New York: Reinhold, 1962.

Williams, Raymond. *The Country and the City*. New York: Oxford University Press, 1973.

Wood, Michael. *In Search of the Trojan War*. New York: Facts on File Publications, 1985.

Woodham-Smith, Cecil. *The Great Hunger*. New York: Harper and Row, 1962.

Wordsworth, William. "The Prelude." In *English Romantic Writers*, edited by David Perkins. New York: Harcourt Brace, 1967.

Yeats, W. B. *Autobiographies*. London: Macmillan, 1979.

———. *The Autobiography of William Butler Yeats*. New York: Macmillan, 1938.

———. *The Collected Letters of W. B. Yeats*. Vol. 1. Edited by John Kelly and Eric Domville. New York: Oxford University Press, 1986.

———. *The Poems of W. B. Yeats*. New York: Macmillan, 1983.

———. *The Variorum Edition of the Plays of W. B. Yeats*. Edited by Russell K. Alspach. London: Macmillan, 1966.

———. *A Vision*. New York: Collier, 1966.

Index

241